Key Issues

ON MORAL SENTIMENTS
Contemporary Responses to Adam Smith

Key Issues

ON MORAL SENTIMENTS

Contemporary Responses to Adam Smith

Edited and Introduced by

JOHN REEDER

Universidad Complutense de Madrid

Series Editor

ANDREW PYLE

University of Bristol

THOEMMES PRESS

© Thoemmes Press 1997

Published in 1997 by
Thoemmes Press
11 Great George Street
Bristol BS1 5RR, England

US office: Distribution and Marketing
22883 Quicksilver Drive
Dulles, Virginia 20166, USA

ISBN
Paper : 1 85506 550 9
Cloth : 1 85506 549 5

On Moral Sentiments
Key Issues No. 18

British Library Cataloguing-in-Publication Data

A catalogue record of this title is available
from the British Library

Printed in Great Britain by Antony Rowe Ltd., Chippenham

CONTENTS

INTRODUCTION

I

Although perhaps not enjoying the *succès de scandale* of certain other philosophical works of its time,[1] Adam Smith's *Theory of Moral Sentiments* was to appear in no fewer than twenty-six editions in English between 1759 and 1825, together with six editions of three separate translations into French and two editions of two separate translations into German in the same period.[2] We have evidence that Smith's book was read by a fairly comprehensive sample of the leading philosophers during this period, from his friends David Hume and Edmund Burke, fellow Scots philosophers such as Lord Kames, Thomas Reid, Adam Ferguson and Dugald Stewart, French *philosophes* such as D'Holbach and the Condorcets, Antoine and Sophie, to Herder and Kant in Germany.[3] A later generation of Scots thinkers, disciples of Dugald Stewart at Edinburgh such as Thomas Brown and Sir James Mackintosh, were to continue to include detailed, if critical, analyses of Smith's philosophical theories in their lectures and writings. Similarly, in France in the earlier decades of the nineteenth century, the *Theory of Moral Sentiments* was still being discussed from the period of the Restoration up until the end of the 1830s by French philosophers such as Victor Cousin or Théodore-Simon Jouffroy who

---

[1] That 'silly bigotted fellow' (Hume *dixit*) Beattie's *Essay on the Nature and Immutability of Truth in opposition to Sophistry and Scepticism* (1779), for example, went through six editions in as many years.

[2] For bibliographical studies see Charles J. Bullock, *The Vanderblue Memorial Collection of Smithiana* (Boston, 1939); and T. E. Jessop, *A Bibliography of David Hume and of Scottish Philosophers from Francis Hutcheson to Lord Balfour* (London, 1938).

[3] See Samuel Fleischaker, 'Philosophy in Moral Practice: Kant and Adam Smith', *Kant-Studien*, vol. 82 (1991), pp. 249–69.

had inherited through Royer-Collard part of the legacy of the Scottish tradition of 'Common Sense' philosophy. Indeed, Jouffroy's lengthy analysis of the *Theory of Moral Sentiments* marks the end of the book's life as a work of relevant *contemporary* philosophy.

Exactly how much this prolonged interest in the book is attributable not solely to the continuing philosophical significance of what became known as 'Smith's Theory of Sympathy', but is rather a by-product of Smith's other roles as author of the *Wealth of Nations*, founding father of the science of economics, and champion of the cause of economic liberty, is difficult to say. Inevitably, the popularity of the *Wealth of Nations*, above all throughout the nineteenth century, lead to revived interest in the earlier philosophical work.

As the present anthology of critical responses shows, Smith's 'Theory of Sympathy' continued to be deemed worthy of consideration – or refutation – as an interesting philosophical idea in its own right up until the 1830s. It is only later, in the 1870s, with the discussion of what came to be known as '*Das Adam Smith Problem*' in the German speaking world (and above all in the writings of Skarzynski), and the formulation of the notorious *Umschwungstheorie* (the hypothesis that the theory of sympathy set out in the *Theory of Moral Sentiments*, is in some way incompatible with the self-interested, profit-maximizing ethic which supposedly underlies the *Wealth of Nations*), that the earlier philosophical work came to be seen as of interest only insofar as it revealed supposed ambiguities in the mind of the author of the later work of economics.

More recently, ideas such as those related to problems concerning the unintended social outcomes of conscious and intentional human actions (associated with Karl Popper and Friedrich von Hayek), and the fascination on the part of free market-orientated economists with the metaphor and mechanism of the invisible hand, first clearly set out in the *Theory of Moral Sentiments* (part IV, chapter 1), together with the publication of Raphael and Macfie's monumental Glasgow variorum edition (1976) of the work, have all lead to a revival of interest, both scholarly and philosophical, in Smith's first book of philosophy.

II

The first response to the publication of the *Theory of Moral Sentiments* (henceforth TMS),[4] was David Hume's famous teasing letter of 12 April 1759 where he recounts the book's success amongst the 'Mob of Literati' and the 'Retainers to Superstition'. In a more serious vein, in a second letter from Hume, dated 28 July 1759, he makes the objection that in TMS, Smith was inconsistent in arguing that all acts of sympathizing are pleasurable: 'It is always thought a difficult Problem to account for the Pleasure receiv'd from the Tears and Grief and Sympathy of Tragedy: which would not be the Case, if all Sympathy was agreeable' (*Correspondence*, no. 36).[5] Sympathy with grief, for instance, is the sharing of something painful, although a feeling to be approved of as proper. Smith, in a footnote added to the revised second edition of TMS (p. 46), clarified his position by redefining the 'sentiment of approbation' and distinguishing between sympathy and approval. So pleased was he with his reply that he was to remark in a subsequent letter to Gilbert Elliot, 'I think I have entirely discomfitted him [i.e. Hume]' (*Correspondence*, no. 40).

It has been alleged by David Raynor[6] that Hume was the author of the anonymous review of TMS which appeared in Smollett's *Critical Review* for May 1759. The evidence for such an attribution does not seem, however, to be entirely convincing. The review follows the normal eighteenth-century practice of quoting large chunks of the work reviewed and offering a minimum of interpretation and analysis. What are strangely out of place, if the review is indeed Hume's work, are the incongruous sentiments expressed in the concluding paragraph:

---

[4] TMS: this refers to the Glasgow variorum edition of Adam Smith, *The Theory of Moral Sentiments*, edited by D. D. Raphael and A. L. Macfie, corrected reprint (Oxford, 1979).

[5] *Correspondence*: the Glasgow edition of *The Correspondence of Adam Smith*, edited by Ernest Campbell Mossner and Ian Simpson Ross, revised edition (Oxford, 1987).

[6] David Raynor, 'Hume's *Abstract of Adam Smith's Theory of Moral Sentiments*', *Journal of the History of Philosophy*, vol. 22 (1984) pp. 51–79.

The second advantage to be found in this work, is the strict regard which the writer everywhere preserves to the principles of religion: however some pretenders to science may endeavour to separate the philosopher from the lover of religion, it will always be found, that truth being everywhere uniform and consistent, it is impossible for a man to divest himself of the one character, without renouncing all just claim to the other.

Given Hume's notorious scepticism in matters religious, how are we intended to interpret this? Irony? A private joke? Is this perhaps a convention amongst more sceptical writers to fend off the suspicions of the Church party? This normal practice of the eighteenth-century review, of publishing not what we in the twentieth century would consider as critical assessments, but rather abstracts of the work in question, liberally larded with extensive extracts, has meant that in this anthology we have in the interests of avoiding tedium decided to include only two of these anonymous reviews: the above-mentioned attributed to Hume, and a second anonymous review of the first edition of TMS, purportedly written by Edmund Burke.

Burke's adulatory review in the *Annual Register* for 1759 – 'one of the most beautiful fabrics of Moral Theory that has perhaps ever appeared' – was preceded by a letter to Smith dated 10 September 1759 where he wrote of TMS in a similarly eulogistic tone, allowing himself only one minor criticism of form rather than content: 'I will take the liberty to mention too what appeared to me as a sort of Fault. You are in some few Places, what Mr Locke is in most of his writings, rather a little too diffuse' (*Correspondence*, no. 38). This was a criticism which, as we shall see, was to be repeated later with greater severity by both Dugald Stewart and Sir James Mackintosh.

Less indulgent perhaps, and more pertinent, must have been the objection raised by his friend, the cultured Scottish peer, politician and amateur philosopher Sir Gilbert Elliot of Minto. Elliot's letter to Smith which contained his comments has, unfortunately, not survived and all we have is Smith's reply of 10 October 1759 and a manuscript of the Draft Amendment Smith later introduced into the revised second edition of 1761 in response to Elliot's criticism (*Correspondence*, no. 40). From an analysis of Smith's letter and the Draft Amendment, D. D. Raphael has offered the following plausible reconstruction of Elliot's missing objection: 'if moral judgement on our own actions were a reflection of the approval and disapproval of society, then it would be impossible for a man to form a moral judgement which he knows is contrary to popular opinion' (*Correspondence*, p. 48, note 1). As can be seen from Smith's reply and his revisions, Elliot's objection forced Smith into redefining with greater precision the role of the impartial spectator. Although he still retains in the second edition the idea that conscience has its origins in popular opinion, he begins here to establish more and more clearly the distinction between the impartial spectator as final arbiter of the individual conscience and the purely secondary role of popular opinion, which lead him finally in the 1790 sixth edition to separate out completely the function of each: 'the jurisdictions of those two tribunals are founded upon principles which, though in some respects resembling and akin, are, however, in reality different and distinct' (TMS, p. 130). Already in his letter to Elliot, Smith is at great pains to emphasize that virtue is not dependent on popular opinion: '...our judgements concerning our own conduct always have a reference to the sentiments of some other being, and to shew that, notwithstanding this, real magnanimity and conscious virtue can support itselfe under the disapprobation of all mankind' (*Correspondence*, no. 40).

Less philosophically significant perhaps, but of particular interest as representative of the opinions of a well-read layman, are the entries in the diary of the moderate Scots churchman, George Ridpath, recording his reading of TMS. Ridpath was the minister of the Border parish of Stitchel, a graduate of Edinburgh University, friend of both Robertson and Hume, his near-neighbour at Ninewells, and author of a *History of the Borders*. His diary for September and October 1759 shows him not to have been overly impressed with Smith's book, and he is especially harsh in his strictures on the prolixity and oratorical style of the work.

More considered opinions of TMS were to be forthcoming in the years that followed the publication of the revised second edition (1761). Openly critical responses came from fellow

Scots philosophers such as Henry Home, Lord Kames, formerly Smith's patron; Thomas Reid, formerly Professor at Aberdeen and, after 1764, Smith's successor in the Chair of Moral Philosophy at Glasgow, critic of Hume and founder of what came to be known as the Common Sense school of philosophy; Adam Ferguson, sometime Professor of Moral Philosophy at Edinburgh; and Dugald Stewart, in his youth friend and admirer of Smith, later highly influential Professor of Moral Philosophy at Edinburgh and Smith's first biographer.

Lord Kames's objections to Smith's Theory of Sympathy, added to the third edition of his *Essays on the Principles of Morality and Natural Religion* (1779), which, it would appear, were sent in transcript to Smith at the end of 1778, came down to two basic points. Firstly, our moral sentiments with respect to our own actions cannot be explained by sympathy, and secondly, by placing ourselves in the position of a sufferer our feelings of pity actually diminish, not increase. Smith, as befits a reply to a former benefactor, was in his letter suitably deferential and declined to enter into discussion (*Correspondence*, no. 195).

Reid's antipathy towards TMS was altogether more profound. Although he never expressed these differences in print, we have two principal manuscript sources which make quite clear his opinions. Firstly, a letter sent in 1778 to Kames, by this time protector of Reid, on receipt of what was presumably a copy of the same transcript of the objections sent to Smith which were to be included in the new edition of Kames's *Essays*. Reid here states his conviction that Smith's theory is 'indeed only a refinement of the selfish system', a view he enlarges upon in some detail in his unpublished, undated notes for a lecture delivered at Glasgow University sometime during his tenure as Professor between 1763 and 1790. These notes, our second source for Reid's opinion of TMS, recently transcribed by Stewart-Robertson and Fate-Norton,[7] are the fullest expression of Reid's views of what he refers to as Smith's 'System of Sympathy' which he associates with self-love: 'As this

---

[7] J. C. Stewart-Robertson and David Fate Norton, 'Thomas Reid on Adam Smith's Theory of Morals', *Journal of the History of Ideas*, vol. 41 (1980), pp. 381–98; vol. 45 (1984), pp. 309–21.

Author resolves all Sympathy into self-love variously modified by certain operations of the Imagination. So he resolves all moral Approbation and Disapprobation into Sympathy.'[8] Reid then moves from accusing Smith of terminological imprecision to identifying the System of Sympathy with hypocrisy: 'Another observation which I would make upon this System of Sympathy is that it seems rather to account for men's putting on the Appearance of Virtue than for their being really virtuous.'[9] Finally, Reid's argument, together with obvious distaste for Smith's theory, lead him to draw the conclusion that 'the Ultimate Measure and Standard of Sympathy, is not any fixed Judgement grounded on Truth or upon the dictates of a well-informed conscience but the variable opinions and passions of Men',[10] which Reid directly associates with Epicureanism in a pointed quotation from Cicero.[11]

One cannot but suspect that Reid's identification of Smith's philosophy with the Selfish System and Epicureanism, theories normally associated in eighteenth-century England with their supposed disciples Hobbes and Mandeville, and underlying connotations of atheism and materialism, was a widely held view of Smith's opinions. This would account in some measure for Smith's attempts to clarify his position and distance himself from these associations in the sixth edition, above all in chapter IV, 'Of Licentious Systems', of the completely rewritten seventh section.

Perhaps the most remarkable response to TMS, in form if not in content, was Adam Ferguson's unpublished imaginary dialogue between David Hume, Robert Clerk and Adam Smith.[12] Probably written around 1761, this is a hugely enter-

---

[8] See p. 72 below.

[9] See p. 74 below.

[10] See p. 79 below.

[11] Although Smith claimed to have clarified this problem in the second edition (1761) of TMS, since Reid makes no reference to the edition he is using, we cannot be sure whether his argument was based on an examination of the text of this revised second edition (or indeed later editions which contain the same or further corrections, ie. the third, fourth or fifth editions, all published prior to 1790) or the original uncorrected first edition.

[12] See pp. 86–95 below.

taining, no-holds-barred, far from Socratic piece, in which after
a maliciously accurate caricature of Smith's mannerisms – '...the
Servant announced Mr Adam Smith, who at the same time
entered the Room with a smile on his countenance and
muttering somewhat to himself' – Ferguson subjects Smith to
the most forthright of criticisms by the aggressive soldier,
Robert Clerk, later General Clerk:

> Smith: ....I should be glad to know your opinion.
> Clerk: I don't much like to trouble authors with my opinion
> of their works.
> Smith: Ah, Do, you will oblige me!
> Clerk: If you insist upon it. I must be plain and leave no
> doubt.
> Smith: Surely. Surely.
> Clerk: Your Book is to me a Heap of absolute Nonsense.
> Smith seemed to be stunn'd.[13]

More seriously, Ferguson, in the persona of Clerk – or possibly
Clerk himself, if we believe the scene to be the representation
of a real discussion – accuses Smith of circularity, a criticism as
we shall see later, taken up by Thomas Brown.

> You began with calling Sympathy to explain Moral
> Sentiment. You now call up moral sentiment to explain itself:
> what is a well-informed and impartial observer, but a
> Virtuous Person whose Sympathy may be relied on as a Test
> of Virtue?[14]

There is probably no need to introduce the persona of Clerk in
order to explain the peculiarly aggressive tone of the dialogue
since Ferguson himself, a famously hot-headed and irascible
eccentric, a Gaelic-speaking Highlander, former army chaplain,
and holder in succession of no fewer than three different Chairs
at Edinburgh University – Natural Philosophy (1759),
Pneumatics and Moral Philosophy (1764) and Mathematics
(1785) – was quite capable of a similar outburst.

Before going on to examine the part played by the last of
Smith's contemporaries, Dugald Stewart and his disciples at

---

[13] Pages 89–90 below.

[14] Page 90 below.

Edinburgh University, in the discussion of Smith's ethical theories, this is probably the best point to consider the reaction of Christian churchmen to TMS. This book as first published appears to have enjoyed a reputation as an unexceptionable (from the Christian standpoint), and indeed, praiseworthy, work of ethics. Several reviewers remarked on what they saw as Christian, or at least, strongly religious undertones in the work – the reviewer for the *Journal encyclopédique*, for instance, goes out of his way to stress this aspect of the work: '...mais ce qui le rend encore plus précieux, c'est que tout y respire la vertu la plus pure, et que la réligion y est par-tout respectée'[15] – and few were as observant as Reid in detecting secularist undercurrents. The essentially secular system of ethics contained in TMS and the gradual toning down or indeed removal of what might have been taken as the more explicitly Christian references, almost imperceptibly in the revised second edition of 1761 and much more noticeably in the rewritten sections of the sixth edition of 1790, failed to attract the attention of what Hume used to call the 'scurrilous Warburtonian school', the guardians of religious orthodoxy ever ready to denounce secularist trends.

It was the publication of Smith's *Letter...to William Strahan, Esq.* of 9 November 1776 (*Correspondence*, no. 178), together with Hume's posthumous autobiographical sketch, a eulogy of his friend, which was to directly antagonize the Church party and prompt a reaction on the part of the orthodox to Smith's ethical theories. Smith himself was to remark in a letter to a Danish correspondent on the virulence of this reaction, largely verbal we are to suppose, as written observations by offended Christians are scarce: 'A single, and, as I thought, a very harmless sheet of paper, which I happened to Write concerning the death of our late friend, Mr Hume, brought upon me ten times more abuse than the very violent attack I had made upon the whole commercial system of Great Britain' (*Correspondence*, no. 208). Smith's own personal unorthodox religious views – he appears to have believed in some sort of natural religion, something at most approaching an abstract

---

[15] *Journal encyclopédique*, October 1760, quoted by Raphael and Macfie in the Introduction to TMS, p. 29.

Stoic deism, certainly non-Christian, although probably not the radical and mischievous anti-Christian scepticism upheld by his friend Hume – thanks to extreme caution on his part, remained hidden from most of his readers, buried beneath layers of euphemism and circumspection. The Master of Magdalen College, Oxford, later Bishop of Norwich, the Hutchinsonian fundamentalist George Horne, in a squib directed at Smith for eulogizing a notorious unbeliever (*Correspondence*, no. 189) seems, however, to have picked up on the essentially non-Christian nature of Smith's ethics: '...one would think, the belief of the soul's existence and immortality could do no harm if it did not good in a Theory of Moral Sentiments.' Horne is, of course, correct. In Smith's theory the hope of immortality, one of the principal inducements to virtuous behaviour in orthodox Christianity, makes its appearance only ambiguously, as 'a doctrine in every respect so venerable, so comfortable to the weakness, so flattering to the grandeur of human nature, that the virtuous man who has the misfortune to doubt of it cannot possibly avoid wishing most earnestly and anxiously to believe it' (TMS, p. 132).

With the exception of these remarks by Horne, however, Smith's unorthodox religious views (the expression of which were accentuated in the clearly more Stoic sections of the revised sixth edition of TMS where an anti-religious vein is made more apparent)[16] seemed largely to have escaped notice or at least did not give rise to much written comment.

---

[16] See, for instance, the omission of perhaps the most Christian paragraph in the book (pt II, sect. ii, chap. 3, para. 12 in editions 1 to 5, TMS, pp. 91–2) which includes phrases such as 'the holiness of God' and 'the doctrines of revelation coincide, in every respect, with those original anticipations of nature'. This whole long paragraph is replaced in the sixth edition by a single, curt Humean sentence, which characteristically couples religion and superstition: 'In every religion and in every superstition that the world has ever beheld, accordingly, there has been a Tartarus as well as an Elysium; a place provided for the punishment of the wicked, as well as one for the reward of the just.' For the controversy over the removal of the so-called 'Passage on Atonement', see TMS, Appendix II, pp. 383–401.

III

Without derogation from his writings, it may be said that his disciples were among his best works.[17]

Thus one of these disciples, Sir James Mackintosh, expressed himself about his mentor, Dugald Stewart. Stewart was the last of Smith's contemporaries to comment extensively on TMS and constitutes a natural bridge between these eighteenth-century philosophers and the new nineteenth-century generation of Scots, his disciples. His long period of tenure as Professor of Moral Philosophy at Edinburgh, 1785–1820 (although he effectively gave up teaching between 1809 and 1820 when Brown was named conjoint Professor), and his direct knowledge of the teachings of Reid and Ferguson, together with his personal friendship with Smith, made Stewart the perfect link between the two generations. His 'Account of Smith', as he always referred to his biography, the first version of which was written in 1792, then first published in 1794, to be re-edited on countless occasions as the prologue to innumerable nineteenth-century editions of the *Wealth of Nations*, includes an extensive commentary on TMS which he describes as 'a singular effort of invention, ingenuity and subtilty'. A disciple himself of Reid, he could not, however, agree with Smith's theory, nor with the manner in which it was expressed, disapproving of Smith's looseness of expression and terminological imprecision. In his last work, published only weeks before his death in 1828, the *Philosophy of the Active and Moral Powers of Man*, according to Stewart himself a rewriting of his lectures delivered between 1792/3 and 1809, he enlarges on his criticisms of Smith's ethical theories:

> It may be objected to Mr Smith's theory, that it confounds the means or expedients by which nature enables us to correct our moral judgements, with the principles in our constitution to which our moral judgements owe their origin.[18]

---

[17] *Dissertation on the Progress of Ethical Philosophy* (Edinburgh, 1836), p. 315.

[18] Dugald Stewart, *Collected Works*, edited by Sir William Hamilton (Edinburgh, 1854–60), vol. 6, p. 330.

Amongst Stewart's most important philosophical disciples were Thomas Brown and Sir James Mackintosh, both of whom were to devote sections of their published works to a more or less detailed analysis of TMS. Brown was to succeed Stewart as conjoint Professor of Moral Philosophy at Edinburgh on Stewart's effective retirement from teaching in 1809 following a stroke. A prolific poet, and an ingenious eclectic in his philosophical views, Brown alienated his former patron by his attacks on the ideas of Reid and, by extension, on Stewart himself. Brown was a facile, rather verbose, lecturer in philosophy who enjoyed a brilliant reputation in his time, a reputation which has long since evaporated.

In his lectures *On Dr. Smith's System*,[19] Brown takes up Reid and Stewart's objections:

> This essential error, the greatest of all possible systematic errors is no less than the assumption, in every case, of those moral feelings, which are supposed to flow from sympathy, – the assumption of them as necessarily existing before that very sympathy in which they are said to originate...the process to which he ascribes the origins of these moral sentiments cannot even be understood, without the belief of their previous existence.[20]

Brown's early and unexpected death in 1820 reopened the question of who was to succeed Stewart in the Chair at Edinburgh. Stewart's candidate was Mackintosh, but he, something of a social and intellectual gadfly, declined to present himself, preferring to pursue his career in politics. Mackintosh's most important contribution to philosophy was his *Dissertation on the Progress of Ethical Philosophy* (1836), originally written as part of the introductory volume of the seventh edition of the *Encyclopedia Britannica*, which contains a chapter on Smith in which he echoes much of the earlier criticism of Reid and Stewart. After describing Smith's style as 'graceful fulness falling into flaccidity' and objecting to the confusing discursive structure of TMS, 'an ingenious contrivance of cycles and epicycles, which perplex the mind too much to satisfy it, and

---

[19] Lectures 80 and 81 in volume 4 of *Lectures on the Philosophy of the Human Mind* (Edinburgh, 1820).

[20] See p. 137 below.

seem devised to evade difficulties which cannot be solved',
Mackintosh, in his sixth and final objection, offers a variation
on Reid's earlier and more precise point:

> This ingenious system renders all morality *relative* – by
> referring it to the pleasure of an agreement of our feelings with
> those of others, by confining itself entirely to the question of
> moral approbation, and by providing no place for the consid-
> eration of that quality which distinguishes all good from all
> bad actions.[21]

Another of those who attended Stewart's lectures, although
briefly and apparently unnoticed by the philosopher, was James
Mill, and it is interesting how, in his later work of philosophy,
The Analysis of the Phenomena of the Human Mind (1829), he
offers a description of Smith's *Theory of Sympathy* similar to
the Reid/Stewart interpretation:

> ...that remarkable phenomenon in nature, eloquently
> described, but not explained, by Adam Smith, that in minds
> happily trained, the love of Praiseworthiness the dread of
> Blameworthiness is a stronger feeling than the love of actual
> Praise, the Dread of actual Blame.[22]

IV

> Si l'histoire de la PHILOSOPHIE SENSUALISTE AU DIX-HUITIEME
> SIECLE, en montrant quelle triste morale et quelle triste
> politique sortent invinciblement de la metaphysique de la
> sensation avait ruiné le principe dans ses conséquences auprés
> de notre jeune et généreux auditoire, l'étude de la PHILOSOPHIE
> ECOSSAISE venait à propos pour achever de le conquérir à la
> cause opposée. Là, en effet, une saine métaphysique, appuyée
> sur une psychologie sévère, conduit naturellement à une
> esthéthique, à une théodicée, à une morale, à une politique qui
> satisfont à la fois les esprits les plus scrupuleux et les, mes
> éclarées.[23]

---

[21] See p. 159 below.

[22] 1869 edition, edited by J. S. Mill, vol. 2, p. 298.

[23] Victor Cousin, *Philosophie Ecossaise*, 3rd edition (Paris, 1857),
Avertissement, pp. i–ii.

Thus, Victor Cousin succinctly describes why Royer-Collard introduced the Scottish philosophy of Common Sense, essentially that of Reid and Dugald Stewart, into the French university philosophy curriculum after the Restoration. Thought then to be the perfect antidote to combat the 'philosophie sensualiste' of Condillac, the root of all the evils of the Revolution, according to the post-Napoleonic generation, it was to be Royer-Collard's disciples, the eclectic Cousin and Théodore-Simon Jouffroy who were to write the last extended commentaries on TMS as a work of relevant *contemporary* philosophy. Thereafter, TMS was to be seen increasingly as an interesting, if outdated, study of ethics of largely historical significance or as evidence in favour of supposed ambiguities in the ethics underlying the *Wealth of Nations*.

The ethical theories of Adam Smith sit uncomfortably amongst the writings of the so-called French Spiritualist School, studies devoted principally to the anti-sceptical Common Sense philosophy of Reid and Dugald Stewart.[24] (Jouffroy was responsible for the French translation of the works of Reid (1829–36) and Stewart's *Outlines of Moral Philosophy* (1826).) Thus, the chapters of Cousin's *Philosophie Ecossaise* (1845), a course of lectures originally delivered in 1819, which he devotes to Smith and TMS are, not surprisingly given Smith's radically different approach to ethics from Reid's, rather uninspired and not particularly illuminating. Théodore-Simon Jouffroy, who taught at the Ecole Normale and was later Professor of Greek and Roman Philosophy at the Collège de France, seems to have been attracted to TMS because of his interest in the new philosophical trend of psychologism, which he had been drawn to through his reading of Dugald Stewart, rather than because of any proximity to Smith's ethical position. Nevertheless, his lengthy, altogether more perceptive and sympathetic critique of TMS, first published in French in 1834, constitutes a complete compendium of all the objections and criticisms of the work made to date.

Finally, it was to be left to J. A. Farrer, in a volume entitled simply *Adam Smith* (1881), part of a series incongruously named English Philosophers, to present what was the most

---

[24] See James W. Manns, *Reid and his French Disciples* (Leiden, 1994).

detailed study of TMS written in the nineteenth century. Largely exegetic, the work concludes with a final chapter which conveniently passes review of all the principal opinions and objections to the book expressed in the earlier part of the century, from Dugald Stewart to Jouffroy.[25]

John Reeder
Universidad Complutense
de Madrid, 1997

---

[25] At this point I should like to acknowledge the obvious debt owed by the editor of this anthology to Ian Simpson Ross's indispensable biography, *The Life of Adam Smith* (Oxford, 1995).

ABBREVIATIONS

Burke Corr.	*The Correspondence of Edmund Burke*, ed. Thomas W. Copeland et al. (Cambridge and Chicago, 1958–)
GUL	Glasgow University Library
HL	*The Letters of David Hume*, ed. J. Y. T. Greig, 2 vols. (Oxford, 1932)
NHL	*New Letters of David Hume*, ed. Raymond Klibansky and Ernest C. Mossner (Oxford, 1954)
NLS	National Library of Scotland
Rae	John Rae, *Life of Adam Smith* (London, 1895)
RSE	Royal Society of Edinburgh
Scott	W. R. Scott, *Adam Smith as Student and Professor* (Glasgow, 1937)
SRO	Scottish Record Office, H. M. General Register House, Edinburgh

Acknowledgements

Reproduction of items from *The Correspondence of Adam Smith* (revised edition, 1987), edited by E. C. Mossner and Ian S. Ross, is by permission of Oxford University Press.

Reproduction of 'Letter from Thomas Reid to Lord Kames, 30 October 1778' is by permission of Ian S. Ross and the University of Texas Press.

The Publisher wishes to thank the University of Aberdeen, Directorate of Information Systems and Services: Library Division for permission to reproduce MS 2131/2/II/6 that appears in 'A Sketch of Dr Smith's Theory of Morals'.

The Initial Response

LETTER FROM DAVID HUME*
12 April 1759

MS., NLS Acc. 776 (Robertson Papers); NHL 51–5.

Lisle Street, Leicester Fields, 12 Apr. 1759

Dear Smith

I give you thanks for the agreeable Present of your Theory[1] Wedderburn[2] and I made Presents of our Copies to such of our Acquaintance as we thought good Judges, and proper to spread the Reputation of the Book. I sent one to the Duke of Argyle,[3] to Lord Lyttleton,[4] Horace Walpole,[5] Soames Jennyns,[6] and Burke,[7] an Irish Gentleman, who wrote lately a very pretty Treatise on the Sublime. Millar desird my Per-

---

* From *Correspondence of Adam Smith*, edited by E. C. Mossner and Ian S. Ross, revised edition (Oxford, 1987), no. 31, pp. 33–6. The notes of the original editors have been retained.

[1] TMS which Millar had just brought out; see Letter 33 from Andrew Millar, dated 26 Apr. 1759.

[2] Alexander Wedderburn.

[3] Archibald Campbell, 3rd Duke of Argyll.

[4] Sir George, afterwards Lord, Lyttleton (1709–73); politician, patron, and man of letters; Lord of Treasury 1744–54; Chancellor of Exchequer 1756; author of *Dialogues of the Dead* (1760), and *History of the Life of Henry the Second* (1767–71).

[5] Horace Walpole (1717–97) of Strawberry Hill, Mdx., 3rd s. of Sir Robert Walpole; 4th Earl of Orford, 1791; dilettante memorialist and famous letter writer, also remembered for his 'Gothic' novel, *The Castle of Otranto* (1764); educ. Eton and Cambridge; on the Grand Tour with Thomas Gray, 1739–41; M.P. 1741–68; played a conspicuous part in the Hume-Rousseau quarrel of 1766.

[6] Soame Jenyns (1704–87), M.P. 1742–60; author of *Free Enquiry into the Nature and Origin of Evil* (1757) and *View of the Internal Evidence of the Christian Religion* (1777).

[7] Edmund Burke (1729–97), author and statesman, by this time had written a *Vindication of Natural Society* (1756) and *A Philosophical Enquiry into the Origin of Our Ideas of the Sublime and Beautiful* (1757). See Letter 38 from Edmund Burke dated 10 Sept. 1759, reproduced on page 12 of this anthology.

mission to send one in your Name to Dr Warburton.[8] I have delayd writing to you till I cou'd tell you something of the Success of the Book, and could prognosticate with some Probability whether it shoud be finally damnd to Oblivion, or shoud be registerd in the Temple of Immortality. Tho' it has been published only a few Weeks, I think there appear already such strong Symptoms, that I can almost venture to fortell its Fate. It is in short this —— But I have been interrupted in my Letter by a foolish impertinent Visit of one who has lately come from Scotland. He tells me, that the University of Glasgow intend to declare Rouets Office Vacant upon his going abroad with Lord Hope.[9] I question not but you will have our Friend, Ferguson, in your Eye, in case another Project for procuring him a Place in the University of Edinburgh shou'd fail. Ferguson has very much polishd and improved his Treatise on Refinement,[10] and with some Amendments it will make an admirable Book, and discovers an elegant and a singular Genius. The Epigoniad, I hope, will do; but it is somewhat uphill Work. As I doubt not but you consult the Reviews sometimes at present, you will see in the critical Review a Letter upon that Poem; and I desire you to employ your Conjectures in finding out the Author. Let me see a Sample of your Skill in knowing hands by your guessing at the Person.[11] I am afraid of Lord Kaims's Law Tracts.[12] A man might as well think of

---

[8]   William Warburton (1698–1779), churchman (Dean of Bristol 1757; Bp. of Gloucester 1759–79) and controversialist; castigated by Hume in *My Own Life*; 'I found by Dr Warburton's Railing that [my] Books were beginning to be esteemed in good Company', and again, '. . the illiberal Petulance, Arrogance, and Scurrility which distinguishes the Warburtonian School'. See E. C. Mossner, 'Hume's *Four Dissertations*', *Modern Philogy* xlviii (1950) 37–57, and A. W. Evans, *Warburton and the Warburtonians* (London, 1932).

[9]   William Rouet (Rouat, Ruet), Professor of Oriental Languages, Glasgow, 1751; Professor of Church History 1752; travelling tutor to Lord Hope (d. 1765) 1759; resigned from Glasgow University, 1762, amid controversy; see Letter 59 from Lord Erroll, dated 27 Oct. 1761, and Scott 190–5.

[10]   No work of Ferguson's by this title was published, but the reference may be to an early draft or part of *An Essay on the History of Civil Society*.

[11]   Hume wrote this letter, see *Critical Review*, Apr. 1759, reprinted. Hume, *Phil. Wks.* iv. 425–37.

[12]   *Historical Law-Tracts*, 2 vols. (Edinburgh, 1758).

making a fine Sauce by a Mixture of Wormwood and Aloes as
an agreeable Composition by joining Metaphysics and Scotch
Law. However, the Book, I believe, has Merit; tho' few People
will take the Pains of diving into it. But to return to your
Book, and its Success in this Town, I must tell you —— A
Plague of Interruptions! I orderd myself to be deny'd; and yet
here is one that has broke in upon me again. He is a man of
Letters, and we have had a good deal of literary Conversation.
You told me, that you was curious of literary Anecdotes, and
therefore I shall inform you of a few, that have come to my
Knowledge. I believe I have mentioned to you already Helvet-
ius's Book de l'Esprit.[13] It is worth your Reading, not for its
Philosophy, which I do not highly value, but for its agreeable
Composition. I had a Letter from him a few days ago, wherein
he tells me that my Name was much oftener in the Manuscript,
but that the Censor of Books at Paris oblig'd him to strike it
out.[14] Voltaire[15] has lately publishd a small Work calld
Candide, ou L'optimisme. It is full of Sprightliness and Impiety,
and is indeed a Satyre upon Providence, under Pretext of criti-
cizing the Leibnitian System. I shall give you a Detail of it ——
But what is all this to my Book? say you. —— My Dear Mr
Smith, have Patience; Compose yourself to Tranquillity: Show
yourself a Philosopher in Practice as well as Profession: Think
on the Emptiness, and Rashness, and Futility of the common
Judgements of Men: How little they are regulatd by Reason in
any Subject, much more in philosophical Subjects, which so
far exceed the Comprehension of the Vulgar. *Non si quid
improba Roma, Elevet, accedas examenque improbum in illa,*

[13] Claude-Adrien Helvétius (1715–71), philosopher, author of *De l'esprit*
(1758), which was condemned by the Parlement of Paris and burnt, 10 Feb.
1762.

[14] Dated 1 Apr. 1759; MS., RSE v. 50: 'Votre nom honore mon livre, et je
l'aurois cité plus souvent, si la sévérité du censeur me l'eût permis.' The
censor was Chrétien-Guillaume de Lamoignon de Malesherbes (1721–94),
who carried out his duties with restraint, seeing to it, for example, that the
Encyclopédie was published despite its subversive tendencies.

[15] François-Marie Arouet (1694–1778), under the pen name of Voltaire, the
great French man of letters whose *Candide* had just appeared. Smith met
him at Ferney and was his lifelong admirer.

Perpendas trutina, nec te quaesiveris extra.[16] A wise man's Kingdom is his own Breast: Or, if he ever looks farther, it will only be to the Judgement of a select few, who are free from Prejudices, and capable of examining his Work. Nothing indeed can be a stronger Presumption of Falshood than the Approbation of the Multitude; and Phocion, you know, always suspected himself of some Blunder, when he was attended with the Applauses of the Populace.

Supposing, therefore, that you have duely prepard yourself for the worst by all these Reflections; I proceed to tell you the melancholy News, that your Book has been very unfortunate: For the Public seem disposd to applaud it extremely. It was lookd for by the foolish People with some Impatience; and the Mob of Literati are beginning already to be very loud in its Praises. Three Bishops calld yesterday at Millar's Shop in order to buy Copies, and to ask Questions about the Author: The Bishop of Peterborough[17] said he had passd the Evening in a Company, where he heard it extolld above all Books in the World. You may conclude what Opinion true Philosophers will entertain of it, when these Retainers to Superstition praise it so highly. The Duke of Argyle is more decisive than he uses to be in its Favour: I suppose he either considers it as an Exotic, or thinks the Author will be serviceable to him in the Glasgow Elections. Lord Lyttleton says, that Robertson[18] and Smith and

---

[16] Persius, *Sat.* I, 5–7;

> ... non, si quid turbida Roma
> elevet, accedas examenque improbum in illa
> castiges trutina, nec te quaesiveris extra.

[If confused Rome makes light of anything, do not go up and correct the deceitful tongue in that balance of theirs, or look to anyone beside yourself.]

[17] Richard Terrick (1710–77), Bishop of Peterborough 1757–64, and of London 1764–77.

[18] William Robertson (1721–93), historian, Church statesman, and university administrator; had just published his *History of Scotland* (1759); to come were his *History of Charles V* (1769) and *History of America* (1771), also an unfinished *History of India* (1791). He was principal of Edinburgh University, from 1762, and Moderator of the General Assembly of the Church of Scotland, from 1763, for most of the remainder of his life.

Bower[19] are the Glories of English Literature. Oswald[20] protests he does not know whether he has reap'd more Instruction or Entertainment from it: But you may easily judge what Reliance can be put on his Judgement, who has been engagd all his Life in public Business and who never sees any Faults in his Friends. Millar exults and brags that two thirds of the Edition are already sold, and that he is now sure of Success. You see what a Son of the Earth that is, to value Books only by the Profit they bring him. In that View, I believe it may prove a very good Book.

Charles Townsend,[21] who passes for the cleverest Fellow in England, is so taken with the Performance, that he said to Oswald he wou'd put the Duke of Buccleugh under the Authors Care, and would endeavour to make it worth his while to accept of that Charge.[22] As soon as I heard this, I calld on him twice with a View of talking with him about the Matter, and of convincing him of the Propriety of sending that young Nobleman to Glasgow: For I could not hope, that he coud offer you any Terms, which woud tempt you to renounce your Professorship: But I missd him. Mr Townsend passes for being a little uncertain in his Resolutions; so perhaps you need not build much on this Sally.

In recompense for so many mortifying things, which nothing but Truth could have extorted from me, and which I coud easily have multiply'd to a greater Number; I doubt not but you are so good a Christian as to return good for evil and to flatter my Vanity, by telling me, that all the Godly in Scotland

---

[19] Archibald Bower (1686–1766) pamphleteer and author of a *History of the Popes* (1748–66); a protégé of Lyttleton's.

[20] James Oswald of Dunnikier.

[21] The Hon. Charles Townshend (1725–67) of Adderbury, Oxon.; statesman; his troubled personality is now believed to have been affected by an epileptic tendency; M.P. 1747–d.; Lord of Admiralty 1754; Treasurer of the Chamber 1756; Secretary-at-War 1761–2; President of the Board of Trade 1763; Paymaster-General 1765; Chancellor of the Exchequer 1766–d.; md. Lady Dalkeith, 1755, and became stepfather of her children: the later 3rd Duke of Buccleuch, the Hon. Hew Campbell Scott, and Lady Frances Scott.

[22] This came about in 1764–6, when Smith was made tutor of Henry Scott (1746–1812), 3rd Duke of Buccleuch, and, from 1810, 5th Duke of Queensberry. The Duke took no direct part in public life other than becoming the first President, 1783, of the Royal Society of Edinburgh. His extensive estates, however, gave him a considerable electoral interest.

abuse me for my Account of John Knox and the Reformation etc. I suppose you are glad to see my Paper end, and that I am obligd to conclude with

Your humble Servant
David Hume

LETTER FROM DAVID HUME*
28 July 1759

MS., RSE ii. 30; HL i. 311–14.

London, 28 July 1759

Dear Sir

Your Friend, Mr Wilson,[1] calld on me two or three days ago when I was abroad, and he left your Letter: I did not see him till to day. He seems a very modest, sensible, ingenious Man. Before I saw him, I spoke to A. Millar about him, and found him very much dispos'd to serve him. I proposd particularly to Mr Millar, that it was worthy of so eminent a Bookseller as he to make a compleat elegant Set of the Classics, which might set up his Name equal to the Alduses, Stevens, or Elzivirs; and that Mr Wilson was the properest Person in the World to assist him in such a Project. He confest to me, that he had sometimes thought of it; but that his great Difficulty was to find a Man of Letters, who cou'd correct the Press. I mentioned the Matter to Wilson, who said he had a Man of Letters in his Eye; one Lyon,[2] a nonjuring Clergyman at Glasgow. He is probably known to you, or at least may be so: I wou'd desire your Opinion of him.

Mr Wilson told me of his Machines, which seem very ingenious, and deserve much Encouragement. I shall soon see them.

I am very well acquainted with Bourke,[3] who was much

---

* From *Correspondence of Adam Smith*, edited by E. C. Mossner and Ian S. Ross, revised edition (Oxford, 1987), no. 36, pp. 42–4. The notes of the original editors have been retained.

[1] Alexander Wilson, M.D. (1714–86), educ. at St. Andrews, practiced medicine in London, then became a type-founder; appointed in that capacity to Glasgow University, 1748; Professor of Practical Astronomy, and Observer, Glasgow, 1760; awarded the gold medal of the Royal Society of Sciences, Copenhagen, 1772, for a dissertation on sun-spots. He founded the types for the Foulis Press, Glasgow, his Greek founts being unsurpassed.

[2] Revd. James Lyon.

[3] Edmund Burke: see his Letter 38, dated 10 Sept. 1759.

taken with your Book. He got your Direction from me with a
View of writing to you, and thanking you for your Present:
For I made it pass in your Name. I wonder he has not done
it: He is now in Ireland. I am not acquainted with Jennyns;[4]
but he spoke very highly of the Book to Oswald, who is his
Brother in the Board of Trade. Millar show'd me a few days
ago a Letter from Lord Fitzmaurice;[5] where he tells him, that
he had carryd over a few Copies to the Hague for Presents.
Mr Yorke[6] was much taken with it as well as several others
who had read it.

I am told that you are preparing a new Edition,[7] and propose
to make some Additions and Alterations, in order to obviate
Objections. I shall use the Freedom to propose one, which, if
it appears to be of any Weight, you may have in your Eye. I
wish you had more particularly and fully prov'd, that all kinds
of Sympathy are necessarily Agreeable. This is the Hinge of
your System, and yet you only mention the Matter cursorily
in p. 20. Now it would appear that there is a disagreeable
Sympathy, as well as an agreeable: And indeed, as the Sympathetic Passion is a reflex Image of the principal, it must partake
of its Qualities, and be painful where that is so. Indeed, *when
we converse with a man with whom we can entirely sympathize*, that is, where there is a warm and intimate Friendship,
the cordial openness of such a commerce overpowers the Pain
of a disagreeable Sympathy, and renders the whole Movement
agreeable. But in ordinary Cases, this cannot have place. An
ill-humord Fellow; a man tir'd and disgusted with every thing,
always *ennuié*; sickly, complaining, embarass'd; such a one
throws an evident Damp on Company, which I suppose wou'd
be accounted for by Sympathy; and yet is disagreeable.

It is always thought a difficult Problem to account for the
Pleasure, receivd from the Tears and Grief and Sympathy of
Tragedy; which woud not be the Case, if all Sympathy was
agreeable. An Hospital woud be a more entertaining Place
than a Ball. I am afraid that in p. 99 and 111 this Proposition

---

4   Soame Jenyns.

5   See Letter 27, n. 1.

6   ?Hon. Charles Yorke.

7   TMS ed. 2, 1761: for Smith's revisions, see Letter 40 addressed to Gilbert
Elliot, dated 10 Oct. 1759. See page 12 of this anthology.

has escapd you, or rather is interwove with your Reasonings in that place. You say expressly, *it is painful to go along with Grief and we always enter into it with Reluctance.* It will probably be requisite for you to modify or explain this Sentiment, and reconcile it to your System.

My Dear Mr Smith; You must not be so much engross'd with your own Book, as never to mention mine.[8] The Whigs, I am told, are anew in a Rage against me; tho' they know not how to vent themselves: For they are constrain'd to allow all my Facts. You have probably seen Hurd's Abuse of me.[9] He is of the Warburtonian School and consequently very insolent and very scurrilous; but I shall never reply a word to him. If my past Writings do not sufficiently prove me to be no Jacobite, ten Volumes in folio never would.

I signed yesterday an Agreement with Mr Millar; where I mention that I proposed to write the History of England from the Beginning till the Accession of Henry the VII; and he engages to give me 1400 Pounds for the Copy. This is the first previous Agreement ever I made with a Bookseller. I shall execute this Work at Leizure, without fatiguing myself by such ardent Application as I have hitherto employd. It is chiefly as a Resource against Idleness, that I shall undertake this Work: For as to Money, I have enough: And as to Reputation, what I have wrote already will be sufficient, if it be good: If not, it is not likely I shall now write better. I found it impracticable (at least fancy'd so) to write the History since the Revolution. I am in doubt whether I shall stay here and execute the Work; or return to Scotland, and only come up here to consult the Manuscripts. I have several Inducements on both Sides. Scotland suits my Fortune best, and is the Seat of my principal Friendships; but it is too narrow a Place for me, and it mortifies

---

[8] *History of England: The Tudors,* 2 vols. 1759.

[9] See the postscript to Richard Hurd's *Moral and Political Dialogues,* ed. 1, 1759: 'For having undertaken to conjure up the spirit of absolute power, he [Hume] judged it necessary to the charm, to reverse the order of things, and to evoke this frightful spectre by writing (as witches use to say their prayers) *backwards.* . . . Accordingly, while one half of his pains is laid out in exposing the absurdities of *reformed religion,* the other half is suitably employed in discrediting the cause of *civil liberty.*' Later eds. omitted the postscript and presented a footnote in which Hurd gave some qualified praise to the first part of Hume's History (*Julius Caesar to Henry VII*) as distinguished from the other parts.

me that I sometimes hurt my Friends. Pray write me your Judgement soon. Are the Bigots much in Arms on account of this last Volume? Robertson's Book[10] has great Merit; but it was visible that he profited here by the Animosity against me. I suppose the Case was the same with you. I am

Dear Smith
Yours sincerely
David Hume.

[10] William Robertson's *History of Scotland* (1759).

SMITH'S REPLY TO HUME*

It has been objected to me that as I found the sentiment of approbation, which is always agreeable, upon sympathy, it is inconsistent with my system to admit any disagreeable sympathy. I answer, that in the sentiment of approbation there are two things to be taken notice of; first, the sympathetic passion of the spectator; and, secondly, the emotion which arises from his observing the perfect coincidence between this sympathetic passion in himself, and the original passion in the person principally concerned. This last emotion, in which the sentiment of approbation properly consists, is always agreeable and delightful. The other may either be agreeable or disagreeable, according to the nature of the original passion, whose features it must always, in some measure, retain.

* Footnote added to the 2nd edition of *The Theory of Moral Sentiments* (London, 1761), pt I, sect. iii, chap. 1, para. 9.

LETTER FROM EDMUND BURKE*
10 September 1759

MS., James M. and Marie-Louise Osborn Collection, Yale University Library; *Burke Corr.* i. 129–30.

Wimple Street, Cavendish Square,

Sir   Westminster, 10 Sept. 1759

I am quite ashamed that the first Letter I have the honour of writing to you should be an apology for my conduct. It ought to be entirely taken up with my thanks to you for the satisfaction I received from your very agreeable and instructive work, but I cannot do that pleasing act of Justice without apologising at the same time for not having done it much earlier. When I received the Theory of Moral Sentiments from Mr Hume, I ran through it with great eagerness; I was immediately after hurried out of Town, and involved ever since in a Variety of troublesome affairs.[1] My resolution was to defer my acknowledgements until I had read your book with proper care and attention; to do otherwise with so well studied a piece would be to treat it with great injustice. It was indeed an attention extremely well bestowed and abundantly repaid. I am not only pleased with the ingenuity of your Theory; I am convinced of its solidity and Truth; and I do not know that it ever cost me less trouble to admit so many things to which I had been a stranger before.[2] I have ever thought that the old

---

* From *Correspondence of Adam Smith*, edited by E. C. Mossner and Ian S. Ross, revised edition (Oxford, 1987), no. 38, pp. 46–7. The notes of the original editors have been retained.

[1] See Letter 36 from Hume, dated 28 July 1759, reproduced on page 12. Hume thought Burke was in Ireland at this time but there is no other evidence of this.

[2] Burke's review of the book in the *Annual Register* for 1759 praises particularly Smith's originality: 'this author has struck out a new, and at the same time a perfectly natural road of speculation on this subject . . . We conceive , that here the theory is in all its essential parts just, and founded on truth and nature. The author seeks for the foundation of the just, the fit, the proper, the decent, in our most common and most allowed passions; and making approbation and disapprobation the tests of virtue and vice,

Systems of morality were too contracted and that this Science could never stand well upon any narrower Basis than the whole of Human Nature. All the writers who have treated this Subject before you were like those Gothic Architects who were fond of turning great Vaults upon a single slender Pillar; There is art in this, and there is a degree of ingenuity without doubt; but it is not sensible, and it cannot long be pleasing. A theory like yours founded on the Nature of man, which is always the same, will last, when those that are founded on his opinions, which are always changing, will and must be forgotten. I own I am particularly pleased with those easy and happy illustrations from common Life and manners in which your work abounds more than any other that I know by far. They are indeed the fittest to explain those natural movements of the mind with which every Science relating to our Nature ought to begin. But one sees, that nothing is less used, than what lies directly in our way. Philosophers therefore very frequently miss a thousand things that might be of infinite advantage, though the rude Swain treads daily on them with his clouted Shoon.[3] It seems to require that infantine simplicity which despises nothing, to make a good Philosopher, as well as to make a good Christian. Besides so much powerful reasoning as your Book contains, there is so much elegant Painting of the manners and passions, that it is highly valuable even on that account. The stile is every where lively and elegant, and what is, I think equally important in a work of that kind, it is well varied; it is often sublime too, particularly in that fine Picture of the Stoic Philosophy towards the end of your first part which is dressed out in all the grandeur and Pomp that becomes that magnificent delusion. I have mentioned something of what affected me as Beauties in your work. I will take the Liberty to mention too what appeared to me as a sort of Fault. You are in some few Places, what Mr Locke is in most of his writings, rather a little too diffuse. This is however a fault of the generous kind, and infinitely preferable to the dry sterile

and shewing that those are founded on sympathy, he raises from this simple truth, one of the most beautiful fabrics of moral theory, that has perhaps ever appeared.'

[3] *Comus*, II. 634–5. Burke uses the quotation in a similar way in his *Speech on Conciliation with the Colonies* (*Works*, Bohn edn. i. 489).

manner, which those of dull imaginations are apt to fall into. To another I should apologise for a freedom of this Nature.

My delay on this occasion may I am afraid make it improper for me to ask any favour from you. But there is one, I have too much at heart not to sacrifice any propriety to attain it. It is, that whenever you come to Town, I may have the honour of being made personally known to you.[4] I shall take the Liberty of putting this office on our friend Mr. Hume who has already so much obliged me by giving me your Book. I am Sir with the truest esteem for your Work and your Character

your most obliged and
obedient Servant
Edm. Burke.

---

[4] Smith and Burke do not appear to have met until 1777.

LETTER FROM WILLIAM ROBERTSON*
14 June [1759]

Address: To Mr Adam Smith, Professor of Moral Philosophy, Glasgow
MS., GUL Gen. 1035/139; Scott 238–9.

Edinburgh, 14 June [1759]

My Dear Sir

Our friend John Home arrived here from London two days ago. Tho' I dare say you have heard of the good reception of the *Theory* from [m]any different people, I must acquaint you with the intelligence Home brings. He assures me that it is in the hands of all persons of the best fashion; that it meets with great approbation both on account of the matter and stile; and that it is impossible for any book on so serious a subject to be received in a more gracious manner. It comforts the English a good deal to hear that you were bred at Oxford, they claim some part of you on that account. Home joins with me in insisting that your next work shall be on some subject less abstruse. I still wish you would think on the History of Philosophy.[1] I write this in great haste, as Johnstone[2] is waiting me that we may go to walk. When shall we see you in town. I ever am

Yours most faithfully
William Robertson

---

* From *Correspondence of Adam Smith*, edited by E. C. Mossner and Ian S. Ross, revised edition (Oxford, 1987), no. 34, p. 40. The notes of the original editors have been retained.

[1] In the 1750s, Smith read to the Literary Club of Glasgow papers on 'Taste, Composition and the History of Philosophy' which he had previously delivered while a lecturer on rhetoric in Edinburgh (R. Duncan, *Notes and Documents Illustrative of the Literary History of Glasgow* (Maitland Club, Glasgow, 1831, 16). See EPS for 'The History of Ancient Logics and Metaphysics', 'The History of Astronomy', and 'The History of the Ancient Physics', the extant parts of the work Robertson desired.

[2] William Johnstone.

LETTER FROM ADAM SMITH TO GILBERT ELLIOT*
10 October 1759

MS., NLS Minto Collection; unpubl.

Glasgow, 10 Oct. 1759

Dear Sir

I know not what apology to make for having so long delayed
to write to you. I thought myselfe infinitely obliged to you for
the objection which you made to a Part of my system,[1] and
immediately began to write a philosophical letter to you to
show that the consequence which you seemed to fear would
follow from it, had no necessary connection with it. Upon
second thoughts, however, I thought it would be better to alter
the 2d Section of the 3d part of my book[2] so as to obviate
that objection and to send you this alteration. This cost me
more time and thought than you could well imagine the composition of three sheets of Paper would stand me; for nothing
is more difficult than to insert something into the middle of
what is already composed and to connect it cleverly at both
ends. Before you read it I will begg of you to read over the
first paragraphs of the second Section of the third part, then
pass over the three next paragraphs, and read the sixth and

---

* From *Correspondence of Adam Smith*, edited by E. C. Mossner and Ian S.
Ross, revised edition (Oxford, 1987), no. 40, pp. 48–57. The notes of the
original editors have been retained.

[1] Elliot had philosophical interests, e.g. Hume assigned him in 1751 the task
of strengthening the part of Cleanthes, the empirical theist, in *Dialogues
Concerning Natural Religion* (HL i. 150–8). Professor David Raphael, communicates the following note: 'From the evidence of this letter and its
enclosure, we can infer the general drift of Elliot's objection: if moral
judgement on our own actions were a reflection of the approval and disapproval of society, then it would be impossible for a man to form a moral
judgement which he knows is contrary to popular opinion. The second and
longer of the amendments which Smith enclosed with this letter answers the
objection by developing Smith's theory of the impartial spectator.'

2 TMS ed. 1, April 1759: Part III, Section ii, of that edition is entitled 'In
what manner our own judgments refer to what ought to be the judgment
of others: And of the origin of general rules'.

seventh till you come to the paragraph at the bottom of page 260 which begins with the word, *Unfortunately*; instead of that paragraph insert the second of those additions which you will receive by this Post under another cover. I will be greatly obliged to you if you will send me your opinion of it. You will observe that it is intended both to confirm my Doctrine that our judgements concerning our own conduct have always a reference to the sentiments of some other being, and to shew that, notwithstanding this, real magnanimity and conscious virtue can support itselfe under the disapprobation of all mankind. I should be glad to know how far you think I have made out both; if you do not think it quite satisfactory I can make it still a great deal plainer, by a great number of new illustrations. I would likewise beg of you to read what I say upon Mandevilles system and then consider whether upon the whole I do not make Virtue sufficiently independent of popular opinion.

I think, I have made it sufficiently plain that our judgements concerning the conduct of others are founded in Sympathy. But it would seem very odd if we judged of our own conduct by one principle and of that of other men by another.

You will find too in the Papers I have sent you an answer to an objection of D. Humes.[3] I think I have entirely discomfitted him.

I am now about publishing a new edition of my Book[4] and would be greatly obliged to you for any criticisms you could make upon it. If you see Colonel Clerk I should be glad to know his opinion and would wish you to communicate the papers I have sent you to him.[5] I am fully sensible how much

---

[3] See Letter 36 from Hume, dated 28 July 1759, reproduced on page 7: 'I wish you had more particularly and fully prov'd, that all kinds of Sympathy are necessarily Agreeable.' For Smith's answer, see the TMS note for insertion below (Glasgow TMS, I.iii.1.9).

[4] TMS ed. 2, in print by 30 Dec. 1760: see Letter 54 addressed to Strahan on that date. The ed. is dated 1761.

[5] Robert Clerk (?1724–97), educ. Edinburgh University, *c.* 1737–40; entered army, Col. 1762, Maj. Gen. 1772, Lt. Gen. 1793. He became a protégé of Lord Shelburne: Carlyle of Inveresk (473) called him 'truly the greatest siccatore in the world'; and Hume, 'that Meteor' (NHL 87). Adam Ferguson represented Clerk as opposed to Smith's doctrine of sympathy: see *Journal of the History of Ideas* xxi (1960) 222–32.

trouble I am giving you by all this. I know, however, your friendship will excuse it.

Boscawens Victory gave everybody here the greatest satisfaction.[6] We look upon it as a preventative of the threatened invasion, about the event of which few people seem very anxious. I thought myself equally honoured and obliged by the letter you was so good as to write to me upon it.[7]

The only news here relates to elections. Mr. Crawfurd has lost the town of Air. Sir Adam Ferguson and Lord Loudoun have got the better of him there. Your friend Mr. Muir of Caldwell is in some danger from Mr. Cunningham of Craigen[d]s. The head court of the Shire was held yesterday in which everything was carried for Mr. Muir, and all the new votes, that were made to oppose him, rejected. The decision of that affair will depend, I hear, on the Duke of Argylle.[8] I ever am

---

[6] In 1758–9 the French collected troops and flat-bottomed boats for an invasion of Britain. When de la Clue ventured out of Toulon with his fleet he was caught off Lagos and defeated on 18 August 1759 by Admiral Hon. Edward Boscawen (1711–61), known as Wry-necked Dick or Old Dreadnought to his sailors. In November Conflans was defeated by Hawke at Quiberon Bay, which finally ended the invasion threat.

[7] Not traced: perhaps the letter in which Elliot advanced his 'objection' to TMS: dated, very likely, early in September, as it would take two to three weeks for news of Boscawen's victory to reach London.

[8] Parliamentary affairs at this date in some areas of Scotland were at a critical phase. Management had been firmly in the hands of the 3rd Duke of Argyll, to whom Elliot owed his seat in Selkirkshire, but Elliot also had links with Bute whose star was rising in view of his influence over the Prince of Wales and the imminence of George II's death. The manager of Bute's affairs in Scotland was William Mure of Caldwell (1718–76), M.P. for Renfrewshire 1742–61. In 1759 Mure supported as candidate for Ayr burghs, Patrick Craufurd of Auchenames (c. 1704–78), thus opposing the wishes of Argyll and John Campbell, 4th Earl of Loudoun (1705–82), who had been superseded the year before as Commander-in-Chief in America. In consequence, Mure was opposed in Renfrewshire by the Earl of Glencairn, who supported as candidate William Cuninghame of Craigends, son of a former member. At the Michaelmas head court – when the list of voters for Renfrewshire was established on the basis of property ownership – the roll stood as follows: 13 freeholders for Mure; 6 for Cuninghame; and 7 neutral, waiting for Argyll's instructions. Mure wrote to Bute on 16 Oct.: 'I had the good fortune to out-number my opponents by more than two to one, so we kept off the roll the whole of Glencairn's new creations and are preparing to stand a law suit in defence of our proceedings' (Bute MSS., HP i.493). In 1760 Argyll backed Mure, then a place was found for him as a Baron of the Exchequer Court of Scotland, and Craufurd was forced on the county. In Ayr in 1759 Argyll supported Sir Adam Fergusson (1733–1812), son of Lord Kilkerran, but when Bute came to power in 1760, Argyll compromised

Dear Sir

Your most obliged and
most obedient humble Servt
Adam Smith

[MS. Draft Amendments for Edition 2 of TMS, 1761][9]

Page 99. Line 12.[10] After the following Sentence: *But it is painful to go along with grief, and we always enter into it with reluctance:*
Make a reference and insert the following note at the bottom of the page.

Note.

It has been objected to me that as I found the Sentiment of Approbation, which is always agreable, upon Sympathy, it is inconsistent with my System to allow of any disagreeable Sympathy. I answer that in the sentiment of approbation, there are two things to be taken notice of; first, the Sympathetic passion of the Spectator; and, secondly, the emotion which arises from his observing the perfect coincidence between this sympathetic passion in himself and the original passion in the person principally concerned. This last emotion, in which the Sentiment of approbation properly Consists, is always agre-

---

with him and sought to get Fergusson to withdraw. The Ayr council were angered by the Argyll-Bute deal and refused to replace Fergusson, but in 1761 the election went to Alexander Wedderburn, a supporter of Bute.

[9] The draft amendments are in the hand of the amanuensis who produced the MS. of the 'Early Draft of the *Wealth of Nations*' (Scott 386–7). The same hand is found in GUL University Records, vol. 30, pp. 166–84, Minutes of University Meeting of 13 Aug. 1762, 'Report of the Committee on the Rector's and Principal's Powers' (see Scott 203–5, for the text). The document accompanying the letter of 10 Oct. 1759 is presumably a copy of a draft prepared for the printer. The text of this was subsequently altered before publication; see notes 2 and 3. The draft amendments are written on three double folio sheets, the kind Smith customarily used. The water-mark is the same as that of the fragment on Justice (GUL, MS., Gen. 1035/227).

[10] The first draft amendment relates to a paragraph which in edition 1 was Part I, Section iv, Chapter 1, c 9. In ed. 2 this became Part I, Section iii, Chapter 1, c 9, and that is how it remained in ed. 6 (Glasgow edn., I.iii.1.9). In ed. 2 the footnote was added pretty well as in the draft amendment, but with slight revision. The final sentence of the note was deleted in ed. 6, 1790.

able and delightful. The other may either be agreable or disagreable, according to the nature of the original passion, whose features it must always, in some measure, retain. Two Sounds, I suppose, may, each of them taken singly, be austere, and yet, if they are perfect concords, the perception of this harmony and coincidence may be agreable.

page 260 At the bottom.[11]

Instead of the erased passage in this and the following page insert what follows into the Text.

When I endeavour to examine my own conduct, when I endeavour to pass sentence upon it and either to approve or condemn it, it is evident that, in all such cases, I divide myself, as it were, into two persons, and that I, the examiner and Judge, represent a different character from that other I, the person whose conduct is examined into and judged of. The first is the Spectator whose sentiments with regard to my own conduct I endeavour to enter into, by placing myself in his Situation, and by considering how it would appear to me when seen from that particular point of view. The second is the Agent, the person whom I properly call myself, and of whose conduct, under the Character of a Spectator, I was endeavouring to form some oppinion. The first is the Judge; the

---

[11] Like the first draft amendment, this one received a slight revision here and there, but in addition it received very ample supplementation towards the end when it was actually printed in the second edition. Smith in his letter asks Elliot to pass over paragraphs 3–5 in Part III, Section ii. Two of these deleted paragraphs are in fact reproduced, with slight revision, in the second and third paragraphs of the amendment. In the sixth edition, and consequently in the Glasgow edition, the first two paragraphs of the amendment are printed at III.1.6–7. The third paragraph of the amendment was deleted in ed. 6. Paragraphs 4–7 of the amendment ('The Great Judge . . . disadvantageous Judgement') were replaced in ed. 6, at III.1. cc 31–2, by a revised and condensed statement of their thought. The 8th and 9th paragraphs of the amendment, and part of the 10th paragraph ('It is only . . . inequality of our sentiments') are at III.3. cc 1–3. The remainder of the 10th paragraph of the amendment was amplified in ed. 2, and the amplification appears in ed. 6 at III.3. cc 4–5, 7–9, 11. The 11th paragraph of the amendment was amplified in ed. 2, but the amplification was omitted in ed. 6, which has itself an extensive addition in this part of the book. The 12th and last paragraph of the amendment, which was of course in ed. 1, is to be found in the 6th (Glasgow edn., III.4.2).

Second, the pannel. But that the Judge should, in every respect, be the same with the pannel, is as impossible, as that the cause should, in every respect, be the same with the effect.

To be amiable and to be meritorious, that is, to deserve Love and to deserve reward, are the great Characters of virtue, and to be odious and punishable, of vice. But all these characters have an immediate reference to the sentiments of others. Virtue is not said to be amiable or to be meritorious, because it is the object of its own Love or of its own gratitude; but because it excites those sentiments in other men. The consciousness that it is the object of such favourable regards is the source of that inward tranquillity and self satisfaction with which it is naturally attended, as the Suspicion of the contrary gives occasion to the torments of vice. What so great happiness as to be beloved, and to know that we deserve to be beloved? What so great misery as to be hated, and to know that we deserve to be hated?

Man is considered as a moral, because he is regarded as an accountable being. But an Accountable being, as the word expresses, is a being that must give an Account of its actions to some other, and that, consequently, must regulate them according to the good liking of this other. Man is accountable to God and his fellow creatures. But tho' he is, no doubt, principally accountable to God, in the order of time, he must necessarily conceive himself as accountable to his fellow creatures, before he can form any idea of the Deity, or of the rules by which that Divine Being will judge of his conduct. A Child, surely, conceives itself as accountable to its parents, and is elevated or cast down by the thought of their merited approbation or disapprobation, long before it forms any idea of its Accountableness to the Deity, or of the rules by which that Divine being will judge of its conduct.

The Great Judge of the World, has, for the wisest reasons, thought proper to interpose, between the weak eye of human reason and the throne of his eternal justice, a degree of obscurity and darkness which, tho it does not entirely cover that great tribunal from the view of mankind, yet renders the impression of it faint and feeble in comparison of what might be expected from the grandeur and importance of so mighty an object. If those infinite rewards and punishments, which the almighty has prepared for those who obey or transgress his will, were perceived as distinctly as we foresee the frivolous and temporary retaliations which we may expect from one another, the weakness of human nature, astonished at the immensity of objects so little fitted to its comprehension, could no longer attend to the little affairs of this world; and it is absolutely impossible that the business of society could have been carried on, if, in this respect, there had been a fuller revelation of the intentions of providence than that which has already been made. That men, however, might never be without a rule to direct their conduct by, nor without a judge whose authority should enforce its observation, the author of nature has made man the immediate judge of mankind, and has, in this respect, as in many others, created him after his own image, and appointed him his vicegerent upon earth to Superintend the behaviour of his brethren. They are taught by Nature to acknowledge that power and jurisdiction which has thus been confered upon him, and to tremble or exult according as they imagine that they have either merited his Censure or deserved his Applause.

But whatever may be the authority of this inferior tribunal, which is continually before their eyes, if at any time it should decide contrary to these rules and principles which nature has established for regulating its Judgements, men appeal from this unjust decision, and call upon a Superior tribunal established in their own minds, to redress the unjustice of this weak or partial judgement.

There are certain principles established by nature for governing our judgements concerning the conduct of those we live with. As long as we decide according to those principles, and neither applaud nor condemn any thing which nature has not rendered the proper object of Applause or condemnation, nor any further than she has rendered them such, the person, concerning whom we form these Judgements must himself necessarily approve of them. When he puts himself into our situation, he cannot avoid entering into those views of his own conduct which, he feels, must naturally occur to us, and he is obliged to Consider it himself in the very same light in which we represent it. Our sentiments, therefore, must necessarily produce their full effect upon him, and he cannot faill to conceive all the triumph of self approbation from what appears to him such merited applause, as well as all the horrors of Shame from what, he is sensible, is such deserved condemnation. But it is otherwise if we have either applauded or condemned him, contrary to those principles and rules which nature has established for the direction of our judgements concerning every thing of this kind. If we have either applauded or Condemned him for what, when he puts himself in our Situation, does not appear to him to be the object either of applause or Condemnation; as, in this case, he cannot enter into our Sentiments, if he has any constancy or firmness, he is little affected by them, and can neither be elevated by the favourable nor mortified by the unfavourable decision. The applause of the whole world will avail but little if our own conscience condemns us; and the disapprobation of all mankind is not capable of oppressing us when we are absolved by the tribunal within our own breast, and when our own mind tells us that mankind are in the wrong.

But tho this tribunal within the breast be thus the supreme arbiter of all our actions, tho' it can reverse the decisions of all mankind with regard to our character and Conduct, tho it can mortify us amidst the Applauses and Support us under the Censure of the world, yet if we enquire into the origin of its institution, its jurisdiction, we shall find, is in a great measure derived from the authority of that very tribunal, whose decisions it so often and so justly reverses. When we first come into the world, being desireous to please those we live with, we are accustomed to Consider what behaviour is likely to be agreeable to every person we converse with, to our parents, to our masters, to our companions. We address ourselves to individuals, and for some time fondly pursue the impossible and absurd project of rendering ourselves universally agreable, and of gaining the good will and approbation of every body. We soon Learn, however, from experience, that this universal approbation is altogether unattainable. As soon as we come to have more important interests to manage, we find, that by pleasing one man we almost certainly disoblige another, and that by humouring an individual, we may often irritate a whole people. The fairest and most equitable conduct must frequently obstruct the interests or thwart the inclinations of particular persons, who will seldome have candour enough to enter into the propriety of our motives, or to see that our conduct, how disagreable soever to them, is perfectly suitable to our situation. We soon learn, therefore, to sett up in our own minds a judge between ourselves and those we live with. We conceive ourselves as acting in the presence of a person

quite candid and equitable, of one who has no particular
relation, either to ourselves, or to those whose interests are
affected by our conduct; who is neither father, nor Brother,
nor friend, either to them, or to us; but is meerly a man in
general, an impartial Spectator who considers our conduct
with the same indifference with which we regard that of other
people. If when we place ourselves in the Situation of such a
person, our own actions appear to us under an agreable aspect,
if we feel that such a Spectator cannot avoid entering into all
the motives which influenced us, whatever may be the judgements of the world, we cannot help being pleased with our
own behaviour, and regarding ourselves, in spite of the Censure
of our companions, as the just and proper objects of approbation. On the contrary, if the man within condemns us, the
loudest acclamations of mankind appear but as the noise of
ignorance and folly, and whenever we assume the Character
of this impartial judge, we cannot avoid viewing our own
actions with his distaste and dissatisfaction. The weak, the
vain and the frivolous, indeed, may be mortified by the most
groundless Censure or elated by the most absurd applause.
Such persons are not accustomed to consult the judge within
concerning the oppinion which they ought to form of their
own conduct. This inmate of the breast, this abstract man, the
representative of mankind and Substitute of the Deity, whom
nature has appointed the Supreme arbiter of all their actions
is seldome appealed to by them. They are contented with the
decision of the inferior tribunal. The approbation of their
companions, of the particular persons whom they have lived
and conversed with, has generally been the ultimate object of
all their wishes. If they Succeed in this their Joy is compleat;
and if they faill they are entirely disappointed. They never
think of appealing to the Superior court. They have Seldome
enquired after its decisions and are altogether unacquainted
with the rules and forms of its procedure. When the world
injures them, therefore, they are incapable of doing themselves
Justice and are in consequence necessarily the Slaves of the
world. But it is otherwise with the man who has, upon all
occasions, been accustomed to have recourse to the judge
within and to consider, not what the world approves or disapproves of, but what appears to this impartial Spectator the
natural and proper object of approbation and disapprobation.
The judgement of this supreme arbiter of his conduct is the

applause which he has been accustomed principally to court, is the Censure which he has been accustomed principally to fear. Compared with this final decision, the sentiments of all mankind, tho' not altogether indifferent, appear to be but of small moment; and he is incapable of being either much elivated by their favourable, or greatly depressed by their most disadvantageous Judgement.

It is only by consulting this judge within that we can see whatever relates to ourselves in its proper shape and dimensions, or that we can make any proper comparison between our own interests and those of other men.

As to the eye of the body objects appear great or small, not so much according to their real dimensions, as according to the nearness or distance of their situation; so do they likewise to, what may be called, the natural eye of the mind: and we remedy the defects of both these organs pretty much in the same manner. In my present situation an immense landscape of Lawns and woods and distant mountains, seems to do no more than cover the little window which I write by, and to be out of all proportion less than the chamber in which I am sitting. I can form a just comparison between those great objects and the little objects around me, in no other way, than by transporting myself, at least in fancy, to a different station, from whence I can survey both at nearly equal distances, and thereby form some judgement of their real proportions. Habit and experience have taught me to do this so easily and so readily, that I am scarce sensible that I do it; and a man must be, in some measure, acquainted with the philosophy of vision, before he can be thoroughly convinced, how little those distant objects would appear to the eye, if the imagination, from a knowledge of their real magnitudes, did not swell and dilate them.

In the same manner to the selfish and original passions of human nature, the loss or gain of a very small interest of our own, appears to be of vastly more importance, excites a much more passionate joy or sorrow, a much more ardent desire or aversion, than the greatest concern of another with whom we have no particular connection. His interests as long as they are surveyed from this station, can never be put into the ballance with our own, can never restrain us from doing whatever may tend to promote our own, how ruinous soever to him. Before we can make any proper comparison of those opposite interests we must change our position. We must view them, neither from our own place, nor yet from his, neither with our own eyes nor yet with his, but from the place and with the eyes of a third person, who has no particular connection with either and who judges with impartiality between us. This is the only station from which both can be seen at equal distances, or from which any proper comparison can be made between them. Here too habit and experience have taught us to assume this station so easily and so readily that we are scarce sensible that we assume it; and it requires, in this case too, some degree of reflection and even of philosophy to convince us, how little interest we should take in the greatest concerns of our neighbour, how little we should be affected by whatever relates to him, if the sense of propriety and justice did not correct the other wise natural inequality of our sentiments. It is from this station only that we can see the propriety of generosity and the deformity of injustice; the propriety of resigning the greatest interests of our own for the yet more important interests of others, and the deformity of doing the smallest injury to another in order to obtain the greatest benefite to ourselves. The real littleness of ourselves and of whatever relates to ourselves can be seen from this Station only; and it is here only that we can learn the great lesson of Stoical magnanimity and firmness, to be no more affected by what befalls ourselves than by what befalls our neighbour, or, what comes to the same thing, than our neighbour is capable of being affected by what befalls us. 'When our neighbour, says Epictetus, loses his wife or his son, there is nobody who is not sensible that this is a human calamity, a natural event altogether according to the ordinary course of things. But, when the same thing happens to ourselves, then we cry out, as if we had suffered the most dreadful misfortune. We ought, however, to remember how we were affected when this accident happened to another, and such as we were in his case such ought we to be in our own.'

It is not upon all occasions, however, that we are capable of judging with this perfect impartiality between ourselves and others. Even the judge within is often in danger of being corrupted by the violence and injustice of our selfish passions, and is often induced to make a report very different from what the real circumstances of the case are capable of authorizing.

There are two different occasions upon which we examine our conduct, and endeavour to view it in the light in which the impartial spectator would view it. First, when we are about to act; and secondly &c. continue as in page 261.

DIARY OF GEORGE RIDPATH*
29 September–11 October 1759

Saturday, September 29th. – Shaved after dinner and rode to
Eccles, where I found Mrs. Dysart up and a good deal better,
but still in warm keeping. Got Smith's *Theory of Moral Senti-*
ments from Matthew, of which I read a little in the evening,
but was more inclined to doze.

Sunday, September 30th. – Lectured on Acts xxiv. 17–fin.
Preached on Jerem. ix. 23, 24. Gave over preaching in the
forenoon.

Munday, October 1st. – Saw sick at Home a.m. W. Dickson's
wife and her little niecie here in the afternoon. Read in the
evening about a fourth part of Smith's *Theory.* Got letter from
Richard Edgar inviting me to the burial of his brother Andrew
who died on Sabbath morning.

Tuesday, October 2nd. – Set out for Eymouth a little after
8. Got to Edrom betwixt 10 and 11. Thought Will would have
been gone before me, but had him to wait for. Eat some dinner
in Adam Ridpath's, where Will seems to be rightly enough
situated. Spoke about some things he wanted, and some things
proper to be done to the room. Adam having been also invited
to the burial, we all set out together and got to Eymouth
betwixt 2 and 3. A great many people at the burial. Drank
some wine in Paton's with Dr. Balderstone, W. Hall, J. Stanton,
etc. Supped and lay all night in Mrs. Edgar's. Mr. Hall lost his
election on Saturday by 16 votes. Hodgson had got a great
start of him.

Wednesday, October 3rd. – Breakfasted with Mrs. Crow,
and rode afterwards to Berwick with Philip. Dined in Mr.
Waite's, and was nowhere else. Set out after 3 and got here
betwixt 7 and 8. Look'd out for something for to-morrow at
Ednam.

Friday, October 5th. – Went to Kelso to dine with Mr. Lundy,
where was also Robert Turnbull. The Presbytery had appointed
us, together with Mr. Pollock, to wait on W. Ramsay about

* From *Diary of George Ridpath, 1755–1761* (Edinburgh, 1922), pp. 273–6.

the affair of Robert Turnbull's reparations, which the Clerk is still refractory in executing. We went over to Waldie's to him in the afternoon, and after some little prequeerings, prevailed with him to consent to the things being done. Drank tea in Mr. Lundy's and came home betwixt 7 and 8.

Saturday, October 6th. – Mild day. Attended at Edrom, where Messrs. Turnbull and Dysart preached. Walked to and again with Nancy. Will went to Edrom after dinner. Had a letter from Philip in the evening, in which he informs me that he has a letter from a man at Greenock informing him that Mr. Home of St. Kitts has consigned to him a tierce of sugar to be sold for Philip's use, which accordingly he is to sell, and remit the money. A tierce is only $\frac{2}{3}$ of a hogshead. How so small a matter should be sent, when so much is due, is somewhat strange. But as the Fleet from the Islands is in the Channel it is probable the thing will be soon explained by a letter from Home himself.

Tuesday, October 9th. – Tongue and adjacent part of the throat uneasy in swallowing, spitting, etc. Kept almost wholly within doors and read without interruption Smith's *Theory*. Got to the end of it and went over again with more attention than before about 100 pages in the beginning. At night revised some of the *Review*. Got from Philip in the morning the good news of his getting a letter at last from Home with two bills enclosed, one on Glasgow for £100 and one on London for £10, 10s. The tierce of sugar sent to Greenock was part of the cargo he received from Bridgewater, but being somewhat damaged he could not dispose of it at St. Kitts. This is a most happy event to Philip and a just cause of thankfulness to us all.

Wednesday, October 10th. – Read Smith most of the day; also the Edinburgh newspapers. In the evening read in the 6th Volume of Dodsley's *Miscellanies* which Nancy has pickt up somewhere, a very good translation of Cebes's[1] *Table* by Scott, also some other things. Tongue growing better by abstemiousness, water and warmth.

Thursday, October 11th. – Read over a good deal more of Smith's *Theory of Moral Sentiments* and looked over the rest. The work shows him to be a man of knowledge and of genius

---

[1] Cebes, a Theban, disciple of Socrates and the reputed author of the *Pinax* or 'votive tablet,' a philosophical dialogue.

too, but yet I can by no means join in the applauses I have heard bestowed on it. What is new in it is perhaps of no great moment in itself, and is neither distinctly explained nor clearly established. An extravagant turn to declaim and embellish leads him quite astray from that study of accuracy, precision, and clearness that is so essentially necessary to the delivering of any theory, especially a new one; and his indulging of this humour for playing everywhere the orator, tho' his oratorical talents are far from being extraordinary, has made him spin out to the tedious length of 400 pages what in my opinion might be delivered as fully and with far more energy and perspicuity in 20. What can this arise from but the man's being used all his life to declaim to boys and not attending to the distinction necessary to be made betwixt a circle of *them* as auditors and a world of cool and reasonable men as readers? The most valuable part of the work, tho' not altogether free from the fault taken notice of, is the account given in the end of the different systems of Moral Philosophy, Ancient and Modern. Read some more things in Dodsley's *Miscellanies* and what I had not read before of the August magazine.

HUME'S ABSTRACT*

The Theory of Moral Sentiments. By Adam Smith, professor
of moral philosophy in the university of Glasgow
The philosophical writers, who enlighten the world by their
reasonings and discoveries, are entitled to great praise; and so
much the more as they seldom, in their own time, meet with
that renown and reputation, which it is natural for an author
of genius to propose to himself as the reward of his labours.
Men of a philosophical turn alone are the proper judges of such
performances; and as these are but few in all ages, profound
reasonings make their way but slowly with the public, and are
often overlooked, till the author can no longer reap pleasure
or advantage from the reputation which he acquires by them.
Nor is this the only obstacle to the progress of philosophical
writings. Even the few who are entitled to judge of their merit,
have often their sentiments warped by innocent, because
unavoidable prejudices; and having previously embraced some
system of their own, with regard to these objects of enquiry,
receive with reluctance, if not with aversion, any attempt to
overturn those opinions, which they have been accustomed
to look upon as certain and indisputable. An historian or
poet, or any author, who proposes to give us entertainment,
is favourably received; and we consider him as a man who
endeavours to add to our stock of pleasure and enjoyment;
but a writer, who attempts to convey instruction, appears not
to us under so favourable an aspect; and his very undertaking
seems to imply a tacit reproach, either of our ignorance or
mistake; an insinuation which no man, much less a philosopher, can hear of with pleasure.
   As these difficulties retard the success of all philosophical
writings, we may observe, that moral researches lie under peculiar disadvantages, and are addressed to a much thinner
auditory, and meet with more numerous prejudices, than attend

* From 'Hume's *Abstract of Adam Smith's Theory of Moral Sentiments*' (May
   1759), edited by David Raynor, first published in the *Journal of the History
   of Philosophy*, vol. 22, no. 1 (January 1984), pp. 65–79.

any other species of science or enquiry. The objects of such theories, tho' seemingly familiar and common, are, in reality, obscure and intricate. Every man of letters, almost without exception, has formed some kind of system with regard to them; and even men of the world, hearing that these subjects have been canvassed ever since the commencement of literature, are apt to think, that if human understanding could reach any certainty in such subjects, it must long ago have fixed on the true system.

The author of this *Theory of Moral Sentiments*, of which we propose to give some account to the public, has overlooked or neglected these discouragements, with that boldness which naturally accompanies genius; and after all the systems of moral philosophy, which have been advanced both in antient and modern times, has not feared to propose new principles and new deductions to the world. The ingenuity, and (may we venture to say it) the solidity of his reasonings ought to excite the languid attention of the public, and procure him a favorable reception. He needs but be hearkened to: his first principles appear so clear, the chain of his arguments so close, his argumentation, and even his style, so forcible and vigorous, that there is no danger of our confounding him with that numerous class of metaphysicians, who, rather from their incapacity for every other branch of learning, than from their peculiar talents for philosophy, have in all nations and ages, but never more than in this, given disgust to the studious part of mankind.

We shall endeavour to form an abstract of the reasonings of this very ingenious writer. However difficult to reduce into a small compass a system of this nature, we must necessarily give a view of the whole, in order to do justice to the author and to the public.

Our author seems to be fully sensible, that the only method by which moral philosophy can be improved, and acquire that solidity and conviction, in which it has been commonly found so deficient, is to follow the practice of our modern naturalists, and make an appeal every moment to fact and experience. He begins with observing, that, however selfish men may sometimes be supposed, there is a principle in their nature which interests them in the fortunes of others, and gives them a sympathy with the movements and affections of their fellow-creatures. This sympathy he endeavours to account for, by supposing, that while we survey the pains or pleasure of others, we enter into them by the force of imagination, and form so lively an idea of these feelings, that it approaches by degrees to the feelings themselves.

'That this is the source of our fellow-feeling for the misery of others, that it is by changing places in fancy with the sufferer, that we come either to conceive or to be affected by what he feels, may be demonstrated by many obvious observations, if it should not be thought sufficiently evident of itself. When we see a stroke aimed and just ready to fall upon the leg or arm of another person, we naturally shrink and draw back our own leg or our own arm; and when it does fall, we feel it in some measure, and are hurt by it as well as the sufferer. The mob, when they are gazing at a dancer on the slack rope, naturally writhe and twist and balance their own bodies, as they see him do, and as they feel that they themselves must do if in his situation. Persons of delicate fibres and a weak constitution of body complain, that in looking on the sores and ulcers which are exposed by beggars in the streets, they are apt to feel an itching or uneasy sensation in the correspondent part of their own bodies. The horror which they conceive at the misery of those wretches affects that particular part in themselves more than any other; because that horror arises from conceiving what they themselves would suffer, if they really were the wretches whom they are looking upon, and if that particular part in themselves was actually affected in the same miserable manner. The very force of this conception is sufficient, in their feeble frames, to produce that itching or uneasy sensation complained of. Men of the most robust make, observe that in looking upon sore eyes they often feel a very sensible soreness in their own, which proceeds from the same reason; that organ being in the strongest man more delicate, than any other part of the body is in the weakest.' [I.i.1.3]

This account seems very natural and probable; but whether it be received or not, is not of great importance to our author's Theory. It is sufficient to his purpose, if sympathy, whence ever it proceeds, be allowed to be a principle in human nature, which surely, without the greatest obstinacy, cannot be disputed. This spring, this movement, this power, is the chief foundation of his system. By means of it he hopes to explain all the species of approbation or disapprobation, which are excited by human action or behaviour. It is indeed the principle which runs through all his theory of morals; and if his deductions be as simple and convincing as his first fact or postulatum is evident and unquestionable, we may venture to give him the preference above all writers who have made any attempt on this subject.

There is a pleasure which attends all sympathy. 'As the person who is principally interested in any event is pleased with our sympathy, and hurt by the want of it, so we, too, seem to be pleased when we are able to sympathize with him, and to be hurt when we are unable to do so. We run not only to congratulate the successful, but to condole with the afflicted; and the pleasure which we find in conversing with a man whom we can entirely sympathize with in all his passions, seems to do more than compensate the painfulness of that sorrow with which the view of his situation affects us. On the contrary, it is always disagreeable to feel that we cannot sympathize with him, and instead of being pleased with this exemption from sympathetic pain, it hurts us to find that we cannot share his uneasiness. If we hear a person loudly lamenting his misfortunes, which, however, upon bringing the case home to ourselves, we feel, can produce no such violent effect upon us, we are shocked at his grief; and, because we cannot enter into it, call it pusillanimity and weakness. It gives us the spleen, on the other hand, to see another too happy or too much elevated, as we call it, with any little piece of good fortune. We are disobliged even with his joy, and, because we cannot go along with it, call it levity and folly. We are even put out of humour if our companion laughs louder or longer at a joke than we think it deserves; that is, than we feel that we ourselves could laugh at it.' [I.i.2.6]

Having found that we feel pleasure when any passion or emotion appears in another with which we can sympathize, and a pain whenever the contrary happens, our author thinks, that this pleasure or pain will account for all our approbation or disapprobation of human action or behaviour. In order to try the solidity of this system, we need but examine, whether it be really the case, that sympathy and approbation are always found united towards the same objects, and the want of sympathy and disapprobation.

'When the original passions of the person principally concerned are in perfect concord with the sympathetic emotions of the spectator, they necessarily appear to this last just and proper, and suitable to their objects; and, on the contrary, when, upon bringing the case home to himself, he finds that they do not coincide with what he feels, they necessarily appear to him unjust and improper, and unsuitable to the causes which excite them. To approve of the passions of another, therefore, as suitable to their objects, is the same thing, as to observe that we entirely sympathize with them; and not to approve of them as such, is the same thing as to observe that we do not entirely sympathize with them. The man who resents the injuries that have been done to me, and observes that I resent them precisely as he does, necessarily approves of my resentment. The man whose sympathy keeps time to my grief, cannot but admit the reasonableness of my sorrow. He who admires the same poem, or the same picture, and admires them exactly as I do, must surely allow the justness of my admiration. He who laughs at the same joke, and laughs along with me, cannot well deny the propriety of my laughter. On the contrary, the person who, upon these different occasions, either feels no such emotion as that which I feel, or feels none that bears any proportion to mine, cannot avoid disapproving my sentiments on account of their dissonance with his own. If my animosity goes beyond what the indignation of my friend can correspond to; if my grief exceeds what his most tender compassion can go along with; if my admiration is either too high or too low to tally with his own; if I laugh loud and heartily at what he only smiles, or, on the contrary, only smile when he laughs loud and heartily; in all these cases, as soon as he comes from considering the object, to observe how I am affected by it, according as there is more or less disproportion between his sentiments and mine, I must incur a greater or less degree of his disapprobation: and upon all occasions his own sentiments are the standards and measures by which he judges of mine. [I.i.3.1]

'When we judge in this manner of any affection, as proportioned or disproportioned to the cause which excites it, it is scarce possible that we should make use of any other rule or canon but the correspondent affection in ourselves. If, upon bringing the case home to our own breast, we find that the sentiments which it gives occasion to coincide and tally with our own, we necessarily approve of them as proportioned and suitable to their objects: if otherwise, we necessarily disapprove of them, as extravagant and out of proportion. [I.i.3.9]

'Every faculty in one man is the measure by which he judges

of the like faculty in another. I judge of your sight by my sight, of your ear by my ear, of your reason by my reason, of your resentment by my resentment, of your love by my love. I neither have, nor can have, any other way of judging about them.' [I.i.3.10]

Our author next proceeds to explain, that there is a double sympathy, which attends all our judgments concerning human sentiments and behaviour. We first consider the feelings of the person who is actuated by any passion, and next the feelings of the person who is the object of it. These sometimes are opposite to each other. When a man meets with any insult which, we feel, would provoke us to anger, we sympathize with his anger; it appears to us to have propriety; we approve of it; it is thought consistent with the rules of duty and morality: but when we turn our eyes to the object of this anger, we have not the same pleasant feeling of approbation. To be the object of anger is always disagreeable and shocking; and the pain which thence arises to the person, tho' it does not destroy, is able at least to diminish the sympathetic satisfaction of the indifferent spectator. On the contrary, all the benevolent passions are supported by a double sympathy: the propriety of the sentiment in the person, who feels it, gives us a high degree of satisfaction: the pleasing sentiments of the person, who is the object of it, encreases this satisfaction, and,consequently, this approbation. Hence, it proceeds, that the angry passions in order to be approved of, must be much more reduced and tamed, and mollified, than the benevolent ones. A tendency towards love, friendship, humanity, is the characteristic of virtue: a propensity towards anger, resentment, jealousy, is a comprehensive description of vice. Every one is sensible, that this observation is founded on fact and experience; and such an evident concurrence of daily observation with our author's theory, must be regarded as a strong proof of its solidity.

This reasoning, which seems so conclusive, our author fortifies by a great number of other curious and ingenious observations. He remarks very justly, that we cannot sympathize fully with the bodily appetites of hunger and thirst, or transfer them to ourselves, as we do the passions of the mind. 'Hence it is indecent (says our author) to express any strong degree of those passions which arise from a certain situation or disposition of the body; because the company, not being in the same disposition, cannot be expected to sympathize with them. Violent hunger, for example, though upon many occasions not only natural, but unavoidable, is always indecent, and to eat voraciously is universally regarded as a piece of ill manners. There is, however, some degree of sympathy, even with hunger. It is agreeable to see our companions eat with a good appetite, and all expressions of loathing are offensive. The disposition of body which is habitual to a man in health makes his stomach easily keep time, if I may be allowed to coarse an expression, with the one, and not with the other. We can sympathize with the distress which excessive hunger occasions, when we read the description of it in the journal of a siege, or of a sea voyage. We imagine ourselves in the situation of the sufferers, and thence readily conceive the grief, the fear and consternation, which must necessarily distract them. We feel, ourselves, some degree of those passions, and therefore sympathize with them: but as we do not grow hungry by reading the description, we cannot properly, even in this case, be said to sympathize with their hunger. [I.ii.1.1]

'It is the same case with the passion by which nature unites the two sexes. Though naturally the most furious of all the passions, all strong expressions of it are upon every occasion indecent, even between persons in whom its most complete indulgence is acknowledged by all laws, both human and divine, to be perfectly innocent. There seems, however, to be some degree of sympathy even with this passion. To talk to a woman as we would to a man is improper: it is expected that their company should inspire us with more gaiety, more pleasantry, and more attention; and an intire insensibility to the fair sex, renders a man contemptible in some measure even to the men. [I.ii.1.2]

'Such is our aversion for all the appetites which take their origin from the body: all strong expressions of them are loathsome and disagreeable. According to some antient philosophers, these are the passions which we share in common with the brutes, and which having no connection with the characteristical qualities of human nature, are upon that account beneath its dignity. But there are many other passions which we share in common with the brutes, such as resentment, natural affection, and even gratitude, which do not, upon that account, appear to be so brutal. The true cause of the peculiar disgust which we conceive for the appetites of the body, when we see them in other men, is that we cannot enter into them. To the person himself who feels them, as soon as they are gratified, the object that excited them ceases to be agreeable: even its presence often becomes offensive to him; he looks round to no purpose for the charm which transported him the moment before, and he can now as little enter into his own passion as another person. When we have dined, we order the covers to be removed; and we should treat in the same manner the objects of the most ardent and passionate desires, if they were the objects of no other passions but those which take their origin from the body. [I.ii.1.3]

'Even of the passions derived from the imagination, those which take their origin from a peculiar turn or habit it has acquired, tho' they may be acknowledged to be perfectly natural, are, however, but little sympathized with. The imaginations of mankind, not having acquired that particular turn, cannot enter into them; and such passions, tho' they may be allowed to be almost unavoidable in some part of life, are always in some measure ridiculous. This is the case with that strong attachment which naturally grows up between two persons of different sexes, who have long fixed their thoughts upon one another. Our imagination not having run in the same channel with that of the lover, we cannot enter into the eagerness of his emotions. If our friend has been injured, we readily sympathize with his resentment, and grow angry with the very person with whom he is angry. If he has received a benefit, we readily enter into his gratitude, and have a very high sense of the merit of his benefactor. But if he is in love, though we may think his passion just as reasonable as any of the kind, yet we never think ourselves bound to conceive a passion of the same kind, and for the same person for whom he has conceived it. The passion appears to every body, but the man who feels it, entirely disproportioned to the value of the object; and love, though it is pardoned in a certain age because we know it is natural, is always laughed at, because we cannot enter into it. All serious and strong expressions of it appear ridiculous to a third person; and if the lover is not good company to his mistress, he is to no body else. He himself is sensible of this; and as long as he continues in his sober senses, endeavours to treat his own passion with raillery and ridicule. It is the only stile in which we care to hear of it; because it is the only stile in which we ourselves are disposed to talk of it. We grow weary of the grave, pedantic, and long-sentenced love of Cowley and Propertius, who never have done with exaggerating the violence of their attachments; but the gaiety of Ovid, and the gallantry of Horace, are always agreeable.' [I.ii.2.1]

There is something similar in the selfish passions, hope, fear, grief, sorrow: these may be sympathized with by the spectator, and consequently, may be allowed to possess a degree of propriety; but they are never sympathized with to the full extent of what is felt by the person himself, who is actuated by them.

'It is upon account of this full sensibility (says our author) to the afflictions of others, that magnanimity amidst great distress appears always so divinely graceful. His behavior is genteel and agreeable who can maintain his chearfulness amidst a number of frivolous disasters. But he appears to be more than mortal who can support in the same manner the most dreadful calamities. We feel what an immense effort is requisite to silence those violent emotions which naturally agitate and distract those in his situation. We are amazed to find that he can command himself so intirely. His firmness, at the same time, perfectly coincides with our insensibility. He makes no demand upon us for that more exquisite degree of sensibility which we find, and which we are mortified to find, that we do not possess. There is the most perfect correspondence between his sentiments and ours, and on that account the most perfect propriety in his behavior. It is a propriety too, which, from our experience of the usual weakness of human nature, we could not reasonably have expected he should be able to maintain. We wonder with surprise and astonishment at that strength of mind which is capable of so noble and generous an effort. The sentiment of complete sympathy and approbation, mixed and animated with wonder and surprise, constitutes what is properly called admiration, as has already been more than once taken notice of. Cato, surrounded on all sides by his enemies, unable to resist them, disdaining to submit to them, and reduced, by the proud maxims of that age, to the necessity of destroying himself; yet never shrinking from his misfortunes, never supplicating with the lamentable voice of wretchedness, those miserable sympathetic tears which we are always so unwilling to give; but on the contrary, arming himself with manly fortitude, and the moment before he executes his fatal resolution, giving, with his usual tranquillity, all necessary orders for the safety of his friends; appears to Seneca, that great preacher of insensibility, a spectacle which even the gods themselves might behold with pleasure and admiration.' [I.iii.1.13]

By this obvious, yet ingenious, theory, the author accounts for the origin and distinction of the amiable and respectable virtues. He who has a tender feeling for the sufferings of others, possesses the former; he who enjoys an unalterable firmness in bearing his own misfortunes, is entitled to the praise of the latter.

The sentiments and affections of others may be considered in two lights; either with a reference to their cause or their effect. When we consider them with a reference to their cause, we approve or disapprove of them according as we find ourselves capable or incapable of sympathizing with them; of entering into them, or of going along with them; and we thence denominate them proper or improper. When we consider them with regard to their effect, to the good or ill which they produce towards others, we ascribe to them *merit* or *demerit*; we wish to reward or punish the person; we feel a species of gratitude or resentment towards him. The explication of those sentiments forms the second part of our author's theory. As we have a direct sympathy with the agent in any virtuous conduct, and thence approve of it, so have we an indirect sympathy with the gratitude of the person who profits by it; and thence esteem his conduct meritorious, and wish to reward it.

'We sympathize with the sorrow of our fellow-creature whenever we see his distress; we likewise enter into his abhorrence and aversion for whatever has given occasion to it. Our heart, as it adopts and beats time to his grief, so is it likewise animated with that spirit by which he endeavours to drive away or destroy the cause of it. The indolent and passive fellow-feeling, by which we accompany him in his sufferings, readily gives way to that more vigorous and active sentiment by which we go along with him in the effort he makes, either to repel them, or to gratify his aversion to what has given occasion to them. This is still more peculiarly the case, when it is man who has caused them. When we see one man oppressed or injured by another, the sympathy which we feel with the distress of the sufferer seems to serve only to animate our fellow-feeling with his resentment against the offender. We are rejoiced to see him attack his adversary in his turn, and are eager and ready to assist him whenever he exerts himself for defence, or even for vengeance within a certain degree. If the injured should perish in the quarrel, we not only sympathize with the real resentment of his friends and relations, but with the imaginary resentment which in fancy we lend to the dead, who is no longer capable of feeling that or any other human sentiment. But as we put ourselves in his situation, as we enter, as it were, into his body, and in our imaginations, in some measure, animate anew the deformed and mangled carcass of the slain, when we bring home in this manner his case to our own bosoms, we feel upon this, as upon many other occasions, an emotion which the person principally concerned is incapable of feeling, and which yet we feel by an illusive sympathy with him. The sympathetic tears which we shed for that immense and irretrievable loss, which in our fancy he appears to have sustained, seem to be but a small part of the duty which we owe him. The injury which he has suffered demands, we think, a principal part of our attention. We feel that resentment which we imagine he ought to feel, and which he would feel, if in his cold and lifeless body there remained any consciousness of what passes upon earth. His blood, we think, calls aloud for vengeance. The very ashes of the dead seem to be disturbed at the thought that his injuries are to pass unrevenged. The horrors which are supposed to haunt the bed of the murderer, the ghosts which, superstition imagines, rise from their graves to demand vengeance upon those who brought them to an untimely end, all take their origin from this natural sympathy with the imaginary resentment of the slain. And with regard, at least, to this most dreadful of all crimes, nature, antecedent to all reflections upon the utility of punishment, has in this manner stamped upon the human heart, in the strongest and most indelible characters, an immediate and instinctive approbation of the sacred and necessary law of retaliation.' [II.i.2.5]

Our very ingenious author, after having bestowed some considerations on the sense of duty, on conscience and remorse, proceeds to consider the effect of utility upon the sentiment of approbation.

'That utility is one of the principal sources of beauty has been observed by every body, who has considered with any attention what constitutes the nature of beauty. The conveniency of a house gives pleasure to the spectator as well as its regularity, and he is as much hurt when he observes the contrary defect, as when he sees the correspondent windows of different forms, or the door not placed exactly in the middle of the building. That the fitness of any system or machine to produce the end for which it was intended, bestows a certain propriety and beauty upon the whole, and renders the very thought and contemplation of it agreeable, is so very obvious that nobody has overlooked it.' [IV.1.1]

The reason for this pleasure, which we receive from the contemplation of utility, is assigned by our author, to be a species of *sympathy* with the persons who reap that advantage. 'The characters of men, as well as the contrivances of art, or the institutions of civil government, may be fitted either to promote or to disturb the happiness both of the individual and of the society. The prudent, the equitable, the active, resolute and sober character promises prosperity and satisfaction, both to the person himself and to every one connected with him. The rash, the insolent, the slothful, effeminate and voluptuous, on the contrary, forebodes ruin to the individual, and misfortune to all who have any thing to do with him. The first turn of mind has at least all the beauty which can belong to the most perfect machine that was ever invented for promoting the most agreeable purpose: and the second, all the deformity of the most aukward and clumsy contrivance. What institution of government could tend so much to promote the happiness of mankind as the general prevalence of wisdom and virtue? All government is but an imperfect remedy for the deficiency of these. Whatever beauty, therefore, can belong to civil government upon account of its utility, must in a far superior degree belong to these. On the contrary, what civil policy can be so ruinous and destructive as the vices of men? The fatal effects of bad government arise from nothing, but that it does not sufficiently guard against the mischiefs which human wickedness gives occasion to.' [IV.2.1]

But though the author admits, that the consideration of usefulness enhances and enlivens the perception of moral beauty or merit; he very justly maintains, that that perception is originally and essentially different from any view of utility. It seems impossible, that the approbation of virtue should be a sentiment of the same kind with that, by which we approve of a convenient and well contrived building; or that we should have no other reason for praising a man than that for which we commend a chest of drawers.

Our author subjoins many irrefragable arguments, by which he refutes the sentiments of Mr. Hume, who founded a great part of his moral system on the consideration of public utility. The compass to which we are confined, will not allow us to explain them at full length; but the reader, who will consult the author himself, will find, that philosophy scarce affords any thing more undeniable and conclusive.

Some philosophers, whom we shall venture to call fantastical, have ascribed all sense of beauty, external as well as internal, to fashion and custom. Our author rejects this absurd opinion, but he allows these principles to have some influence; and he endeavours, in the fifth part of this Theory, to explain it.

'When two objects have frequently been seen together, the imagination acquires a habit of passing easily from the one to the other. If the first appears, we lay our account that the second is to follow. Of their own accord they put us in mind of one another, and the attention glides easily along them. Tho' independent of custom, there should be no real beauty in their union, yet when custom has thus connected them together, we feel an impropriety in their separation. The one we think is aukward when it appears without its usual companion. We miss something which we expected to find, and the habitual arrangement of our ideas is disturbed by the disappointment. A suit of cloaths, for example, seems to want something if they are without the most insignificant ornament which usually accompanies them, and we find a meanness or aukwardness in the absence even of a haunch button. When there is any natural propriety in the union, custom increases our sense of it, and makes a different arrangement appear still more disagreeable than it would otherwise seem to be. Those who have been accustomed to see things in a good taste are more disgusted by whatever is clumsy or aukward. Where the conjunction is improper, custom either diminishes or takes away altogether our sense of the impropriety. Those who have been accustomed to slovenly disorder lose all sense of neatness or elegance. The modes of furniture or dress which seem ridiculous to strangers, give no offence to the people who are used to them. [V.1.2]

'Since our sentiments concerning beauty of every kind, are so much influenced by custom and fashion, it cannot be expected, that those, concerning the beauty of conduct, should be entirely exempted from the dominion of those principles.

Their influence here, however, seems to be much less than it is every where else. There is, perhaps, no form of external objects, how absurd and fantastical soever, to which custom will not reconcile us, or which fashion will not render even agreeable. But the characters and conduct of a Nero, or a Claudius, are what no custom will ever reconcile us to, what no fashion will ever render agreeable; but the one will always be the object of dread and hatred; the other of scorn and derision. The principles of the imagination, upon which our sense of beauty depends, are of a very nice and delicate nature, and may easily be altered by habit and education: but the sentiments of moral approbation and disapprobation, are founded on the strongest and most vigorous passions of human nature; and tho' they may be somewhat warpt, cannot be entirely perverted. [V.2.1]

'But tho' the influence of custom and fashion, upon moral sentiments, is not altogether so great, it is, however, perfectly similar to what it is every where else. When custom and fashion coincide with the natural principles of right and wrong, they heighten the delicacy of our sentiments, and increase our abhorrence for every thing that approaches to evil. Those who have been educated in what is really good company, not in what is commonly called such, who have been accustomed to see nothing in the persons whom they esteemed and lived with, but justice, modesty, humanity, and good order, are more shocked with whatever seems to be inconsistent with the rules which those virtues prescribe. Those, on the contrary, who have had the misfortune to be brought up amidst violence, licentiousness, falsehood and injustice, lose, though not all sense of the impropriety of such conduct, yet all sense of its dreadful enormity, and of the vengeance and punishment due to it. They have been familiarized with it from their infancy, custom has rendered it habitual to them, and they are very apt to regard it as what is called the way of the world, something which either may or must be practiced to hinder us from being the dupes of our own integrity. [V.2.2]

'Fashion too will sometimes give reputation to a certain degree of disorder, and, on the contrary, discountenance qualities which deserve esteem. In the reign of Charles II, a degree of licentiousness was deemed the characteristic of a liberal education. It was connected, according to the notions of those times, with generosity, sincerity, magnanimity, loyalty, and proved that the person who acted in this manner, was a gentleman, and not a puritan. Severity of manners, and regularity of conduct, on the other hand, were altogether unfashionable, and were connected, in the imagination of that age, with cant, cunning, hypocrisy, and low manners. To superficial minds, the vices of the great seem at all times agreeable. They connect them, not only with the splendour of fortune, but with many superior virtues, which they ascribe to their superiors; with the spirit of freedom and independency, with frankness, generosity, humanity, and politeness. The virtues of the inferior ranks of people, on the contrary, their parsimonious frugality, their painful industry, and rigid adherence to rules, seem to them mean and disagreeable. They connect them, both with the meanness of the station to which those qualities commonly belong, and with many great vices, which, they suppose, usually accompany them; such as an abject, cowardly, ill-natured, lying, pilfering disposition. [V. 2.3]

'The objects with which men in the different professions and states of life are conversant, being very different, and habituating them to very different passions, naturally form in them very different characters and manners. We expect in each rank and profession, a degree of those manners, which, experience has taught us, belong to it. But as in each species of things, we are particularly pleased with the middle conformation, which, in every part and feature, agrees most exactly with the general standard which nature seems to have established for things of that kind; so in each rank, or, if I may so, in each species of men, we are particularly pleased, if they have neither too much, nor too little of the character which usually accompanies their particular condition and situation. A man, we say, should look like his trade and profession; yet the pedantry of every profession is disagreeable. The different periods of life have, for the same reason, different manners assigned to them. We expect in old age, that gravity and sedateness which its infirmities, its long experience, and its worn out sensibility seem to render both natural and respectable, and we lay our account to find in youth that sensibility, that gaiety and sprightly vivacity which experience teaches us to expect from the lively impressions that all interesting objects are apt to make upon the tender and unpractised senses of that early period of life. Each of those two ages, however, may easily have too much of the peculiarities which belong to it. The flirting levity of youth, and the immovable insensibility of old age, are equally disagreeable. The young, according to the common saying, are most agreeable when in their behaviour there is something of the manners of the old, and the old, when they retain something of the gaiety of the young. Either of them, however, may easily have too much of the manners of the other. The extreme coldness, and dull formality, which are pardoned in old age, make youth ridiculous. The levity, the carelessness, and the vanity, which are indulged in youth, render old age contemptible.' [V.2.4]

Our author concludes his ingenious Theory with some reflections on the different systems of moral philosophy, which have been advanced both in antient and modern times. Here he discovers the extent of his erudition, as well as the depth of his philosophy. He runs over with great perspicuity, both the speculative and practical systems of morality, which have obtained reputation in different ages; and he justly observes, that no one of them could ever have met with success, did it not bear some resemblance to the truth, and was not, in some particulars, conformable to fact and daily experience.

'A system of natural philosophy may appear very plausible, and be for a long time very generally received in the world, and yet have no foundation in nature, nor any sort of resemblance to the truth. The vortices of Des Cartes were regarded by a very ingenious nation, for near a century together, as a most satisfactory account of the revolutions of the heavenly bodies. Yet it has been demonstrated to the conviction of all mankind, that these pretended causes of those wonderful effects, not only do not actually exist, but are utterly impossible, and if they did exist, could produce no such effects as are ascribed to them. But it is otherwise with systems of moral philosophy, and an author who pretends to account for the origin of our moral sentiments, cannot deceive us so grossly, nor depart so very far from all resemblance to the truth. When a traveller gives us an account of some distant country, he may impose upon our credulity the most groundless and absurd fictions as the most certain matters of fact. But when a person pretends to inform us of what passes in our neighborhood, and of the affairs of the very parish which we live in, tho' here too, if we are so careless as not to examine things with our own eyes, he may deceive us in many respects, yet the greatest falsehoods which he imposes upon us must bear some resemblance to the truth, and must even have a considerable mixture of truth in them. An author who treats of natural philosophy, and pretends to assign the causes of the great phaenomena of the universe, pretends to give an account of the affairs of a very distant country, concerning which he may tell us what he pleases, and as long as his narration keeps within the bounds of seeming possibility, he need not despair of gaining our belief. But when he proposes to explain the origin of our desires and affections, of our sentiments of approbation and disapprobation, he pretends to give an account, not only of the affairs of the very parish that we live in, but of our own domestic concerns. Tho' here too, like indolent masters who put their trust in a steward who deceives them, we are very liable to be imposed upon, yet we are incapable of passing any account which does not preserve some little regard to the truth. Some of the articles, at least, must be just, and even those which are most overcharged must have had some foundation, otherwise the fraud would be detected even by that careless inspection which we are disposed to give. The author who should assign, as the cause of any natural sentiment, some principle which neither had any connection with it, nor resembled any other principle which had some such connection, would appear absurd and ridiculous to the most injudicious and unexperienced reader.' [VII.i.4.14]

If there be any part of our author's valuable performance, which will give both entertainment and instruction to the careless reader (such as most readers are at present) it is this disquisition of the different systems of philosophy. We should but mangle it, by attempting to give an abridgement of it. We shall therefore conclude our account of this *Theory of Moral Sentiments*, by remarking, that the performance contains two kinds of merit, which are but too seldom found in works of abstract and speculative reasoning.

The first is the advantage of a lively, perspicuous, manly, unaffected stile. His discourse, animated by the sentiments of virtue, flows along, like a full and rapid stream, and carries us through many entertaining scenes of common life, and many curious disquisitions of literature. Though he penetrates into the depths of philosophy, he still talks like a man of the world; and after accounting for every part of his theory, by the abstract principles of human nature, he illustrates his argument every moment by appeals to common sense and experience. Whether his philosophical topics be solid or not, we dare not venture to pronounce: Time alone, the great test of truth, must affix his seal to subjects of such nice and curious disquisition. But his illustrations, being more within the reach of ordinary reason, fall under the apprehension of every reader, and form a strong presumption in favour of the solidity and force of our author's genius.

The second advantage to be found in this work, is the strict regard which the writer every where preserves to the principles of religion: however some pretenders to science may endeavour to separate the philosopher from the lover of religion, it will always be found, that truth being every where uniform and consistent, it is impossible for a man to digest himself of the one character, without renouncing all just claim to the other. As it is a familiar rule with logicians to conclude, that if any argument is attended with absurd consequences, it must itself be absurd; it ought no less to be established as a certain principle, that every topic, however specious, which leads into impiety or infidelity, should be rejected with disdain and contempt. Our author seems every where sensible of so fundamental a truth; and by keeping this great object in view, he secures himself, if not against all error, which it is impossible for human nature entirely to avoid, at least against all error that is dangerous or pernicious.

[REVIEW OF] *THE THEORY OF MORAL SENTIMENTS*, BY ADAM SMITH*
[Purportedly by Edmund Burke]

It is very difficult, if not impossible, consistently with the brevity of our design, to give the reader a proper idea of this excellent work. A dry abstract of the system would convey no juster idea of it, than the skeleton of a departed beauty would of her form when she was alive; at the same time the work is so well methodised, the parts grow so naturally and gracefully out of each other, that it would be doing it equal injustice to shew it by broken and detached pieces. There will, in a work of this kind, always be great deficiencies; but we are far from professing to make our accounts stand to the reader in the place of the books on which we remark. Had we thought that this in any degree would happen, we should certainly think ourselves obliged totally to omit this article in the Register, as it would be an effect the farthest in the world from our design, which is in the strongest manner to recommend to the attention of our readers, some of these books which we think deserving of it; we chuse none which we cannot recommend; we give our judgment with candour and impartiality; but never aiming to impose our opinions dogmatically on the public, we think it but justice to the authors and the readers, to give some specimen, however imperfect, of each writer's way of thinking and expression. We mean to raise, not to satisfy curiosity.

There have been of late many books written on our moral duties, and our moral sensations. One would have thought the matter had been exhausted. But this author has struck out a new, and at the same time a perfectly natural road of speculation on this subject. Had it been only an ingenious novelty on any other subject, it might have been praised; but with regard to morals, nothing could be more dangerous. We conceive, that here the theory is in all its essential parts just, and founded on truth and nature. The author seeks for the foundation of the just, the fit, the proper, the decent, in our

* From *Annual Register*, vol. 2 (1759), pp. 484–9.

most common and most allowed passions; and making approbation and disapprobation the tests of virtue and vice, and
shewing that those are founded on sympathy, he raises from
this simple truth, one of the most beautiful fabrics of moral
theory, that has perhaps ever appeared. The illustrations are
numerous and happy, and shew the author to be a man of
uncommon observation. His language is easy and spirited, and
puts things before you in the fullest light; it is rather painting
than writing. We insert the first section, as it concerns sympathy, the basis of his theory; and as it exhibits equally with
any of the rest, an idea of his style and manner.

Of Sympathy

'How selfish soever man may be supposed, there are evidently
some principles in his nature, which interest him in the fortune
of others, and render their happiness necessary to him, though
he derives nothing from it except the pleasure of seeing it. Of
this kind is pity or compassion, the emotion which we feel for
the misery of others, when we either see it, or are made to
conceive it in a very lively manner. That we often derive sorrow
from the sorrow of others, is too obvious to require any
instances to prove it; for this sentiment, like all the other
original passions of human nature, is by no means confined to
the virtuous and humane, though they perhaps may feel it
with the most exquisite fensibility. The greatest ruffian, the
most hardened violator of the laws of society, is not altogether
without it.

As we have no immediate experience of what other men feel,
we can form no idea of the manner in which they are affected,
but by conceiving what we ourselves should feel in the like
situation. Though our brother is upon the rack, as long as we
are at our own ease, our senses will never inform us of what
he suffers. They never did, nor ever can carry us beyond our
own persons, and it is by the imagination only, that we can
form any conception of what are his sensations. Neither
can that faculty help us to this any other way, than by representing to us what would be our own, if we were in his case.
It is the impressions of our own senses only, not those of his,
which our imaginations copy. By the imagination we place
ourselves in his situation, we conceive ourselves enduring all
the same torments, we enter as it were into his body, and

become in some measure him, and thence form some idea of his sensations, and even feel something, which, tho' weaker in degree, is not altogether unlike them. His agonies, when they are thus brought home to ourselves, when we have thus adopted and made them our own, begin at last to affect us, and we then tremble and shudder, at the thought of what he feels. For as to be in pain or distress of any kind excites the most excessive sorrow, so to conceive or to imagine that we are in it, excites some degree of the same emotion, in proportion to the vivacity or dulness of the conception.

That this is the source of our fellow-feeling for the misery of others, that it is by changing places in fancy with the sufferer, that we come either to conceive or be affected by what he feels, may be demonstrated by many obvious observations, if it should not be thought sufficiently evident of itself. When we see a stroke aimed and just ready to fall upon the leg or arm of another person, we naturally shrink and draw back our own leg, or our own arm; and when it does fall, we feel it in some measure, and are hurt by it as well as the sufferer. The mob, when they are gazing at a dancer on the slack rope, naturally writhe and twist, and balance their own bodies, as they see him do, and as they feel that they themselves must do in his situation. Persons of delicate fibres, and a weak constitution of body, complain, that in looking on the sores and ulcers that are exposed by beggars in the streets, they are apt to feel an itching or uneasy sensation in the corresponding part of their own bodies. The horror which they conceive at the misery of those wretches affects that particular part in themselves, more than any other; because that horror arises from conceiving what they themselves would suffer, if they really were the wretches whom they are looking upon, and if that particular part in themselves was actually affected in the same miserable manner. The very force of this conception is sufficient, in their feeble frames, to produce that itching or uneasy sensation complained of. Men of the most robust make, observe that in looking upon sore eyes they often feel a very sensible soreness in their own, which proceeds from the same reason; that organ being in the strongest man more delicate than any other part of the body is in the weakest.

Neither is it those circumstances only, which create pain or sorrow, that call forth our fellow-feeling. Whatever is the passion which arises from any object in the person principally concerned, an analogous emotion springs up, at the thought of his situation, in the breast of every attentive spectator. Our joy for the deliverance of those heroes of tragedy or romance who interest us, is as sincere as our grief for their distress, and our fellow-feeling with their misery is not more real than with their happiness. We enter into their gratitude towards those faithful friends, who did not desert them in their difficulties; and we heartily go along with their resentment against those perfidious traitors, who injured, abandoned, or deceived them. In every passion, of which the mind of man is susceptible, the emotions of the by-stander always correspond to what, by bringing the case home to himself, he imagines, should be the sentiments of the sufferer.

Pity and compassion are words appropriated to signify our fellow-feeling with the sorrow of others. Sympathy, though its meaning was, perhaps, originally the same, may now, however, without much impropriety, be made use of to denote our fellow-feeling with any passion whatever.

Upon some occasions sympathy may seem to arise merely from the view of a certain emotion in another person. The passions, upon some occasions, may seem to be transfused from one man to another, instantaneously, and antecedent to any knowledge of what excited them in the person principally concerned. Grief and joy, for example, strongly expressed in the look and gestures of any one, at once affect the spectator with some degree of a like painful or agreeable emotion. A smiling face is, to every body that sees it, a chearful object; as a sorrrowful countenance, on the other hand, is a melancholy one.

This, however, does not hold universally with regard to every passion. There are some of which the expressions excite no sort of sympathy, but before we are acquainted with what gave occasion to them, serve rather to disgust and provoke us against them. The furious behaviour of an angry man is more likely to exasperate us against himself, than against his enemies. As we are unacquainted with his provocation, we cannot bring his case home to ourselves, nor conceive any thing like the passions which it excites. But we plainly see what is the situation of those with whom he is angry, and to what violence they may be exposed from so enraged an adversary. We readily, therefore, sympathize with their fear or resentment, and are immediately disposed to take part against the man, from whom they appear to be in so much danger.

If the very appearances of grief and joy inspire us with some degree of the like emotions, it is because they suggest to us the general idea of some good or bad fortune that has befallen the person in whom we observe them: and in these passions this is sufficient to have some little influence upon us. The effects of grief and joy terminate in the person who feels those emotions, of which the expressions do not, like those of resentment, suggest to us the idea of any other person for whom we are concerned, and whose interests are opposite to his. The general idea of good or bad fortune, therefore, creates some concern for the person who has met with it; but the general idea of provocation excites no sympathy with the anger of the man who has received it. Nature, it seems, teaches us to be more averse to enter into this passion, and, till informed of its cause, to be disposed rather to take part against it.

Even our sympathy with the grief or joy of another, before we are informed of the cause of either, is always extremely imperfect. General lamentations, which express nothing but the anguish of the sufferer, create rather a curiosity to enquire into his situation, along with some disposition to sympathize with him, than actual sympathy that is very sensible. The first question that we ask is, What has befallen you? 'Till this be answered, tho' we are uneasy, both from the vague idea of his misfortune, and still more from torturing ourselves with conjectures about what it may be, yet our fellow-feeling is not very considerable.

Sympathy, therefore, does not arise so much from the view of the passion, as from that of the situation which excites it. We sometimes feel for another a passion of which he himself seems to be altogether incapable; because when we put ourselves in his case, that passion arises in our breast from the imagination, though it does not in his from the reality. We blush for the impudence and rudeness of another, though he himself appears to have no sense of the impropriety of his own behaviour, because we cannot help feeling with what confusion we ourselves should be covered, had we behaved in so absurd a manner.

Of all the calamities to which the condition of mortality exposes mankind, the loss of reason appears, to those who have the least spark of humanity, by far the most dreadful, and they behold that last stage of human wretchedness with deeper commiseration than any other. But the poor wretch, who is in it, laughs and sings perhaps, and is altogether insensible of his own misery. The anguish which humanity feels, therefore, at the sight of such an object, cannot be the reflection of any sentiment of the sufferer. The compassion of the spectator must arise altogether from the consideration of what he himself would feel if he was reduced to the same unhappy situation, and, what perhaps is impossible, was at the same time able to regard it with his present reason and judgment.

What are the pangs of a mother when she hears the moaning of her infant, that during the agony of disease cannot express what it feels? In her idea of what it suffers, she joins, to its real helplessness, her own consciousness of that helplessness, and her own terrors for the unknown consequences of its disorder; and out of all these forms, for her own sorrow, the most complete image of misery and distress. The infant, however, feels only the uneasiness of the present instant, which can never be great. With regard to the future it is perfectly secure, and in its thoughtlessness and want of foresight, possesses an antidote against fear and anxiety, the great tormentors of the human breast, from which reason and philosophy will in vain attempt to defend it when it grows up to a man.

We sympathize even with the dead, and overlooking what is of real importance in their situation, that aweful futurity which awaits them, we are chiefly affected by those circumstances which strike our senses, but can have no influence upon their happiness. It is miserable, we think, to be deprived of the light, of the fun; to be shut out from life and conversation; to be laid in the cold grave a prey to corruption and the reptiles of the earth; to be no more thought of in this world, but to be obliterated in a little time from the affections and almost from the memory of their dearest friends and relations. Surely, we imagine, we can never feel too much for those who have suffered so dreadful a calamity. The tribute of our fellow-feeling seems doubly due to them now when they are in danger of being forgot by every body: and, by the vain honours which we pay to their memory, we endeavour, for our own misery, artificially to keep alive our melancholy remembrance of their misfortune. That our sympathy can afford them no consolation, seems to be an addition to their calamity; and to think that all we can do is unavailing, and that, what alleviates all other distress, the regret, love, and the lamentation of their friends, can yield no comfort to them, serves only to exasperate our sense of the misery. The happiness of the dead, however, most assuredly is affected by none of these circumstances; nor is it the thought of these things which can ever disturb the security of their repose. The idea of that dreary and endless melancholy, which the fancy naturally ascribes to their condition, arises altogether from our joining to the change which has been produced upon them, our own consciousness of that change, from our putting ourselves in their situation, and from our lodging, if I may be allowed to say so, our own living souls in their inanimated bodies, and thence conceiving what would be our emotions in this case. It is this very illusion of the imagination which renders the foresight of our own dissolution so terrible to us, and the idea of those circumstances, which undoubtedly can give us no pain when we are dead, makes us miserable while we are alive. And from thence arises one of the most important principles in human nature, the dread of death, the great poison to the happiness, but the great restraint upon the injustice of mankind, which, while it afflicts and mortifies the individuals, guards and protects the society.'

Smith's Contemporaries

[FROM] ESSAYS ON THE PRINCIPLES OF MORALITY AND NATURAL RELIGION*
Henry Home, Lord Kames

A system that resolves every moral sensation or sentiment into sympathy, shall next be introduced. Listen to the author himself. 'As we have no immediate experience of what other men feel, we can form no idea of it but by imagining what we ourselves would feel in the like situation. Our senses will never inform us of what a man suffers on the rack. They cannot carry us beyond our own persons; and it is by the imagination only that we can form any perception of what he suffers. Neither can that faculty help us to this, any other way than by representing to us what would be our own sufferings if we were in his place. His agonies when thus brought home to ourselves, begin at last to affect us; and we then tremble and shudder at the thought of what he feels.'[1] The foundation here assigned for the various sentiments of morality, ought to have been very strictly examined before venturing to erect so weighty a superstructure upon it. Is it certain that this play of imagination will necessarily raise the passion of sympathy? The celebrated Rousseau affirms the contrary. 'Pity is sweet, says he, because in putting ourselves in place of the person who suffers, we feel the pleasure of not suffering as he does.'[2] And considering that the rack is a punishment reserved for atrocious criminals, I should be inclined to think with Rousseau, that the sight of an odious wretch on the rack, instead of sympathizing in his pain, would make one feel pleasure in not suffering as he does; precisely as a ship in a storm makes the spectators at land rejoice in their own security.

But however that may be, my respect to the author of this system as a man of genius and learning, cannot make me blind to a difficulty that appears unsurmountable. If the torments of a man on the rack be not obvious to my sight from his violent

---

* 3rd edition (Edinburgh, 1779), chap. 11, pp. 109–13.

[1] Theory of Moral Sentiments, p. 2.

[2] Emile, liv. 4.

perturbation, nor to my hearing from dismal screams and groans, what can I learn from imagining myself to be in his place? He may be happy for ought I know. To give that act of imagination any effect, I ought before hand to know that the person on the rack is suffering violently. Then indeed, the bringing his case home to myself, would naturally inflame my sympathy. I have another argument against this system, which, being more simple and popular, will probably be more relished. That a man should conceive himself to be another, is no slight effort of imagination; and to make sympathy depend on that effort, confines it to persons who have given much exercise to a ductile imagination. Dull people and illiterate rustics are intirely excluded; and yet, among such there appears no defect of sympathy to associates and blood-relations. Nay, we find sympathy eminent even in children; and yet, it would be a hard task to make a child imagine itself to be what it is not. This shows clearly, that sympathy must proceed from some natural principle inherent in all human beings, the young as well as the old.

This principle will appear from the following facts, which every thinking person knows to be true. First, every passion stamps on the countenance certain signs appropriated to it by nature. Next, being taught by nature to connect every external sign with the passion that caused it; we can read in every man's countenance his internal emotions. Third, certain emotions, thus made known, raise in beholders the passion of sympathy.[3] With respect to the last, nothing is more natural than that a social being should be affected with the passions of its fellows. Joy is infectious: so is grief. Fear communicates itself to the beholders; and in an army, the fright of a few spreads the infection till it becomes an universal panic. These facts are clear and certain; and applying them to the subject before us, is it not evident, that the distress we read in a person's countenance, directly moves our sympathy, without needing any aid from imagination? I appeal to any man who has seen a person on the rack, whether his sympathy was not raised by sight merely, without any effort of imagination. Thus, in the sympathetic system under examination, an intricate circuit is made in order to account for a passion that is raised by a single glance. The

[3] See Elements of Criticism, vol. I, page 446. Edit. 5th.

system indeed is innocent; but did it hold in fact, its consequences would not be so. Sympathy is but one of many principles that constitute us moral beings; and yet is held forth as the foundation of every moral sentiment. Had not morality a more solid foundation in our nature, it would give very little obstruction to vicious desires or unjust actions. It is observed above, that, according to this system, sympathy would be rare among the lower ranks. And I now add, that if moral sentiments had no foundation but the imagining myself to be another, the far greater part of mankind would be destitute of any moral sentiment.

So much for the sake of truth: in every other view controversy is my aversion. One observation more, and I conclude. This system is far from comprehending all our moral sentiments. It may pretend to account for my sentiments regarding others; but my sentiments regarding myself are entirely left out. My distress upon losing an only son, or my gratitude for a kindly office, are sentiments that neither need to be explained by imagining myself to be another person, nor do they admit of such explanation.

LETTER FROM ADAM SMITH TO LORD KAMES*
16 November 1778

Address: The Right Honble, The Lord Kaimes
MS., SRO GD24/1/586; Rae 341.

Edinburgh, 16 Nov. 1778

My Dear Lord

I am much obliged to your Lordship for the kind communication of the objections you propose to make in your new Edition[1] to my System. Nothing can be more perfectly friendly and polite than the terms in which you express yourself with regard to me; and I should be extremely peevish and ill-tempered if I could make the slightest opposition to their publication I am no doubt extremely sorry to find myself of a different opinion both from so able a judge of the subject and from so old and so good a friend.[2] But differences of this kind are unavoidable;[3] and besides, *partium contentionibus respublica crescit*. I should have been waiting on your Lordship before this time; but the remains of a cold have for these four or five days past made it inconvenient to go out in the evening. Remember me to Mrs Drummond[4] and believe me to be

Your most obliged and most humble Servant.

Adam Smith

---

* From *Correspondence of Adam Smith*, edited by E. C. Mossner and Ian S. Ross, revised edition (Oxford, 1987), no. 195, p. 234. The notes of the original editors have been retained.

[1] *Essays on the Principles of Morality and Natural Religion*, (ed. 3, 1779).

[2] Kames had sponsored Smith's Edinburgh lectures on rhetoric and jurisprudence, 1748–51.

[3] Kames resisted Smith's moral doctrine concerning sympathy on three grounds: putting oneself in the place of a sufferer leads to self-satisfaction and diminution of pity; those with the liveliest imaginations are not the most moral of men; moral sentiments towards our own actions are not explained by sympathy.

[4] Agatha, dau. of James Drummond of Blair Drummond; md. Kames (Henry Home) 1741; unexpectedly became heiress to Blair Drummond 1766, and assumed the name Home Drummond; d. 1795.

LETTER FROM THOMAS REID TO LORD KAMES*
30 October 1778

Glasgow Coll Oct 30 1778

My Lord

I had lately the Honour of two letters from your Lordship, one of them inclosing a Solicitation from Sir Alexander Dick[1] which I must answer with pain. It is indeed very painfull to me to refuse what would be acceptable to so many persons whom I honour & respect, as are the friends of Charles Lindsay, and yet it must be done.

The late Dr. Baillie of our College desired a communing with me last Winter about the disposal of the next vacant Oxford Exhibition.[2] He wished to have it for his Son a young Man of remarkable Merit in all Respects, who is intended for the Medical Line under Dr Hunter his Mothers Brother.[3] The plan of his Education was contrived by Dr. Hunter himself, tho he was so delicate that he would not solicit for him. Dr Baillie knew that I had a Son of my own who had been longer upon the List of Candidates than either his Son or Charles Lindsay, and therefore communicated more to me of the plan respecting his son than he had Authority to communicate to others. I

* From 'Unpublished Letters of Thomas Reid to Lord Kames, 1762–1782', edited by Ian S. Ross, in *Texas Studies in Literature and Language*, vol. 7 (1965), pp. 33–6. The editor's notes have been retained.

[1] Bt., M.D. (1703–1785), president of the Royal College of Physicians, Edinburgh (1756–1763); prominent in Edinburgh intellectual and social circles – Boswell said he dined a thousand guests a year. He furnished Boswell with anecdotes about Kames for a projected life.

[2] For the history of these exhibitions see W. I. Anderson, *Snell Exhibitions* (Glasgow, 1901); they provoked a great deal of litigation in the eighteenth century.

[3] Matthew Baillie, M.D. (1761–1823), son of the Reverend James Baillie, D.D., professor of divinity at Glasgow. The uncle was the famous anatomist Dr. William Hunter. Baillie became a very successful private practitioner after his election as an F.R.S. (1790), and at the height of his popularity earned £10,000 a year. He attended George III in his insanity and finally died from overwork.

consider Dr Hunter as intitled to the Attention of this College
more than any Man whatsoever; and besides am under personal Obligations to him; and therefore I very readily gave up
my own Sons pretensions in favour of Dr. Hunters Nephew.
Dr Hunter knows all this, and all my Colleagues knew nine
months ago, that I had dropped my own Son and declared for
Dr Baillies. No body mentioned Charles Lindsay at that time.
It was thought he had forfeited all hopes. His Friends knew
this & therefore wanted to put him into another Line. And we
were not a little surprized when we heard that he had refused
going into the Army. I hope he may be wiser in time to come,
but I truely do not think Oxford a place for curing habits of
Idleness. And if he should not behave otherwise than he did
last Session, it would hurt himself & dishonour us to send him
there. However that may be, I must stand for Mr Baillie.
I wished to satisfy your Lordship of my Reasons, tho I do
not think myself bound to be so explicit to any other
Person.

I had wrote so far when I had the Honour of your Lordships
Letter of the 27, which requires next to be answered.

I have always thought Dr Smith's System of Sympathy
wrong. It is indeed only a Refinement of the selfish System; &
I think your *Arguments against it solid. Your introductory
Compliment of all possible* deference to the Author, who is a
Man of Genius & an excellent Writer must be very acceptable, & is pouring Balm into the wound, or rather smiting
with a friendly hand, which does not break the head; & I
highly approve of it.

Would it be amiss to shew Dr Smith what you propose to
print relating to his System, & to have a communing with him;
not in order to convince him that he is wrong; but in order to
know from himself that there is nothing said that is offensive
or disagreeable to him. He has too much Sense to take amiss
your arguing against his System, and if there is any expression
not affecting the Argument which he would wish to be altered,
you will have an opportunity of gratifying him. If I was in his
place I would take this as a high Act of Courtesy and Respect.
And if bad Humor may be prevented, & friendship cemented
by this Means, I think it is a great Matter. My Zeal for this,
is the onely Apology I can make to your Lordship, for sug-

gesting what I have said, to one who knows so much better, what Propriety requires of Lord Kames in such a Case.[4]

I congratulate your Lordship on *your having finished* to your Satisfaction the Discourse on Vision. Acti labores jucundi.

Query. Whether is there any pleasure or gratification in a passion directed against myself? As in Terences selftormentor.[5]

Answer. It is a contradiction to say that there is pleasure in Torment. Yet I think there is a Gratification in this kind of Torment. I cannot separate the Idea of Gratification from the accomplishment of what I desire and intend. Desire fullfilled is Gratification, even when the desire is to suffer.

If I have a Mortification in my Arm I may desire very earnestly to have it cut off. I am gratified by having it cut off by a skillful Surgeon. Yet I think it would be improper to say I have any pleasure in having it cut off.

The Principles which lead a Man to chuse Affliction, & voluntarily to afflict himself are two, Remorse & Grief. A Man has done a bad thing which fills him with indignation against himself. Self love would here say, What is done cannot be undone, let me never think of what is past, nor trouble myself about it, but do better for the time to come. But the Language of Remorse is very different. I have done a bad thing says the penitent. I ought to suffer for it. My Soul is stained, how shall I wash out the stain? My Friend whom I have justly offended by my fault, generously forgives it. Alas! this Goodness makes the sting of remorse go deeper, & I can the less forgive myself. I ought to afflict myself, & I will do it because I ought.

If you ask whether there is any Gratification in this? I think there is the gratification of doing what I desire to do & what I think I ought to do. But is there pleasure in it? By no Means.

---

[4] Kames followed Reid's advice, and before he published the third edition of his *Essays on the Principles of Morality* (Edinburgh, 1779), he applied to Adam Smith to see if he would be put out by strictures on his *Theory of Moral Sentiments* (Edinburgh, 1759). In his reply, Smith said that he was sorry to differ from 'so old and so good a friend; but the differences of this kind are inevitable, and, besides, *Partium contentionibus respublica crescit*' (letter of November 16, 1778, Abercairny Collection, No. 586). See two previous items in this anthology.

[5] In the *Heauton Timorumenos* (i.e., *Self-Punisher*), an overstrict father, Menedemus, causes his son to leave home and serve abroad as a mercenary. In remorse, Menedemus moves to the country and lives a life of self-imposed hardship, taking on the heaviest farm work available.

My very intention is [to] put myself to pain. The Gratification is not the Gratification of self Love but of a just Indignation against my self.

Why does a Man afflict himself for the loss of his Dear Friend? Self love would dictate, Your Grief cannot recall him, forget your loss. Eat, drink and be merry. No says Friendship I ought to grieve, it is my Duty I should hate my self if I could forget him. The gratification is in doing what friendship demands and makes your Duty. It is not by any means a selfish Gratification, but a generous and a virtuous one.

I am quite convinced that we have a Natural faculty which makes us Physiognomists antecedent to Experience. In this as in many other Respects it is the Inspiration of the Almighty that gives us Understanding.

I am my Lord with perfect Respect

Your Lordships most humble Servt
Tho Reid.

A SKETCH OF DR SMITH'S THEORY OF MORALS*[1]

Thomas Reid

[MS.2131/2/II/6]   I do not at all pretend in this Sketch of Dr Smith's Theory [to have^c]² to have given a full and adequate Account of his System far less of the Arguments and facts by which he has in a very ingenious manner Supported it. Those who would have a just view of it must consult his own Book which is too well wrote to admit of an abridgment without doing it injustice. I have onely mentioned the chief principles of this System and especially such as I intend to make some remarks upon.

In general I would observe that although in Mr Humes

---

* From 'Thomas Reid on Adam Smith's Theory of Morals', edited by J. C. Stewart-Robertson and David Fate Norton, first published in the *Journal of the History of Ideas*, vol. 45 (1984), pp. 310–21. The editors' notes have been retained.

1 The MSS. which together constitute the fullest known text of Reid's 'objections' to Adam Smith's theory of morals – sc. MSS. 2131/2/II/6 and 3/I/28, – are reproduced here with the kind permission of the Aberdeen University Library. The title, which the editors have supplied, is an amplification of the first line of MS. 2131/2/II/6.

2 The following table of superscript notations, employed throughout our transcription, compromises a portion (only) of that designed for, and currently being used in the editing of Reid's unpublished papers. Its refinement has been a continuing process, accomplished over many years and in the face of a wide assortment of often disparate MSS. Its purpose again is to demonstrate and, in so far as this is possible, to ensure the authenticity of Reid's actual lecture-material on this as on other philosophical subjects.

[^c]: a word or phrase cancelled or stroked out but still decipherable.

^s/ss: a word or phrase superscribed.

[^wo]: a word, in whole or part, omitted from the MS, but here inserted to facilitate the sense.

^os: one word inscribed over another.

^o: as spelled in the original.

[^c cr]: a cancellation where the reading provided is conjectural only.

^n n: a self-instructional note.

[^r]: a word or phrase repeated without cancellation.

( ): a cancellation rendering the original illegible.

^ma ma: the enclosed text is a marginal addendum.

[^m] a mark in the text indicating a re-positioning of words or the location for a marginal addendum.

^cr: the reading of the word is conjectural only.

System we had occasion to take Notice of Some things which border upon licentiousness, there is nothing of this kind to be found in the System now under our consideration. Every branch of Virtue has a just Regard payed to it. Nay these Virtues which Dr Smith calls the awfull & respectable, such as self denial Temperance Fortitude & Magnanimity, have rather a higher rank in this System than in that of Dr Hutcheson,[3] who seems to allow them no other merit than that of Auxiliaries to the Amiable Virtues of Benevolence & kind Affection. I would likewise observe that Doctor Smith has given the most distinct and Accurate Account that is to be found any where[4] of the Several [Systems^c] Theories concerning Morals ^{s}both Ancient & modern^s that were before him, excepting Mr Humes System which he has onely touched upon. He has pointed out with great Judgment both the defects and the excellences of all these Systems. And on this account the book is highly valuable. It is his own Theory contained in [the^{wo}] former part of the book which I propose to offer some remarks upon.

The Author in this System endeavours to reduce Morals to very few original Principles, for as all Our^{os} moral Sentiments are resolved into Sympathy so even this Sympathy seems to be resolved into self love, which receives some change in its direction by an operation of the imagination. I would therefore first of all observe some things upon the manner in which Sympathy is accounted for.

The Sourse^o of Sympathy he makes to be our placing our selves in the Situation of the person with whom we Sympathize, & thence forming an Idea of his Sensations and even feeling something which though weaker in degree is not unlike to them. This account of the cause of Sympathy does not appear to me agreable^o to the Nature of that feeling. When I [imagine^c] conceive^s my self in the condition of the Suffering

---

[3] 'Hutcheson' (i.e. Francis Hutcheson) appears also as 'Hutchison' in the text, sometimes very distinctly (as on f.11, MS 2131/2/II/6), at other times in a manner scarcely distinguishable from its alternate. Reid was not alone in so addressing the former Professor of Moral Philosophy at Glasgow.

[4] The subordinate conjunction, 'that is to be found any where,' is doubly marked – by an 'x' and with appropriate over-scoring, – to follow immediately upon 'Accurate Account,' in place of the phrase, 'of the Several ... Theories.'

person it is not indeed a natural consequence of this that I should imagine my self to suffer what he suffers but I can[s] imagine all this without Suffering any thing at all. For as I can imagine my self to be in france[o] without being one foot nearer to it than when I have no such Imagination. So I can imagine my self to be undergoing a severe chirurgical operation, I can imagine a racking pain to accompany this operation without feeling that pain in the least. To imagine pain and to feel pain are things totally distinct nor does the first imply any degree of the last. The bare imagination of my being in pain is not being in pain as the imagination of my being in france[o] is not being in France.

2 Supposing that the imagination of my being pained gave me some degree of that uneasiness which the pain it self would give, if really felt[,] yet this uneasiness would no wise resemble Sympathy. The uneasiness arising[os] from my own pain whether felt or imagined is totally selfish, & to every one who attends carefully to the emotions of his own Mind will appear of a quite different nature from that uneasiness which we feel from Sympathy with the pains of others which is a social feeling.

3 When I feel this Sympathy with a person that Suffers I am not at all conscious of this change of persons. There are indeed many operations of our minds which escape our notice for want of attentive reflexion. But operations of the imagination ought not to be supposed unless we are conscious of them. This is nothing else but to feign a Hypothesis in order to account for a Phenomenon a Method of Philosophizing indeed to[o] common but against all just rules of Philosophizing. This Hypothesis therefore ought not to be admitted unless it is true in fact and whether it be so or not every man who is capable of accurate Reflexions upon his own feelings may certainly know. When we see a friend racked with a fit of the gout or Stone what do we feel? What are we conscious of? Why as far as appears to me we feel instantaneously & without the least Reflexion without any imaginary change of persons, we feel [that which we[c]] his pain and uneasiness in some degree. The [muscles[c]] features of our face the contortions of our body by a kind of instinct [are[c]] correspond to his, nor is the imagination at all employed at this time about ourselves, our suffering friend occupies all our thoughts, and the Sympathy must be much weakened before it will give us leisure to think what we would suffer in the Same Situation. This imagination while it

lasts puts a stop to the Sympathy altogether by turning our attention to our selves. This notion therefore of our feeling onely for our selves when we seem most disinterestedly to feel for others seems to be a meer Hypothesis unsupported by fact. It is very similar to the hypothesis of those who make the love of our Children and our Friends to be onely a modification of self love. We love ourselves in our Children say they, we consider our children and our friends as parts of our [friends^c] selves[.]^5. I conceive that both Dr Hutcheson & Bishop Butler ^{s}& even Mr Hume^s have fully refuted all the theories by which Social Affection & Sympathy are resolved into self Love variously modified by certain operations of the Imagination.

4 We may observe that Sympathy with the Sufferings of others may signify two things which have commonly been confounded although they ought carefully [to^{wo}] be distinguished by every one who would think justly and accurately with regard to morals. 1 Sympathy signifies a natural instinct in which the will has no share, an instinct that makes us feel uneasiness at the sufferings of others, and prompts or inclines us to relieve them. This Sympathy being a part of our frame implys^o no virtue at all. It may be in the most obdurate heart even in the moment it voluntarly^s inflicts that very Suffering with which it sympathizes[.] An unnatural Mother may feel this Sympathy with the Agonies of her [child^c] ^{s}innocent infant^s while she cruelly puts it to death with her own hands. She does it with reluctance and with uneasiness. This reluctance and [and^c] uneasiness [but he^c] is involuntary & is [not^c] no virtue at all but her^{os} cruel deed is voluntary and is the more criminal that it is done against the admonition of natural affection as well as of Conscience[.] But 2 The Sympathy which can with any propriety be called virtuous is a fixed determination of the will to yield that comfort and relief to the distressed which we our selves would [^{c}derive^{cr}] ^{s}think due

---

^{5} Reid often supplies no period for sentences ending on the right-hand side of his page, sometimes, but not always, because he has no remaining space. (A frayed edge, of which there are many, is not likely to have been Reid's doing, but the two kinds of cases are practically indistinguishable in certain instances.) Of aproximately 25 periods supplied, more than eighty percent are for sentences of this sort. In a much longer manuscript of lecture material (128 pages) 57 marginal periods were clearly omitted, while only 22 were omitted within lines. Hence, Reid's punctuation is not quite so erratic as it might seem.

to us[s] in such Circumstances[.] Now this kind of Sympathy supposes a moral faculty. We immediately perceive Sympathy to be due to the distressed. We claim & expect it our selves in circumstances of distress, & must be self condemned if we do not to others as we think they ought to do towards us in like circumstances. Sympathy when we take it in the first of these senses is a natural affection, resulting immediately from our frame. And requires no imaginary change of persons. When we take Sympathy in the second Sense no change of persons will account for it without supposing a faculty by which we perceive right and wrong.

5 The account which this ingenious Author gives of Sympathy does not seem to me to agree with the Phenomena of that Emotion. We sympathize more with those whom we love & esteem and with whom we are connected, and in the same person we sympathize more with his Grief than with his Joy. and more with the innocent sufferer than the Guilty. Now it is hard to give a reason why we may not imagine a change of person with a Stranger or Enemy, a guilty person, as well as with a friend a Relation an innocent person[.] If it should be said that we have a greater inclination to imagine a change of persons with the later[o] than with the former. I know no cause that can be assigned of this inclination but Sympathy; and if Sympathy because of this inclination it must be [previous[c]] prior[s] to the change of persons and therefore cannot be the effect of it but what should give us a greater inclination to change persons with the miserable than with the happy. No probable cause can be assigned for such an inclination yet we sympathize chiefly with the miserable and very little with the happy. [n]Add A Insert A[n]

MS.2131/3/1/28   Remarks on Smith's Theory page 4

That what has been said with regard to Dr Smiths Account of Sympathy may be better Understood. I shall Add some observations which I conceive may lead us to a right Understanding of this part of the human Constitution, and enable us to judge of Hypotheses that are brought to account for it.

Sympathy seems to me to be inseparably connected with Love Affection and Esteem. I cannot possibly love a Man without being pleased with every good that befals him and uneasy at his misfortune[.] If you ask me why I take so much concern in his good or bad fortune it is because I love him. If

I have no Benevolence or good will towards a Man, I have no Sympathy with him; his good or bad fortune are perfectly indifferent to me. If I hate him, this hatred produces an affection contrary which we may call Antipathy. For it is an inseparable attendant of Malice to be pleased with the misery and displeased with the happiness of those who are objects of hatred[.] And it is on the other hand no less inseparable from benevolen[ce][6] to be pleased with happiness and to grieve for the distresses and afflictions of those whom we wish well to. Nor can I conceive the least degree of Sympathy either with the griefs or Joys of another which has not a proportionable degree of Benevolence for its foundation. As Self love makes us rejoice in every event that tends to promote our own happiness and grieve at every thing of a contrary tendency; so that [as^c] it is impossible for a man who has any affection for himself to be indifferent with regard to his own happiness or misery; [so^c] it is no less impossible to be indifferent with regard to the happiness and misery of others whom we love. If one loves another person as well as himself he will feel the calamities of that person as much as if they were his own. And in all cases the degree of our Sympathy will bear exact proportion to the degree of our affection and good will.

If this is a just account of the Nature of Sympathy, as to me it seems to be; no hypothesis can account for [it^{wo}] which does not at the same time account for benevolence. And if Benevolence be a Natural and Original Principle of the human Mind, Sympathy must be so also. If on the other hand Sympathy is to be resolved into Self Love varied in its direction by some Operations of the Imagination, every kind Affection Gratitude Parental Affe*t*ion Friendship must in like manner be resolved into Self love, & be onely so many different modifications of Selfishness. But this method of accounting for our benevolent affections has been so fully refuted by Cicero in his Second Book de Finibus, by Lord Shaftsbury° Dr Hutcheson Bishop Butler & others, ˢeven by Mr Humeˢ [that^c] I think no more needs be said upon this Subject. ⁿEnd of Aⁿ

MS.2131/3/I/28   As this Author resolves all Sympathy into self love variously modified by certain operations of the Imagination. So he resolves all moral Approbation and Disap-

---

⁶ The last two letters have run off the right-hand edge of f.1 recto.

probation into Sympathy. And this is the next thing in this System which I beg leave to make some remarks upon.

1 I observe that the word Sympathy seems not to have always the same fixed and determinate meaning in this System, nor to be so accurately defined as is necessary to make it the foundation of a distinct Theory of Morals[.] In the beginning of this work the Author observes that in every passion pleasant as well as painfull, the emotions of the bystander correspond to what, by bringing the case home to himself, he imagines should be the sentiments of the Sufferer. And that this disposition of the human mind is what we call Sympathy. I do not find any other definition of Sympathy throughout the Book. And this I think is not what is commonly meant by the word Sympathy[.] The etimology° of the word plainly points out the common means of it in the English Language [.] It supposes some painfull or°ˢ agreable feeling ˢor passionˢ in the person sympathized with, & [implysᶜ] causesˢ a correspondent & similar feeling in the spectator[;] this is what we call Sympathy. But Dr Smith makes his Sympathy to correspond not to what the person sympathized with really ˢ& actually ˢ suffers or [orʳ] enjoys but what he should ˢor oughtˢ suffer or enjoy[.] This if I understand it aright supposes that we first form a judgment how the person to whom any good or evil has befallen ought to be affected with it. And that our Sympathy ˢwith himˢ corresponds not to the feeling which he actually has of what has befallen him but to that which he ought to have. And it appears from many instances brought by the Author that this is his meaning. Thus says he we blush for the impudence or Rudeness of another. Here we judge that the impudent & rude person ought to blush for his own Conduct and therefore we blush for him. I conceive this meaning of the word Sympathy is altogether new & that if one had not a hypothes° to serve by it he would never have dreamed that it is Sympathy that makes us blush for the impudence and rudeness of another. It might I think [asᶜ] moreˢ properly be called Antipathy but that we may not dispute about words, Let us suppose that our feeling that Emotion for another which he ought to feel but does not feel, is to be called Sympathy. It is evident that this Sympathy supposes a moral Judgment and consequently a moral faculty. It is impossible to judge that a man ought to be affected in such a manner in certain circumstances unless we have some faculty by which we perceive that [h]is being

affected in this way is [wrong^c] right^s and that his being affected in such another way is [right^c] wrong^s[.] Now this is what we call a moral faculty. Therefore it appears to me that this definition of Sympathy makes a moral faculty to be necessarily^o antecedent to our Sympathy and consequently our moral Sentiments cannot be the Effect of Sympathy[;] they must go before it, and set bounds to it.

2 When the author observes that our Approbation of the Passions of others as just and proper arises from our perceiving them to [be^{wo}] in accord with what we should feel in like Circumstances; the world *should* here is ambiguous; either it means what we ought to feel in like Circumstances or what we actually would feel in like circumstances. If the first is the meaning it supposes that we have a moral faculty by which we judge of the justness and propriety of our feelings as was already observed[,] but if we take the word *should* here to mean what we actually would feel in like Circumstances, I conceive this account of approbation is very far from the truth. If a man who had an opportunity of enriching himself by a little dishonesty which could not be detected, does in such circumstances nobly withstand the temptation and preserves his integrity the most avaritious^o man approves of his conduct as right while at the same time he is conscious that in the same circumstances he himself would have acted a very different part. Our Approbation of others does not therefore depend upon what we actually would do in such circumstances, but upon what we think we ought to do. There is a measure of right and wrong which we can with equal facility apply to our own conduct or to the conduct of others.

3 We may observe that this Author speaks all along of the passions and the feelings of ourselves and others as being not onely the proper but the onely object of moral Approbation & Disapprobation[.] Now I have endeavoured to shew that neither our o[w]n feelings nor the feelings of others ^sin so far as they are involuntary^s are ( ) at all the Object of Moral Approbation or Disapprobation. A Mans Moral Character depends not upon what he feels but how he Acts. Whatever agreeable or disagreeable involuntary^s feelings he has, it matters not; if it is the fixed determination of his Mind to do what he ought to do he is a man of Virtue; if he has not this determination he is not. Now as the whole of this System by which our moral Sentiments are resolved into Sympathy is

built upon this foundation. That what we call Virtue and what we account the object of Moral Approbation is a certain tone or temperament of our feelings and passions. If that is not true the foundation of it must fail. [n]See B. Insert B[n] and passions. If that is not true the foundation of it must fail. [n]See B. Insert B[n]

MS.2131/3/I/28   [n]B insert this page 6 at B6[n]

I am aware that this Author sometimes places the Nature of Virtue which is the Object of Approbation in an Effort to sympathize with others in their Emotions, and an Effort to regulate our own Emotions so as that others may sympathize with them. Now[s] An Effort is no doubt [s]an Act[s] of the will and is in our Power, & therefore may be an object of moral approbation. But as in most places he seems to place Virtue in a certain tone or temperament of our Passions and Emotions, & not in any voluntary Effort, I think his System is justly liable to the objection I have mentioned. No Man can be a just object either of moral Approbation or disapprobation for what is not in his power. Our passions and Emotions [s]in as far as they are involuntary[s] are not [altogether[c]] in our Power and [in[c]] as far as they are not involuntary[s] they are neither objects of Praise nor blame.

MS.2131/2/II/6.   4 Another observation which I would make upon this System of Sympathy is that it seems rather to account for mens putting[o] on the Appearance of Virtue than for their being really virtuous. The Social Virtues according to this System are resolved into an Effort to Sympathize with others in their Sufferings and Joys. But what is the inducement to make this Effort? According to our Authors System it is this[:] That we desire above all things to act so as that the impartial Spectator may enter into the principles of our Conduct and may Sympathize with them[.] Now all that is necessary to this end is that we have the appearance of Sympathizing with other[s]. It needs onely the Appearance of Virtue to draw the admiration and applause of Mankind which is the inducement to that Effort wherein social Virtue consists. By this Account Social Virtue seems to be resolved either into Vanity or into self interest. But let us next Consider the Account that is given of the Virtues of Self Government. These are resolved into an Effort to regulate our Passions so that others may Sympathize with them. Now as men can judge onely from appearances the appearance of temperance and fortitude will answer all the end[s] for which those virtues are practised.

5. To approve or disapprove of the opinions of others, ˢsays our Authorˢ[,] is acknowledged by every body to mean no more than to observe their agreement, or disagreement with our own. But this is equally the case with respect to our approbation or disapprobation of the passions & sentiments of others. I humbly conceive [there is a fallacy here both in the premises and in the Conclusion drawn from themᶜ] ˢ that mens Opinions are no proper Object either of Approbation or Disapprobation, but if we apply these words to Opinions, to approve the Opinion of another Man is to signify nothing else but to be of the Same Opinionˢ. To approve of an opinion is to observe its agreement with our own. This seems to have a meaning but in reality I cannot find that it has any meaning. To approve an opinion is to adopt it and to adopt it is to approve it[,] as the Author observes. That [whichᶜ] is my own opinion whichˢ I approve and that which I approve is my own Opinion. To say that such an opinion is my own opinion, and to say that it is an opinion which I approve is not saying two things but saying one and the same thing in different words. Therefore to say that to approve an Opinion is no more than [toʷᵒ] observe its agreement with our own Opinion Is in reality to say no more but this[,] That to approve an Opinion is to observe that we approve it and to have an Opinion is to observe that we have it. I acknowledge that no Man approves of an Opinion which is contrary to his own Opinion, for this would be to ᵐᵃhave directlyˢ contrary opinions at one and the same time which is impossible. Butᵐᵃ⁷ The Author Observes that every faculty in one Man is the measure by which he judges of the Like faculty in another. I judge of your sight by my Sight, of your Ear by my Ear, of your Reason by my Reason[.] [So farᶜ] ˢIn these instancesˢ I agree with him. The Eye must be the ultimate Judge of the Objects of Vision. The Faculty of Taste in like manner in objects of Taste and the faculty of Reason in Objects of Reasoning; and I add that in Like manner the Moral Faculty is that by which we must ultimately Judge of Morals. And so it is with regard to Every

---

⁷ The sentence beginning 'I acknowledge that no Man...' and ending with the marginal addendum (so marked in the text) is probably a later insertion. The script is slightly lighter and finer than the foregoing, while Reid has made conjunctive provision for what was to have been the next, and separate, paragraph (on f. 7) with the dangling 'But' at the end of the addenda.

original power of Judging. But this must be confined by[8] our judging powers. And therefore when he adds that I judge of your Resentment by my Resentment, of your Love by my Love, & that I neither have nor can have any other way of judging about them. This I can by no means assent to. To judge by resentment and to judge by Love are ways of speaking altogether new. Neither Resentment nor Love are judging Faculties, and it is impossible to judge of any thing by them. We have indeed a faculty by which we judge whether resentment is proportioned to the cause of it. And by this faculty we judge both of our own Resentment and the Resentment of others. When I say that such an ( ) Offence did not deserve such a degree of Resentment I express by this a Judgment of my Mind. But it is a judgment regarding right and wrong that is a judgment of the Moral Faculty. By this Faculty I judge both of my own resentment and of the resentment of another whether it is excessive and disproportioned to the offence or not. And the same thing may be said of Love.

[There is likewise some fallacy[c]] To say therefore that my resentment is [is[r]] the faculty by which I judge of your Resentment or that my Love is the faculty by which I judge of your Love; this seems to me to be totally irreconcileable[c] to all the notions I have of love or resentment[;] they are in no sense judging faculties [of Judging[c]]. And it might be said as well that I judge of your hunger by my hunger, or of your will by my will.

I must likewise observe that this Author uses the Words Approbation and Disapprobation in too vague and ambiguous a Sense in this reasoning[;] when we speak at one time of approving an Opinion at another of approving an Action of a Moral Agent; the word Approbation is in these two cases taken in quite different Senses. To approve of an opinion is to judge it to be a true opinion. To approve of an action is to judge that the Agent acted virtuously and properly in doing that Action. The approbation of an action implys not onely a judgment of its being right, but it implys some sentiment of inward worth in the Agent, on account of which he merits our benevolent regard and Esteem. The approbation of his opinion implys

---

[8] Does Reid mean 'confined *to* our judging power,' or confined in the sense of 'restricted by . . .'? The sense here is not clear, for 'this' lacks a distinct reference.

nothing of this kind. The word approbation therefore when applyed to opinions and to Actions is equivocal and we can not reason from the one sense of it to the other. So that although it were true, as it is not, that to approve of the opinion of another, [is no m^c] might properly be said to be no more than observing the agreement of his opinion with ours yet it would not follow that to approve of his resentment is no more than to observe its agreement with our own resentment. [X^m]

^{ma}X [Lastly^c] I conceive this System can never Account for our Approbation and Disapprobation of our own Actions. It is evident that we approve or disapprove of our own^s Actions as well as those of others, & by the same principle. Will it be said then that when a Man does a good Action which his heart approves. That this approbation is nothing else but sympathysing^o with himself[?] It would be still more strange if when a Man does an Action which his heart condemns him for, that this disapprobation of his own Mind is an Antipathy to himself. Yet I see no other way Agreable to this System of accounting for our Approbation or disapprobation of our Own Actions. To Judge of the Propriety of my own Passions and feelings, I must change persons with the impartial Spectator and view them with his Eyes. But how shall I know what judgment he would pass upon them[?] Onely by knowing how I my self judge in such cases. This is the onely way in which I can Jud[g]e of them. There must therefore be some faculty of the Mind by which we approve or disapprove of actions without respect to the Judgment of others otherwise we never could Judge whether they will appear in an agreable or in a disagreable light to others.^{ma}

See Cⁿ

MS.2131/3/I/28.   ⁿC end of 7 pageⁿ

6 The Law of Sympathy although it seems at first very simple, and ^sat the same time^s to Account for many Phenomena of human Nature yet in the Progress of this work it becomes very complex, and is modified variously in every passion to suit the Appearances.

Thus we are told that we Sympathize very little with bodily pain, and not in the least with the bodily pleasures of others. We Sympathize highly with the social Passions but not with the unsocial or in a small degree; yet we sympathize not with the passion of love between the Sexes[.] In the Selfish

Passions of others our Sympathy is particularly capricious, it is greatest with small Joys and great Sorrows[.]

We sympathize readily with the rich the great & the power-full, but very little with the poor and mean. Almost every Affection and Passion has a particular Force^{cr} or degree in which degree onely it is in harmony with the Sympathy of the Observer[.] If it is higher or lower it makes a discord. And creates antipathy[.] For he asserts that we have an Antipathy to those Passions or affections of others which we disapprove of as improper[.] Indeed as Approbation and Disapprobation are Contraries if the one be Sympathy the other must be Antipathy. In order therefore to compleat° this System it had been necessary to shew the Original of Antipathy and its Laws as well as those of Sympathy.[9]

^{ma}To conclude these Observations, it is obvious that according to this System there is no fixed Standard of Virtue at all[;] it depends not upon our Actions but upon the Tone^{cr} of our Passions,[10] which in different men is different from Constitution. Nor does it solely depend upon our own Passions but also upon the Sympathetick passions of others. [W]hich may be different in different Persons or in the Same Person at different Times. Nor is there any Standard according to which either the Emotions of the Actor or the Sympathy of the Spectator is to be measured[;] ^sall that is required is that they be in Harmony or Concord^s[.] It is evident that the ultimate Measure & Standard of Right and Wrong in human Conduct according to this System of Sympathy, is not any fixed Judgment grounded upon Truth or upon the dictates of a well informed Conscience but the variable opinions and passions of Men. So that we may apply to this System, what Cicero says of the Epicurean. Ita pro vera certaque Justitia, Simulationem nobis Justitiae traditis; praeciptisque quodammodo, ut

---

[9] The marginal addendum which follows appears in a very minute hand, along the right-hand margin of f. 2. verso (which, incidentally, bears the unaccountable number '6').

[10] We have not been able to determine with complete certainty whether here and in the previous paragraph Reid has written 'Force' or 'Tone.' Nevertheless, the conjectural readings provided seem to represent best the sense of what he is saying, given that there is a quantitative turn in the first instance ('Force or degree'), and that he has earlier (p. 47, lines 11–12) spoken of 'a certain tone or temperament of our feelings and passions.'

nostram Stabilem Conscientiam contemnamus, aliorum errantem opinionem Aucupemur. De Finibus 2.22^{ma11}

MS.2131/2/II/6. Let us endeavour to attend to that operation of our Minds which we call moral Approbation, and examine it on every side. We shall find that it is an operation of its own kind, of a distinct Nature from all the other operations of mind we are conscious of. Yet perhaps it is not so perfectly simple as to have nothing of composition in its nature[.] It may be made up of different Ingredients but we shall find all of them proper to this operation and not^s belonging to it in common with other operations of the Mind. It seems to me upon the most carefull attention to be made up of these three ingredients. Judgment, Affection and Feeling. Let us consider these distinctly, that we may have the more clear and determinate notions concerning this Operation of the Mind, which is of all the operations of the Mind the Most important.

1 In moral Approbation there is a judgment but of a peculiar kind which therefore we may call moral Judgment. Nothing can be the object of moral judgment but some voluntary determination or action of a moral Agent and such actions may be comprehended under these three classes[:] they are either right wrong or indifferent. Between true and false in propositions there is no medium for every proposition must be either true or false; But between right and wrong in Actions there is a medium for an action such [as^{wo}] the turning of a Straw may be perfectly indifferent & neither right nor wrong. We neither approve of such an action nor disapprove of it, yet we pass a moral Judgment concerning it, to wit that there is neither virtue nor vice in it. This kind of Moral judgment is neither accompanied by any Affection nor by any [any^r] feeling. It neither increases nor diminishes our esteem of the Agent; we have neither pleasure nor pain from doing such an action our selves nor in observing another do it. It is otherwise [with App^c] when we judge an action to be morally good. For

---

[11] Reid omits the ill-suited interpolation 'quod certissimum est' after 'ita.' Rackham translates this passage as follows: 'So your school undoubtedly preaches the pretence (*simulationem*) of justice instead of the real and genuine thing. Its lesson amounts to this – we are to despise the trustworthy voice of our own conscience, and to run after the fallible imaginations (*errantem opinionem*) of other men.' (Loeb Classical edition).

2 Such judgment is necessarily accompanied with some benevolent affection to[wards[s]] the Agent. Moral Worth even in a
Stranger with whom we have not the least connexion never
fails to produce some degree of Esteem mixed with good will.
And this Esteem which we have for a man on account of his
moral Worth is different from that which is grounded on
his intellectual accomplishments his birth fortune or particular
connexion with us. Moral Worth when it is not set off by
eminent intellectual Endowments and External advantages is
like a Diamond in the mine while it is rough & unpolished
and perhaps crusted over with some basic Material that takes
away all its lustre. But when it is attended with these advantages it is like a diamond properly cut and polished and set[;]
then its luster[o] & brilliancy attracts every Eye. Yet these things
that contribute so much to its fine appearance add but little to
its real Value. This Esteem that is merited by worthy conduct,
is not lessened when we are conscious of such conduct in
ourselves. We may call this self Esteem. And a man cannot but
esteem himself when he is conscious of these Qualities for
which he esteems others. The consciousness of real Moral
Worth is therefore necessarily accompanied with a pro[por-
[wo]]tionable[cr] degree of self esteem. [When[c]][s] An undue degree
of[s] self esteem [is[c]] when grounded upon external advantages
or the gifts of fortune is Pride; When grounded upon some
vain conceit of inward worth which does not belong to us it
is Arrogance. But when a Man without thinking of himself
more highly than he ought to think, is conscious of that Integrity of heart and uprightness of Conduct which he most highly
esteems in another and values himself duly upon this Account.
This is not Pride, it is so far from being vicious, that there can
be no Virtue without it. He that Esteems Virtue as he ought,
must value himself, and ought to value himself in Proportion
as he is conscious he is possessed of it. If unjust imputations
are thrown upon him, he flings them off with a noble disdain.
It is the natural Language of virtue in such a situation[.] My
Integrity will I hold fast and will not let it go; my heart shall
not reproach my[12] while I live. We may call this the Pride of
Virtue, but it is not a vicious but a Noble, a Magnanimous
Disposition. The Sense of Honour which is so much spoke[o] of

[12] Reid presumably intended to write 'me.'

in the World and so often mistaken and misapplied; this Sense of Honour I say rightly understood is nothing but that Estimation which a good Man ought to have of himself from a Consciousness of his real Worth. A True Sense of Honour will make [X^m] ^ma a man disdain the doing anything that is unworthy or base as much as he disdains the imputation of it.^ma

Let us on the other hand attend to the Affection that accompanies moral disapprobation either of the conduct of others or of our own Conduct. Every thing we disapprove of in the conduct of another lessens him in our Esteem[.] There are some more^s brilliant faults which having a mixture of good and evil in them, may have a very different aspect according to the side on which we view them. In such faults of our friends and much more of our selves we are disposed to view them on the best side; and on the other hand such actions in those to whom we are ill affected, we are apt to view on the worst side. This partiality in taking things by the best or the worst handle is the chief cause of [that^c] wrong Judgment with regard to the character of others and of Self deceit with regard to our selves. But when we take complex Actions to pieces and view every part by itself, ill conduct of every kind lessens our Esteem of a man as much as good conduct increases it. It is apt^s to turn Love into indifference. Indifference into Contempt and Contempt into abhorrence. As all our affections therefore may be distinguished in [to^wo] benevolent and malevolent ^sfavourable and unfavourable^s[,] it appears that as moral approbation of the conduct [of^wo] others is necessarily accompanied with a certain kind of benevolent affection towards them; which we esteem due on account of their worth; so on the other hand, moral Disapprobation as necessarily produces a contrary affection, which if it does not produce hatred yet necessarily lessens love and esteem.

When a Man is conscious of bad conduct in himself this must needs lessen his self esteem, it humbles and depresses his spirit. He could even punish himself for his misbehaviour if that could wipe out the Stain. There is a sense of Dishonour ^sand Worthlessness^s arising from Guilt, as well as a Sense [of^wo] Honour and worth arising from worthy conduct, and this is the case even if^s a man can conceal his guilt from all the World.

3 There is an agreable Feeling attending Approbation & a disagreable attending disapprobation. There is no affection whatsoever that is not attended with some agreable or disagre-

able Emotion. All the benevolent affections give pleasure the contrary ones Pain in one degre° or another. When we contemblate° a noble⁵ Character [of Worthᶜ] though even in ancient History or in Romance; like a beautifull Object it gives a lively and pleasant Emotion to the Spirits. It warms the heart and invigorates the whole frame. Like the Beams of the Sun it enlivens the face of Nature and diffuses [bothᶜ] its light and warmth all around. We feel a real Sympathy with every Noble and worthy Character that is represented to us. We rejoyce° in his prosperity we are afflicted in his Distress. We even catch some sparks of that celestial fire [of Virtueᶜ] that animated his conduct and feel the glow of his Virtue and Magnanimity. This Sympathy however is onely the Effect and the consequence of our Approbation and Esteem[.] For real Sympathy must always be preceeded by [byᶜ] some Benevolent Affection such as Esteem Love or Pity.

When the Person whose conduct we approve is connected with us by acquaintance, Friendship, or Blood, the pleasure we derive from his good Conduct is vastly increased. We claim some property in his worth and value our selves on account of it. This evidences a Stronger degree of Sympathy, which is always increased by every social tie. But the highest pleasure of all is when we are conscious of right Conduct in ourselves. Were we to place the *summum bonum* in any one kind of Enjoyment, surely that which arises from consciousness of Integrity, and of a uniform endeavour to act according to our best moral Judgment, would most justly claim a preference to all other enjoyments that the human Nature is capable of [bothᶜ,] on account of the Dignity of its Nature[,] the intenseness of the happiness it affords, its duration, its being in our power, and ⁵its being⁵ secured from all accidents of time or fortune.

On the other hand the [Contemptᶜ] View of a vicious Character like that of an ugly and deformed Object, is disagreable. It gives Disgust Spleen and Abhorrence, it ¹³chills the blood and makes it run cold.

If the unworthy Person is nearly connected with us we have

---

¹³ The reading here is conjectural only, for both 'it' and 'and' are real possibilities. Nevertheless, although the overscription offers no clear choice, the positioning of the 'i' on the extreme left perhaps tilts the balance in favour of Reid's amendment of 'and' to 'it'.

a very painful Sympathy indeed. We blush for the lesser faults of our near concerns and feel ourselves as it were dishonoured by them. But where there is a high degree of Depravity in any near Concern; we are deeply humbled & depressed by it. The Sympathetick feeling has some resemblance to that of Guilt tho' it be free from all Guilt. We are ashamed to see our acquaintance. We would if possible disclaim all connexion with the Guilty Person. We wish to tear him from our hearts, and to blot him out of our Remembrance.

Time however alleviates those Sympathetick Sorrows which arise from bad conduct in our friends and Connexions, especially if we are conscious that we have no share directly or indirectly in their Guilt. The wisdom of Nature hath intended that this Sympathetick Distress, should interest us the more deeply in the good Behaviour as well as in the good fortune of our friends and Connexions; And there thereby Friendship Relation and every Social Tie among men should be aiding to Virtue and Unfavourable to Vice. We see how common it is even for vicious Parents, to be deeply afflicted when their children enter into those courses [of^c] in which perhaps they themselves have gone before them & by their Example shewn them the way.

If bad Conduct in those in whom we are interested is uneasy & painfull it must be much more so when a man is conscious of it in himself. This uneasy feeling has a Name in all Languages[;] we call it remorse. It has been described so often by writers of every Age, and of persuasions even by the Epicureans themselves that I need not attempt the description of it. It is on account of the uneasiness of this feeling that bad men take so much pains to get rid of it, and to hide even from their own eyes as much as possible the gravity of their Conduct. Hence all the Arts of self deceit, by which men varnish their crimes and endeavour to make the black-moor white. Hence all[s] the various methods of Expiation which [a^c] Superstition[s^c] has[os] invented to solace the Conscience of the criminal and give some cooling to his parched breast. Hence also arise very often the endeavours of men of bad hearts to excell in some amiable quality which may be a kind of counterpoise to their vices both in the opinion of others and in their own[.] For no man can possibly bear the thoughts of being absolutely[s] destitute of all worth. The consciousness of this would make him detest himself and hate the Light of the Sun.

To the truth of this Account which I have endeavoured to give of the Operations of that natural Power of the human Mind which we call Conscience or the Moral Faculty, I hope Gentlemen your hearts & Consciences will bear witness, when you please to reflect cooly and deliberately upon the Subject. It is impossible to have clear and distinct Notions of any power of the human Mind otherwise than by a carefull reflection upon those operations of it of which we are conscious when they are exerted. And surely[s] there is no power of the Mind, which deserves our most serious attention so much as this.

If the account I have given of this faculty be just, we may see from it from what particular and partial views of it the several philosophical Systems concerning it have been derived. Doctor Clark considered it onely as a Judgment of the Understanding. It is a Judgment indeed but of a peculiar kind. As by the Eye we judge of Light and Darkness of Colour and Figure, by the Palate we judge of Sweet and bitter, by the Ear of Harmony and Discord[,] [s]By our Memory we judge of what we did suffered[o] or enjoyed in Time past[3][,] by our Understanding of Truth and Error, by our Taste of Beauty and Deformity[,] so by our Moral Faculty we judge of right and wrong in Conduct. All these are judging Faculties. They have each its distinct Nature & its distinct Objects[;] each of them gives us simple Ideas or Notions which we could not have by any or all the rest. Right and wrong in Conduct are Ideas of their own kind as Sweet and Bitter are[;] they are not to be resolved either into fittness Utility Beauty or Sympathy, any more than the Ideas of Sweet and bitter can be.

Dr. Hutchison[o] saw very clearly and has proved that the Notion of Right and Wrong in Conduct are Ideas of their own Kind and therefore he very justly attributed them to a peculiar Faculty which he calls the moral Sense. He did not perceive however that we have simple Ideas by the Understanding as well as the Senses, and that we judge by the senses as well as by the Understanding. So that in reality it may be called Moral understanding as properly as Moral Sense. The [Errors[c]] [s]wrong notions[s] which have been commonly entertained by Philosophers about the Senses in general, were apt to be applied to the Moral Sense by those who gave it that Name. There is a [great[c]] strong[s] dispos[pos[r]]ition in the modern Philosophy to resolve every thing into Feelings or impressions. And Dr Hutcheson in conformity to this has resolved Moral Approbation and Disapprobation into certain agreable and Uneasy feelings. From the Account I have given I think it appears that tho' there are agreable and uneasy feelings arising from Moral Approbation and Disapprobation, yet these are not the onely operations of the moral Faculty.[14]

---

[14] MS. 2131/2/II/6 ends at this point, approximately one third of the way down the page.

OF THE PRINCIPLE OF MORAL ESTIMATION*
Adam Ferguson

David Hume, Robert Clerk, Adam Smith[1]

When Mr Hume was at London about to publish some volume of the *History of England*, General Clerk called in a morning & soon after Mr Smith came in also.

Mr Clerk & Mr Hume had been talking of the *History* and Mr Clerk after some Compliments on Mr Hume's Stile & Politeness in writing said he was glad he had taken to History in which he could not avoid being instructive and agreeable too.

[2] HUME. I certainly shall not endeavour to avoid either of these Effects, But I hope you don't think I have endeavoured to avoid them in any of my other writings.

CLERK. If you endeavoured, you have not succeeded; you are very much in fashion. I do not mean for your Doctrines, For I think you rather try to pull down other people's Doctrines than Establish any of your own.

HUME. Pardon me, did I not sett out with a complete Theory of Human Nature, which was so ill received that I determind to refrain from System making?[2]

CLERK. That was rash. The world's a system & the best we can do is to assist one another [3] in perceiving and Communicating its parts & their Connexions.

HUME. I don't know what a man of Letters is to get by that, To be writing what every body knows or may hear from every Coffee House acquaintance.

CLERK. That would be very Idle; but I do not think Mr

---

* 'Of the Principle of Moral Estimation' (1761?), edited by Ernest C. Mossner, first published in the *Journal of the History of Ideas*, vol. 21 (1960), pp. 225–32. The editor's notes have been retained.

[1] Edinburgh University MS Dc. 1. 42. No. 25, 31 pages (holograph page numbers will here be bracketed).

[2] 'Never literary Attempt was more unfortunate than my Treatise of human Nature [1739]. It fell *dead-born from the Press*; without reaching such distinction as even to excite a murmur among the Zealots' (Hume, *My Own Life*, reprinted in Mossner, *Life of David Hume*, 611–15).

Hume is in danger of that even if he should discard all paradox and take to the investigation of useful truths.

HUME.   I own I am inclind to Scepticism & would avoid the pedantry of Dogmamatism [*sic*], But have [I] not declared opinions on Commerce, Politics, and Morals?

CLERK.   I like some of your Thoughts on [4] the subject of Commerce. But for Morals and Politics you seem [rather] to play with them than to be serious.

HUME.   You surely think I am Serious in my *Essay on Morals?*[3]

CLERK.   I do not doubt it. But it sounds odd to say that morality is founded on Utility and that Virtue is only a Cow that gives milk of a particular Sort, Alms to the Poor, and every Man's Due to himself. It is very true that these actions are Useful. The good man performs them because they are Usefull and neighbours applaud them for the same reason; but is there any thing more Usefull than a good Corn Field? People say there is a plentiful Crop, but no one says [5] there is a Virtuous Field.

HUME.   No, for a good Reason. Moral Virtue is peculiar to Mind and is the utility or usefulness that proceeds from mind, that is, from a Benevolent or good Intention.

CLERK.   Do we not Esteem a good Intention although from any Circumstance it be prevented of External Effect, and do we not withhold moral approbation from mere utility that comes without Intention? In short, mind is approved without external Effect & External Effect is not approved without mind. And it is the mind we approve not the Utility.

HUME.   Pardon me, it is both when they come [6] together. A man's pretensions to Virtue are very doubtful if it have no effect in his manners or behaviour.

CLERK.   Very doubtful indeed. The Elasticity of a Bow is very doubtful or rather incredible if an Arrow drawn to the Point is not made to fly from the string. Where benevolence is real it will be beneficent. But we are not talking of the Evidence required to evince the reality of Benevolence. We are supposing

---

[3] *An Enquiry concerning the Principles of Morals* (1751), which, writes Hume as above (p. 613), 'in my own opinion (who ought never to judge on that subject) is of all my writings, historical, philosophical, or literary, incomparably the best: It came unnoticed and unobserved into the World.'

Benevolence to be real & know how agreeable it is apart from its external Effects.

HUME. That I own: But to me Virtue is a Course of Life directed, if you will, by Good Intentions But realized in all the Effects of [7] Innocence, Beneficence, Sobriety, and Candour.

CLERK. I understand, & because you conceive a Virtuous [life] & its external Effects together you chuse to ascribe the Approbation of it to the external Effect alone. For my part, I am inclined to consider [it] rather in respect to its Value in the mind that possesses it, than in its Effects towards those who are within reach of its External Influence. To every man, his own happiness is the first & most import[ant] Concern, and nature cannot require of a man what is not of any value to himself.

HUME. Yet Virtue for the most part is admired as a Principle of Self denial.

CLERK. That [8] proceeds from the stupid Notion that Man is to Estimate himself as he Estimates a dead Ox, from his Belly & Four Quarters, so that whatever he does without a View to that Self is said to be self denial, and in this point of View but [*sic*] Happiness itself may be a System of self denial. We sett out with supposing we know what Virtue is without considering whether it be happy or miserable. For my part, I choose to refrain [from] all terms of Praise, till I know what it is to be Happy & this to every Intelligent being is the first & highest Praise. If a Person be a wretch, Praise him who will, He had better be a [9] Clod or a Block of Wood than a Man without the requisites of a happy mind. In this consists the excellence of mind that it may be happy and, if it fail of this, Existence is an Evil.

HUME. Happiness is surely very different from Mind: for every man thinks himself happy in being Gratifyed, Some with a dinner, some with money, and all with respect & a Good name.

CLERK. When I talk of happiness I do not go to the rabble in the street for an account of it. If there be in Nature affections & habits agreeable, others disagreeable, as Benevolence is agreeable, Malice the Reverse, Courage agreeable, Cowardice in all its forms the Reverse, [10] I call that man happy who is habitually Courageous & Benevolent, whose Actions & Thoughts are pleasant, whose very Existence is the Tranquillity of a mind undisturbed with the consequences of Error and

Mistake, or sense of mean[n]ess, degradation, or wrong. If Virtue is a term of peace and felicity, then I fix it on Goodness & Wisdom, on Fortitude, Temperance, and the occupations of a strenuous Mind.

It is well known that there is distinction of Good & Evil in human life & till we have ascertaind that distinction & made our Choice, all our Inquiries & Pretentions to Philosophy are nugatory & absurd.

Here the Conversation was about [11] to terminate when the Servant announced Mr Adam Smith, who at the same time entered the Room with a smile on his Countenance and muttering somewhat to himself. After the first Salutations Mr Hume said, Smith, The General & I have been upon a Subject in you are well versed & I should have been glad of your assistance.

SMITH.   What was it?

HUME.   No less than the Theory of moral sentiment.

SMITH.   My Book.[4] I am sorry to have been away. I should willingly profit by your remarks. General, he said then, observing him for the first time, I have long [12] wished to know your opinion. I think I have removed all the difficulties and made the *Theory* Compleat.

To this the General made no answer tho Mr Smith made some pause as expecting to hear what he would say. But continued, People thought I should never be able to get over the difficulty of supposing a man to sympathize with himself or if he did not chance to take that trouble what means he had of being admonished of his Faults. I have removed both these difficulties & I should be glad to know your opinion.

CLERK.   I don't much like to trouble authors with my opinion of their works.

SMITH.   Ah, Do, you will oblige me!

CLERK.   If you insist [13] upon it. I must be plain & leave no doubts.

SMITH.   Surely. Surely.

CLERK.   Your Book is to me a Heap of absolute Nonsense.

Smith seemed to be stunnd and Clerk went on, You endeavour to explain away the distinction of Right and Wrong

---

[4]   *The Theory of Moral Sentiments* (1759), second edition 1761.

by telling us that all the difference is the Sympathy or want of Sympathy, that is, the Assent or Dissent of some two or more persons of whom some one acts & some other observes the action and agrees or does not agree in the same feeling with the actor. If the Observer agree, sympathise, go along with him, or feel that he would have done the same himself, he cannot but [14] approve of the Action. If, on the Contrary, he does not Sympathise or agree with the Actor, he dissents & cannot but disapprove of him; and you seem to mean that where there is neither assent nor dissent there is neither Right nor wrong, and no one would ever suppose any such thing. Or if you don't deny the reality of the Distinction, you at least furnish but a very inadequate means of discovering it. How can I believe that a person is in the right because I sympathise with him? May not I myself be in the wrong? Does the presence of any sympathy ascertain a good action, or the want, of a bad one?

SMITH.   No! I have cleared up that point. Parties [15] concerned in any transaction may be willing each to flatter himself or both Mutually to flatter one another, But to the monitor may not fail to present himself. The well informed and impartial observer will bring to view what the Ignorant or prejudiced would overlook.

CLERK.   That is convenient, to be able to bring Virtue itself to your aid when actual Sympathy fails. You began with calling Sympathy to explain Moral Sentiment. You now call up moral sentiment to explain itself: what is a well informed & impartial observer, but a Virtuous Person whose Sympathy may be relyed on as a [16] Test of Virtue? If he be well informed, of what is he informed? Not of Astronomy or Geography, for these would be of little use to him in distinguishing the Chara[c]ters of men. For this purpose he must be informed of the distinction of Right, how constituted and applyed in particular Instances. And to be impartial must aim at a fair application without By [bias?] to any Side. Such a Person is not likely to misslead those who confide in him and such a Person every one is concerned to become in himself & instead of acquiesing in Sympathy as the Test of Virtue, appeals to Virtue as the test of Just Sympathy.

Here then ends [17] your System. After beating round a Circle of Objections & Answers, you return to the point from which you set the Phaenomena of moral distinctions, moral sentiments, to be explained. And let us try once more how far sympathy is adequate to this Purpose. You do not fail to tell us that moral Sentiments are real &, we trust, familiar to all men. You inform us that they constitute satisfaction in some cases and distress in others, thus of great importance & the consequence is that we should be careful to obtain the satisfaction and avoid the distress.

I do not see how we can be [18] aided in this by merely resolving these sentiments into some other affection of the mind, especially into any affection differing from themselves. What is this sympathy which you talk of? The word is not new: but the meaning probably is so. It is commonly synonimous with Pity or a fellow feeling for the distresses of others. But who ever heard of Sympathizing with a person who pays his Debts? or if this were said, it would be supposed that we pityd him for being obliged to part with his money: but you tell us of sympathizing with a Hero on having gained a Battle although he escaped unhurt. The word Sympathy in [19] this sense is generally unknown and to explain moral sentiment by sympathy is to explain the known by the unknown, the very reverse of what is required in Theory.

But if sympathy in all the Affections or Passions were as well known as it is in commiseration or Pity to the distressed, I do not see how it could explain moral Sentiment: For when it is best known it does [not] produce any moral Sentiment either of approbation or blame. When we pity a beggar we do not admire him for begging nor think that a person has any merit in the [20] toothache even if the thoughts of it should sett our Teeth on Edge or draw tears from our Eyes. If Sympathy means participation of any Passion without distinction, I do not see how a Passion participated should be any other than some shade or degree of the Passion [*Passion* repeated in MS] participat[e]d. If I participate in a Person's anger, I am angry too; if in his Joy, I too am glad: but neither one nor the other is moral approbation.

SMITH. I do not say it is: but that a man who participates in the Passion of another cannot but approve of it. Every Passion or strong motive urging a Person to act justifies itself and, if others [21] go along with it or Sympathise, they too approve: if they do not go along with it, they dissaprove or condemn his Conduct and so he does himself if, when the occasion is past, he cannot go along with the passion which actuated him.

CLERK. The whole amount then is that what others term Conscience, you Term Sympathy or the want of Sympathy. Every body knows, that under the operation of any strong Passion men are incapable of cool reflection. This you call justifying their Passion; but when it [is] over & they come to reflect, a Crime if committed stares them in the face & they become a prey to [22] remorse or self condemnation. I do not see that your account of the matter is any way more Intelligible than this, or that we are any way nearer the ultimate in the one account than in the other. Most men repose on the Fact that men are by nature endued with a Principle of Conscience. But you say the Fact commonly called Conscience is Sympathy or the want of Sympathy, and the supposed Theory is a mere change of Words or at best an attempt to confound two distinct principles of Nature.

This practice is too common &, when subs[t]itut[e]d for Theory, is insufferable. One great object of study certainly is to distinguish what is different as well as to bring things of a kind together. In morals, [23] Especially, the judgement is badly confounded by substituting one thing for another. A fashionable Philosopher has told us of late that Judgements are but Sensations, that Integrity or Elevation of mind is no more than Pride; he owns indeed that it is enlightened Pride, *orgueil éclairé.*[5] Others have told us that Benevolence is mere self Love or tends alike to personal Gratification whether in his own wellfare or that of his neighbour.[6]

And in both these hopeful Theories, we are cautiond not to be imposed upon by the specious appearances of Magnanimity or Benevolence, for the one is mere Pride, the other mere Selfishness. Thus to [24] bespeak our Animosity to a Friend by announcing him under the name of our Enemy. At the same time the Gentleman Usher takes great merit to himself for his penetration and knowledge of Persons.

I confess I was affraid that your Sympathy might have some such Effects as this or that the difference of right & wrong

---

[5] Presumably David Hartley, *Observations on Man, his frame, his duty, and his expectations* (1749).

[6] Presumably Richard Price, *A Review of the Principal Questions and Difficulties in Morals* (1757).

might vanish into an assent or dissent of two or more Persons who may agree in the wrong as well [as] in the Right: but you relieve us at last by telling us you do not mean any assent or dissent at random but that of a well informed & impartial observer, who we would say in common language is a virtuous man or competent [25] Judge. And the preference due to such a Person is what no one doubts, tho it is the Phaenomenon which you sett out with a Purpose to explain in your Theory, and so have it at last as others do as a self evident Truth which needs no Explanation.

I do not find that Moralists of old ever went into this Question. They observd that human Life was happy or miserable & they were curious to know how one or the other was brought about, or in other words, what was the Good on which men might rely for Happiness or avoid as misery. This was certainly the [26] first of most importan[t] Question to be settled in human Life and it was certainly wise to go into it even if they should mistake the Solution.

Let the Solution however be what it may, if a Chief Good was acknowledged there could no longer be any doubt of the Choice to be made; or if it were found that Conscience concurred with Experience in recommending the same thing, could there be any Question of the Grounds on which Conscience proceeded. I have sometimes been puz[z]led to guess how this Question came to be started in modern times, or [27] how it came to hold such a place in Modern Philosophy.

HUME.   You may believe I do not doubt its importance as I have treated it myself. Yet I believe the introduction of it was in a great Measure accidental. A performance which made some noise, *The Fable of the Bees*[7], calling Virtue the of[f]-spring of Flattery begot upon Pride and pretending that Private Vices were publick Benefits gave a General Allarm to the friends of Morality. And some of them sett about refuting this Sophism. One contended that the disstinction of Virtue & Vice was founded in the [28] Nature & fitness of Things.[8] Another

---

[7] By Bernard Mandeville, 1705, expanded in 1714, further expanded with comments in 1723. It was the 1723 version that began the controversy.

[8] Presumably William Law, *Remarks upon a late Book, entitled The Fable of the Bees* (1724).

that it was founded in Truth.[9] Another that it was founded in the natural principle of Benevolence.[10] Another, in a Specifick Sense, inspired nature, & which to distingish it from mere Corporeal Sensation was called the Moral Sense.[11]

They were all perhaps in the right, and the Author of *The Fable of the Bees* betrayd himself when he maintained that Private Vice was publick benefit: for as Virtue consist in public Utility or Good, how can that which is a publick Good be a Vice? Moral Sense is a mere figurative expression taken from the analogy of our corporeal organs in distinguishing the[i]r respective [29] Objects, but it appears trifling to me to be inquiring for reason to approve what is so useful as all the virtues of Men are in Society or human Life and I hoped to Silence the Question forever by pointing out this very real & important ground of Approbation or Preference in behalf of Virtue.[12]

CLERK. Well done, but while you considered what Virtue was in its Communications & external Effects, which are the objects of Law and in part the recommendation of Good manners, you forgot or overlooked what is the real recommendation of it to the Person who is to embrase it in his own mind & [30] without whose will it is not to exist. If it be happiness to him, as Wisdom, Goodness, Fortitude, and Temperance certainly are, It is certainly a Thing good in itself, not a thing recommended merely by its utility in procuring something else. We are apt to laugh now at the old Distinctions, Divisions, and Definitions of the Schools: but it were well sometimes to mind them. Some things are coveted as means to an End, others as Ends valuable in themselves. And if these were not sometimes such an End, the whole Fabrick of successive means would fall to the Ground. [31] Hence the

---

[9] Presumably George Berkeley, *Alciphron: or, The Minute Philosopher* (1732), second dialogue.

[10] Presumably Joseph Butler, *Fifteen Sermons Preached at the Rolls Chapel* (1726), of which the first three are entitled 'Upon Human Nature.'

[11] Presumably Francis Hutcheson, *An Inquiry in the Original of our Ideas of Beauty and Virtue; In Two Treatises* (1725); *An Essay on the Nature and Conduct of the Passions and Affections. With Illustrations on the Moral Sense* (1728).

[12] See Hume's *Political Discourse* (1752), 'Of Refinement in the Arts,' last two paragraphs.

important & Genuine Question of Moral Philosophy *de finibus*, or what is the End; and I believe that the utility which you point out are not ends but means concurring to the preservation of Society, and thus as means to furnish the Wise [man] [*and* in MS] with the proper Scene & Object of his Enjoyment, in the Condition of his happy Mind whom no false allurements can mislead or dangers deter.

[FROM] A LETTER TO ADAM SMITH LL.D. ON THE LIFE, DEATH, AND PHILOSOPHY OF HIS FRIEND DAVID HUME ESQ. BY ONE OF THE PEOPLE CALLED CHRISTIANS*
[George Horne, Bishop of Norwich]

ADVERTISEMENT

It is of no consequence, gentle Reader, to you, any more than it is to Dr. SMITH, that you should know the name of the person, who now addresseth you. Your mind cannot be biassed, either way, by that, of which you remain ignorant. The remarks in the following pages are not therefore true, or false, because I made them; but I made them, because I thought them to be true. Read, consider, and determine for yourself. If you find no satisfaction, throw the book into the fire; regret (but with moderation, as becometh a philosopher) the loss of your shilling; and take care not to lose another, in the same manner. If, on the contrary, you *should* find satisfaction (and, it is humbly hoped, you will find a great deal) neglect not to communicate to others, what has thus been communicated to you. Speak handsomely of me, wherever you go, and introduce me to your kinsfolk and acquaintance. The enemies of Religion are awake; let not her friends sleep.

I intended a much longer work; but, like the learned editor of Mr. HUME's Life, am necessitated to 'gratify,' with all possible expedition, 'the impatience of the public curiosity;' so eager is it to hear, what they, who believe in GOD, can possibly have to say for themselves. And if this will do the business, why should you be troubled with more? I am far from agreeing with Mr. VOLTAIRE, in all his observations. But there is one, in which it is impossible to disagree with him. 'I have said, and I abide by it,' cries the little hero, 'that the fault of most books is, their being too large.' On reviewing what I have written, I really cannot see there is occasion to add another sentence.

Had I not chosen, for reasons best known to myself, thus to

---

* Oxford, 1777, pp. i–iv, 1–11.

make my appearance *incog*. I would certainly have sate for my picture, and have tried to cast a look at my title page, as lively and good humoured, as that of Mr. HUME himself. My bookseller, indeed, told me, it would have been a much more creditable way of doing the thing; 'and then, you know, Sir,' said he, 'we could have charged the other sixpence.'

A LETTER, &.

SIR,

You have been lately employed in embalming a philosopher; his *body*, I believe I must say; for concerning the other part of him, neither you nor he seem to have entertained an idea, sleeping or waking. Else, it surely might have claimed a little of your care and attention; and one would think, the belief of the soul's existence and immortality could do no harm, if it did no good, in a *Theory of Moral Sentiments*. But every gentleman understands his own business best.

Will you do an unknown correspondent the honour, Sir, to accept a few plain remarks, in a free and easy way, upon the curious letter to Mr. STRAHAN, in which this ever memorable operation of *embalming* is performed? Our Philosopher's account of *his own life* will likewise be considered, as we go along.

Trust me, good Doctor, I am no bigot, enthusiast, or enemy to human learning *Et ego in Arcadiâ* – I have made many a hearty meal, in private, upon CICERO and VIRGIL, as well as Mr. HUME.[1] Few persons (though, perhaps, as Mr. HUME says, upon a like occasion, 'I ought not to judge on that subject') have a quicker relish for the productions of genius, and the beauties of composition. It is therefore as little in my intention, as it is in my power, to prejudice the literary character of your friend. From some of his writings I have received great pleasure, and have ever esteemed his History of England to have been a noble effort of *Matter and Motion*. But when a man takes it into his head to do mischief, you must be sensible, Sir, the Public has always reason to lament his being *a clever fellow*.

I hope it will not be deemed vanity in me likewise to say, that I have in my composition a large proportion of that,

---

[1] LIFE, p. 5.

which our inimitable SHAKESPEARE styles, *the milk of human kindness*. I never knew what envy or hatred was; and am ready, at all times, to praise, wherever I can do it, in honour and conscience. DAVID, I doubt not, was, as you affirm, a social agreeable person, of a convivial turn, told a good story, and played well at 'his favourite game of whist.'[2] I know not that JOHN THE PAINTER did the same. But there is no absurdity in the supposition. If he did not, he might have done it – Doctor, be not offended – I mean no harm. I would only infer thus much, that I could not, on that account, bring myself absolutely to approve his odd fancy of firing all the dockyards in the kingdom.

Concerning the *philosophical opinions* of Mr. HUME you observe,[3] that 'men will, no doubt, judge variously.' They are certainly at liberty so to do, because the author himself did the same. Sometimes, to be sure, he esteemed them ingenious, deep, subtle, elegant, and calculated to diffuse his literary fame to the ends of the world. But, at other times, he judged very differently; very much so, indeed. 'I dine, says he, I play a game at back-gammon, I converse, and am merry with my friends; and when, after three or four hours amusement, I would return to these speculations, they appear so *cold*, so *strained*, and so *ridiculous*, that I cannot find in my heart to enter into them any farther'.[4] Now, Sir, if you will only give me leave to judge, before dinner, of Mr. HUME's philosophy, as he judged of it after dinner, we shall have no farther dispute upon that subject. Only I could wish, if it were possible, to have a scheme of thought, which would bear contemplating, at any time of the day; because, otherwise, a person must be at the expence of maintaining a brace of these metaphysical Hobby-Horses, one to mount in the morning, and the other in the afternoon.

After all, Sir, friend as I am to freedom of opinion (and no one living can be more so) I am rather sorry, methinks, that men should judge so *variously* of Mr. HUME's philosophical

---

[2]   LIFE, &c. p. 43.

[3]   LIFE, &c. p. 59.

[4]   *Treatise of Human Nature.* I. 467. In the Postscript to this Letter, a view will be given of the HUMIAN system, taken exactly as it appeared to it's author at six o'clock in the evening.

speculations. For since the design of them is to banish out of the world every idea of truth and comfort, salvation, and immortality, a future state, and the providence, and even existence of GOD, it seems a pity, that we cannot be all of a mind about them, though we might have formerly liked to hear the author crack a joke, over a bottle, in his life time. And I could have been well pleased to have been informed by you, Sir, that, before his death, he had ceased to number among his happy effusions tracts of this kind and tendency.

For – (let me come a little closer to you, Doctor,if you please, upon this subject – Don't be under any apprehensions – my name does not begin with a B –) Are *you* sure, and can you make *us* sure, that there really exist no such things as a GOD, and a future state of rewards and punishments? If so, all is well. Let us *then*, in our last hours, read LUCIAN, and play at WHIST, and droll upon CHARON and his boat;[5] let us die as foolish and insensible, as much like our brother philosophers, the calves of the field, and the asses of the desart, as we can, for the life of us. But – if such things BE – as they most certainly ARE – Is it right in you, Sir, to hold up to our view, as 'perfectly wise and virtuous',[6] the *character* and *conduct* of one, who seems to have been possessed with an incurable antipathy to all that is called RELIGION; and who strained every nerve to explode, suppress, and extirpate the spirit of it among men, that it's very name, if he could effect it, might no more be had in remembrance? Are we, do you imagine, to be reconciled to a character of this sort, and fall in love with it, because it's owner was *good company*, and knew how to manage his *cards?* Low as the age is fallen, I will venture to hope, it has grace enough yet left, to resent such usage as this.

[5] LIFE, &c. p. 47, et seq.

[6] LIFE, &c. p. 62.

OF THE THEORY OF MORAL SENTIMENTS, AND THE DISSERTATION ON THE ORIGIN OF LANGUAGES*

Dugald Stewart

1 The science of Ethics has been divided by modern writers into two parts; the one comprehending the theory of Morals, and the other its practical doctrines. The questions about which the former is employed, are chiefly the two following. *First*, By what *principle* of our constitution are we led to form the notion of moral distinctions; – whether by that faculty which, in the other branches of human knowledge, perceives the distinction between truth and falsehood; or by a peculiar power of perception (called by some the Moral Sense) which is *pleased* with one set of qualities, and *displeased* with another? *Secondly*, What is the proper *object* of moral approbation? or, in other words, What is the common quality or qualities belonging to all the different modes of virtue?[1] Is it benevolence; or a rational self-love; or a disposition (resulting from the ascendant of Reason over Passion) to act suitably to the different relations in which we are placed? These two questions seem to exhaust the whole theory of Morals. The scope of the one is to ascertain the origin of our moral ideas; that of the other, to refer the phenomena of moral perception to their most simple and general laws.

2   The practical doctrines of morality comprehend all those rules of conduct which profess to point out the proper ends of human pursuit, and the most effectual means of attaining them; to which we may add all those literary compositions, whatever be their particular form, which have for their aim to fortify and animate our good dispositions, by delineations of the beauty, of the dignity, or of the utility of Virtue.

* From 'Account of the Life and Writings of Adam Smith' (1794), in Adam Smith, *Essays on Philosophical Subjects* (Oxford, 1980), sect. 2, pp. 278–92.
[1] [TMS VII.1.1.]

3   I shall not inquire at present into the justness of this division. I shall only observe, that the words Theory and Practice are not, in this instance, employed in their usual acceptations. The theory of Morals does not bear, for example, the same relation to the practice of Morals, that the theory of Geometry bears to practical Geometry. In this last science, all the practical rules are founded on theoretical principles previously established: But in the former science, the practical rules are obvious to the capacities of all mankind; the theoretical principles form one of the most difficult subjects of discussion that have ever exercised the ingenuity of metaphysicians.

4   In illustrating the doctrines of practical morality, (if we make allowance for some unfortunate prejudices produced or encouraged by violent and oppressive systems of policy), the ancients seem to have availed themselves of every light furnished by nature to human reason; and indeed those writers who, in later times, have treated the subject with the greatest success, are they who have followed most closely the footsteps of the Greek and the Roman philosophers. The theoretical question, too, concerning the essence of virtue, or the proper *object* of moral approbation, was a favourite topic of discussion in the ancient schools. The question concerning the *principle* of moral approbation, though not entirely of modern origin, has been chiefly agitated since the writings of Dr Cudworth, in opposition to those of Mr Hobbes; and it is this question accordingly (recommended at once by its novelty and difficulty to the curiosity of speculative men), that has produced most of the theories which characterize and distinguish from each other the later systems of moral philosophy.

5   It was the opinion of Dr Cudworth, and also of Dr Clarke, that moral distinctions are perceived by that power of the mind, which distinguishes truth from falsehood.[2] This system it was one great object of Dr Hutcheson's philosophy to refute, and in opposition to it, to show that the words Right and Wrong express certain agreeable and disagreeable qualities in actions, which it is not the province of reason but of feeling to perceive; and to that power of

---

[2] [TMS VII.iii.2.]

perception which renders us susceptible of pleasure or of pain from the view of virtue or of vice, he gave the name of the Moral Sense.[3] His reasonings upon this subject are in the main acquiesced in, both by Mr Hume and Mr Smith; but they differ from him in one important particular, – Dr Hutcheson plainly supposing, that the moral sense is a simple principle of our constitution, of which no account can be given; whereas the other two philosophers have both attempted to analyze it into other principles more general. Their systems, however, with respect to it are very different from each other. According to Mr Hume, all the qualities which are denominated virtuous, are useful either to ourselves or to others, and the pleasure which we derive from the view of them is the pleasure of utility.[4] Mr Smith, without rejecting entirely Mr Hume's doctrine, proposes another of his own, far more comprehensive; a doctrine with which he thinks all the most celebrated theories of morality invented by his predecessors coincide in part, and from some partial view of which he apprehends that they have all proceeded.

6   Of this very ingenious and original theory, I shall endeavour to give a short abstract. To those who are familiarly acquainted with it as it is stated by its author, I am aware that the attempt may appear superfluous; but I flatter myself that it will not be wholly useless to such as have not been much conversant in these abstract disquisitions, by presenting to them the leading principles of the system in one connected view, without those interruptions of the attention which necessarily arise from the author's various and happy illustrations, and from the many eloquent digressions which animate and adorn his composition.

7   The fundamental principle of Mr Smith's theory is, that the primary objects of our moral perceptions are the actions of other men; and that our moral judgments with respect to our own conduct are only applications to ourselves of decisions which we have already passed on the conduct of our neighbour. His work accordingly ᵇincludes two distinct inquiries, which, although sometimes blended together

[3] [TMS VII.iii.3.]

[4] [TMS IV.1.

in the execution of his general design, it is necessary for the reader to discriminate carefully from each other, in order to comprehend all the different bearings of the author's argument. The aim of the former inquiry is, to explain in what manner we learn to judge of the conduct of our neighbour; that of the latter, to shew how, by applying these judgments to ourselves, we acquire *a sense of duty*, and a feeling of its paramount authority over all our other principles of action.

8   Our moral judgments, both with respect to our own conduct and that of others, include two distinct perceptions: *first*, A perception of conduct as right or wrong; and, *secondly*, A perception of the merit or demerit of the agent. To that quality of conduct which moralists, in general, express by the word Rectitude, Mr Smith gives the name of Propriety; and he begins his theory with inquiring in what it consists, and how we are led to form the idea of it. The leading principles of his doctrine on this subject are comprehended in the following propositions.

9   1. It is from our own experience alone, that we can form any idea of what passes in the mind of another person on any particular occasion; and the only way in which we can form this idea, is by supposing ourselves in the same circumstances with him, and conceiving how we should be affected if we were so situated. It is impossible for us, however, to conceive ourselves placed in any situation, whether agreeable or otherwise, without feeling an effect of the same kind with what would be produced by the situation itself; and of consequence the attention we give at any time to the circumstances of our neighbour, must affect us somewhat in the same manner, although by no means in the same degree, as if these circumstances were our own.

10   That this imaginary change of place with other men, is the real source of the interest we take in their fortunes, Mr Smith attempts to prove by various instances. 'When we see a stroke aimed, and just ready to fall upon the leg or arm of another person, we naturally shrink and draw back our own leg or our own arm; and when it does fall, we feel it in some measure, and are hurt by it as well as the sufferer. The mob, when they are gazing at a dancer on the slack-rope, naturally writhe and twist and balance their

own bodies, as they see him do, and as they feel that they themselves must do if in his situation.'⁵ The same thing takes place, according to Mr Smith, in every case in which our attention is turned to the condition of our neighbour. 'Whatever is the passion which arises from any object in the person principally concerned, an analogous emotion springs up, at the thought of his situation, in the breast of every attentive spectator. In every passion of which the mind of man is susceptible, the emotions of the bystander always correspond to what, by bringing the case home to himself, he imagines should be the sentiments of the sufferer.'⁶

11   To this principle of our nature which leads us to enter into the situations of other men, and to partake with them in the passions which these situations have a tendency to excite, Mr Smith gives the name of *sympathy* or *fellow-feeling*, which two words he employs as synonymous. Upon some occasions, he acknowledges, that sympathy arises merely from the view of a certain emotion in another person; but in general it arises, not so much from the view of the emotion, as from that of the situation which excites it.

12   2. A sympathy or fellow-feeling between different persons is always agreeable to both. When I am in a situation which excites any passion, it is pleasant to me to know, that the spectators of my situation enter with me into all its various circumstances, and are affected with them in the same manner as I am myself. On the other hand, it is pleasant to the spectator to observe this correspondence of his emotions with mine.

13   3. When the spectator of another man's situation, upon bringing home to himself all its various circumstances, feels himself affected in the same manner with the person principally concerned, he approves of the affection or passion of this person as just and proper, and suitable to its object. The exceptions which occur to this observation are, according to Mr Smith, only apparent. 'A stranger, for

⁵   [TMS I.i.1.3.]

⁶   [TMS I.i.1.4.].

example,[7] passes by us in the street with all the marks of the deepest affliction: and we are immediately told, that he has just received the news of the death of his father. It is impossible that, in this case, we should not approve of his grief; yet it may often happen, without any defect of humanity on our part, that, so far from entering into the violence of his sorrow, we should scarce conceive the first movements of concern upon his account.[8] We have learned, however, from experience, that such a misfortune naturally excites such a degree of sorrow; and we know, that if we took time to examine his situation fully, and in all its parts, we should, without doubt, most sincerely sympathize with him. It is upon the consciousness of this conditional sympathy that our approbation of his sorrow is founded, even in those cases in which that sympathy does not actually take place; and the general rules derived from our preceding experience of what our sentiments would commonly correspond with, correct upon this, as upon many other occasions, the impropriety of our present emotions.'[9]

14   By the *propriety* therefore of any affection or passion exhibited by another person, is to be understood its suitableness to the object which excites it. Of this suitableness I can judge only from the coincidence of the affection with that which I feel, when I conceive myself in the same circumstances; and the perception of this coincidence is the foundation of the sentiment of *moral approbation.*

15   4. Although, when we attend to the situation of another person, and conceive ourselves to be placed in his circumstances, an emotion of the same kind with that which he feels naturally arises in our own mind, yet this sympathetic emotion bears but a very small proportion, in point of degree, to what is felt by the person principally concerned. In order, therefore, to obtain the pleasure of mutual sympathy, nature teaches the spectator to strive, as such as he can, to raise his emotion to a level with that which the object would really produce: and, on the other hand, she

---

[7] [The words 'for example' do not occur in the actual text of TMS, nor is the punctuation of this quotation exact.]

[8] [A complete sentence is omitted at this point.]

[9] [TMS I.i.3.4.]

teaches the person whose passion this object has excited, to bring it down, as much as he can, to a level with that of the spectator.

16 · 5. Upon these two different efforts are founded two different sets of virtues. Upon the effort of the spectator to enter into the situation of the person principally concerned, and to raise his sympathetic emotions to a level with the emotions of the actor, are founded the gentle, the amiable virtues; the virtues of candid condescension and indulgent humanity. Upon the effort of the person principally concerned to lower his own emotions, so as to correspond as nearly as possible with those of the spectator, are founded the great, the awful, and respectable virtues; the virtues of self-denial, of self-government, of that command of the passions, which subjects all the movements of our nature to what our own dignity and honour, and the propriety of our own conduct, require.

17 As a farther illustration of the foregoing doctrine, Mr Smith considers particularly the degrees of the different passions which are consistent with propriety, and endeavours to shew, that, in every case, it is decent or indecent to express a passion strongly, according as mankind are disposed, or not disposed to sympathize with it. It is unbecoming, for example, to express strongly any of those passions which arise from a certain condition of the body; because other men, who are not in the same condition, cannot be expected to sympathize with them. It is unbecoming to cry out with bodily pain; because the sympathy felt by the spectator bears no proportion to the acuteness of what is felt by the sufferer. The case is somewhat similar with those passions which take their origin from a particular turn or habit of the imagination.

18 In the case of the unsocial passions of hatred and resentment, the sympathy of the spectator is divided between the person who feels the passion, and the person who is the object of it. 'We are concerned for both, and our fear for what the one may suffer damps our resentment for what the other has suffered.'[10] Hence the imperfect degree in which we sympathize with such passions; and the pro-

---

[10] [TMS I.ii.3.1. The punctuation does not exactly follow the printed text.]

priety, when we are under their influence, of moderating
their expression to a much greater degree than is required
in the case of any other emotions.

19   The reverse of this takes place with respect to all the
social and benevolent affections. The sympathy of the spectator with the person who feels them, coincides with his
concern for the person who is the object of them. It is
this redoubled sympathy which renders these affections so
peculiarly becoming and agreeable.

20   The selfish emotions of grief and joy, when they are
conceived on account of our own private good or bad
fortune, hold a sort of middle place between our social and
our unsocial passions. They are never so graceful as the
one set, nor so odious as the other. Even when excessive,
they are never so disagreeable as excessive resentment;
because no opposite sympathy can ever interest us against
them: and when most suitable to their objects, they are
never so agreeable as impartial humanity and just benevolence; because no double sympathy can ever interest us for
them.

21   After these general speculations concerning the propriety
of actions, Mr Smith examines how far the judgments of
mankind concerning it are liable to be influenced, in particular   cases,   by   the   prosperous   or   the   adverse
circumstances of the agent. The scope of his reasoning on
this subject is directed to shew (in opposition to the
common opinion), that when there is no envy in the case,
our propensity to sympathize with joy is much stronger
than our propensity to sympathize with sorrow; and, of
consequence, that it is more easy to obtain the approbation
of mankind in prosperity than in adversity. From the same
principle he traces the origin of ambition, or of the desire
of rank and pre-eminence; the great object of which passion
is, to attain that situation which sets a man most in the
view of general sympathy and attention, and gives him an
easy empire over the affections of others.

22   Having finished the analysis of our sense of propriety
and of impropriety, Mr Smith proceeds to consider our
sense of merit and demerit; which he thinks has also a
reference, in the first instance, not to our own characters,
but to the characters of our neighbours. In explaining the
origin of this part of our moral constitution, he avails

himself of the same principle of sympathy, into which he resolves the sentiment of moral approbation.

23 The words *propriety* and *impropriety*, when applied to an affection of the mind, are used in this theory (as has been already observed) to express the suitableness or unsuitableness of the affection to its exciting *cause*. The words *merit* and *demerit* have always a reference (according to Mr Smith) to the *effect* which the affection tends to produce. When the tendency of an affection is beneficial, the agent appears to us a proper object of reward; when it is hurtful, he appears the proper object of punishment.

24 The principles in our nature which most directly prompt us to reward and to punish, are gratitude and resentment. To say of a person, therefore, that he is deserving of reward or of punishment, is to say, in other words, that he is a proper object of gratitude or of resentment; or, which amounts to the same thing, that he is to some person or persons the object of a gratitude or of a resentment, which every reasonable man is ready to adopt and sympathize with.

25 It is however very necessary to observe, that we do not thoroughly sympathize with the gratitude of one man towards another, merely because this other has been the cause of his good fortune, unless he has been the cause of it from motives which we entirely go along with. Our sense, therefore, of the good desert of an action, is a compounded sentiment, made up of an indirect sympathy with the person to whom the action is beneficial, and of a direct sympathy with the affections and motives of the agent. – The same remark applies, *mutatis mutandis*, to our sense of demerit, or of ill-desert.

26 From these principles, it is inferred, that the only actions which appear to us deserving of reward, are actions of a beneficial tendency, proceeding from proper motives; the only actions which seem to deserve punishment, are actions of a hurtful tendency, proceeding from improper motives. A mere want of beneficence exposes to no punishment; because the mere want of beneficence tends to do no real positive evil. A man, on the other hand, who is barely innocent, and contents himself with observing strictly the laws of justice with respect to others, can merit only, that

his neighbours, in their turn, should observe religiously the same laws with respect to him.

27   These observations lead Mr Smith to anticipate a little the subject of the second great division of his work, by a short inquiry into the origin of our sense of justice, *as applicable to our own conduct*; and also of our sentiments of remorse, and of good desert.

28   The origin of our sense of justice, as well as of all our other moral sentiments, he accounts for by means of the principle of sympathy. When I attend only to the feelings of my own breast, my own happiness appears to me of far greater consequence than that of all the world besides. But I am conscious, that, in this excessive preference, other men cannot possibly sympathize with me, and that to them I appear only one of the crowd, in whom they are no more interested than in any other individual. If I wish, therefore, to secure their sympathy and approbation (which, according to Mr Smith, are the objects of the strongest desire of my nature), it is necessary for me to regard my happiness, not in that light in which it appears to myself, but in that light in which it appears to mankind in general. If an unprovoked injury is offered to me, I know that society will sympathize with my resentment; but if I injure the interests of another, who never injured me, merely because they stand in the way of my own, I perceive evidently, that society will sympathize with *his* resentment, and that I shall become the object of general indignation.

29   When, upon any occasion, I am led by the violence of passion to overlook these considerations, and, in the case of a competition of interests, to act according to my own feelings, and not according to those of impartial spectators, I never fail to incur the punishment of remorse. When my passion is gratified, and I begin to reflect coolly on my conduct, I can no longer enter into the motives from which it proceeded; it appears as improper to me as to the rest of the world; I lament the effects it has produced; I pity the unhappy sufferer whom I have injured; and I feel myself a just object of indignation to mankind. 'Such,' says Mr Smith, 'is the nature of that sentiment which is properly

called remorse.[11] It is made up of shame from the sense of the impropriety of past conduct; of grief for the effects of it; of pity for those who suffer by it; and of the dread and terror of punishment from the consciousness of the justly provoked resentment of all rational creatures.'[12]

30 The opposite behaviour of him who, from proper motives, has performed a generous action, inspires, in a similar manner, the opposite sentiment of conscious merit, or of deserved reward.

31 The foregoing observations contain a general summary of Mr Smith's principles with respect to the origin of our moral sentiments, in so far at least as they relate to the conduct of others. He acknowleges, at the same time, that the sentiments of which we are conscious, on particular occasions, do not always coincide with these principles; and that they are frequently modified by other considerations, very different from the propriety or impropriety of the affections of the agent, and also from the beneficial or hurtful tendency of these affections. The good or the bad consequences which accidently follow from an action, and which, as they do not depend on the agent, ought undoubtedly, in point of justice, to have no influence on our opinion, either of the propriety or the merit of his conduct, scarcely ever fail to influence considerably our judgment with respect to both; by leading us to form a good or a bad opinion of the prudence with which the action was performed, and by animating our sense of the merit or demerit of his design. These facts, however, do not furnish any objections which are peculiarly applicable to Mr Smith's theory; for whatever hypothesis we may adopt with respect to the origin of our moral perceptions, all men must acknowledge, that, in so far as the prosperous or the unprosperous event of an action depends on fortune or on accident, it ought neither to increase nor to diminish our moral approbation or disapprobation of the agent. And accordingly it has, in all ages of the world, been the complaint of moralists, that the actual sentiments of mankind

[11] [The quotation omits the words '; of all the sentiments which can enter the human breast the most dreadful'.]

[12] [TMS II.ii.2.3]

should so often be in opposition to this equitable and indisputable maxim. In examining, therefore, this irregularity of our moral sentiments, Mr Smith is to be considered, not as obviating an objection peculiar to his own system, but as removing a difficulty which is equally connected with every theory on the subject which has ever been proposed. So far as I know, he is the first philosopher who has been fully aware of the importance of the difficulty, and he has indeed treated it with great ability and success. The explanation which he gives of it is not warped in the least by any peculiarity in his own scheme; and, I must own, it appears to me to be the most solid and valuable improvement he has made in this branch of science. It is impossible to give any abstract of it in a sketch of this kind; and therefore I must content myself with remarking, that it consists of three parts. The first explains the causes of this irregularity of sentiment; the second, the extent of its influence; and the third, the important purposes to which it is subservient. His remarks on the last of these heads are more particularly ingenious and pleasing; as their object is to shew, in opposition to what we should be disposed at first to apprehend, that when nature implanted the seeds of this irregularity in the human breast, her leading intention was, to promote the happiness and perfection of the species.

32   The remaining part of Mr Smith's theory is employed in shewing, in what manner *our sense of duty* comes to be formed, in consequence of an application to ourselves of the judgments we have previously passed on the conduct of others.

33   In entering upon this inquiry, which is undoubtedly the most important in the work, and for which the foregoing speculations are, according to Mr Smith's theory, a necessary preparation, he begins with stating *the fact* concerning our consciousness of merited praise or blame; and it must be owned, that the first aspect of the fact, as he himself states it, appears not very favourable to his principles. That the great object of a wise and virtuous man is not to act in such a manner as to obtain the actual approbation of those around him, but to act so as to render himself the *just* and *proper* object of their approbation, and that his satisfaction with his own conduct depends much more on

the consciousness of *deserving* this approbation than from that of really enjoying it, he candidly acknowledges; but still he insists, that although this may seem, at first view, to intimate the existence of some moral faculty which is not borrowed from without, our moral sentiments have always some secret reference, either to what are, or to what upon a certain condition would be, or to what we imagine ought to be, the sentiments of others; and that if it were possible, that a human creature could grow up to manhood without any communication with his own species, he could no more think of his own character, or of the propriety or demerit of his own sentiments and conduct, than of the beauty or deformity of his own face. There is indeed a tribunal within the breast, which is the supreme arbiter of all our actions, and which often mortifies us amidst the applause, and supports us under the censure of the world; yet still, he contends, that if we inquire into the origin of its institution, we shall find, that its jurisdiction is, in a great measure, derived from the authority of that very tribunal whose decisions it so often and so justly reverses.

34   When we first come into the world, we, for some time, fondly pursue the impossible project of gaining the good-will and approbation of everybody. We soon however find, that this universal approbation is unattainable; that the most equitable conduct must frequently thwart the interests or the inclinations of particular persons, who will seldom have candour enough to enter into the propriety of our motives, or to see that this conduct, how disagreeable soever to them, is perfectly suitable to our situation. In order to defend ourselves from such partial judgments, we soon learn to set up in our own minds, a judge between ourselves and those we live with. We conceive ourselves as acting in the presence of a person, who has no particular relation, either to ourselves, or to those whose interests are affected by our conduct; and we study to act in such a manner as to obtain the approbation of this supposed impartial spectator. It is only by consulting him that we can see whatever relates to ourselves in its proper shape and dimensions.

35   There are two different occasions, on which we examine our own conduct, and endeavour to view it in the light in which the impartial spectator would view it. First, when

we are about to act; and, secondly, after we have acted. In both cases, our views are very apt to be partial.

36   When we are about to act, the eagerness of passion seldom allows us to consider what we are doing with the candour of an indifferent person. When the action is over, and the passions which prompted it have subsided, although we can undoubtedly enter into the sentiments of the indifferent spectator much more coolly than before, yet it is so disagreeable to us to think ill of ourselves, that we often purposely turn away our view from those circumstances which might render our judgment unfavourable. – Hence that self-deceit which is the source of half the disorders of human life.

37   In order to guard ourselves against its delusions, nature leads us to form insensibly, by our continual observations upon the conduct of others, certain general rules concerning what is fit and proper either to be done or avoided. Some of their actions shock all our natural sentiments; and when we observe other people affected in the same manner with ourselves, we are confirmed in the belief, that our disapprobation was just. We naturally therefore lay it down as a general rule, that all such actions are to be avoided, as tending to render us odious, contemptible, or punishable; and we endeavour, by habitual reflection, to fix this general rule in our minds, in order to correct the misrepresentations of self-love, if we should ever be called on to act in similar circumstances. The man of furious resentment, if he were to listen to the dictates of that passion, would perhaps regard the death of his enemy as but a small compensation for a trifling wrong. But his observations on the conduct of others have taught him how horrible such sanguinary revenges are; and he has impressed it on his mind as an invariable rule, to abstain from them upon all occasions. This rule preserves its authority with him, checks the impetuosity of his passion, and corrects the partial views which self-love suggests; although, if this had been the first time in which he considered such an action, he would undoubtedly have determined it to be just and proper, and what every impartial spectator would approve of. – A regard to such general rules of morality constitutes, according to Mr Smith, what is properly called *the sense of duty.*

38   I before hinted, that Mr Smith does not reject entirely
from his system that principle of *utility*, of which the perception in any action or character constitutes, according
to Mr Hume, the sentiment of moral approbation. That
no qualities of the mind are approved of as virtues, but
such as are useful or agreeable, either to the person himself
or to others, he admits to be a proposition that holds
universally; and he also admits, that the sentiment of
approbation with which we regard virtue, is enlivened by
the perception of this utility, or, as he explains the fact, it
is enlivened by our sympathy with the happiness of those
to whom the utility extends: But still he insists, that it is
not the view of this utility which is either the first or
principal source of moral approbation.

39   To sum up the whole of his doctrine in a few words.
'When we approve of any character or action, the sentiments which we feel are[13] derived from four different
sources.[14] First, we sympathize with the motives of the
agent; secondly, we enter into the gratitude of those who
receive the benefit of his actions; thirdly, we observe that
his conduct has been agreeable to the general rules by
which those two sympathies generally act; and, lastly,[15]
when we consider such actions as making a part of a system
of behaviour which tends to promote the happiness either
of the individual or of society,[16] they appear to derive a
beauty from this utility, not unlike that which we ascribe
to any well-contrived machine.'[17] These different sentiments, he thinks, exhaust completely, in every instance
that can be supposed, the compounded sentiment of moral
approbation. 'After deducting, says he, in any one particular case, all that must be acknowledged to proceed from
some one or other of these four principles, I should be glad
to know what remains; and I shall freely allow this over-

---

[13] [TMS reads: 'according to the foregoing system'.]

[14] [TMS reads: 'four sources, which are in some respects different from one
another'.]

[15] [TMS reads: 'last of all'.]

[16] [TMS reads: 'or of the society'.]

[17] [TMS VII.iii.3.16. The punctuation does not exactly follow the printed
texts.]

plus to be ascribed to a moral sense, or to any other peculiar faculty, provided any body will ascertain precisely what this overplus is.'[18]

40   Mr Smith's opinion concerning the nature of virtue, is involved in his theory concerning the principle of moral approbation. The idea of virtue, he thinks, always implies the idea of propriety, or of the suitableness of the affection to the object which excites it; which suitableness, according to him, can be determined in no other way than by the sympathy of impartial spectators with the motives of the agent. But still he apprehends, that this description of virtue is incomplete; for although in every virtuous action propriety is an essential ingredient, it is not always the sole ingredient. Beneficent actions have in them another quality, by which they appear, not only to deserve approbation, but recompense, and excite a superior degree of esteem, arising from a double sympathy with the motives of the agent, and the gratitude of those who are the objects of his affection. In this respect, beneficence appears to him to be distinguished from the inferior virtues of prudence, vigilance, circumspection, temperance, constancy, firmness, which are always regarded with approbation, but which confer no merit. This distinction, he apprehends, has not been sufficiently attended to by moralists; the principles of some affording no explanation of the approbation we bestow on the inferior virtues; and those of others accounting as imperfectly for the peculiar excellency which the supreme virtue of beneficence is acknowledged to possess.*

41   Such are the outlines of Mr Smith's Theory of Moral Sentiments; a work which, whatever opinion we may entertain of the justness of its conclusions, must be allowed by all to be a singular effort of invention, ingenuity, and subtilty. For my own part I must confess, that it does not coincide with my notions concerning the foundation of Morals: but I am convinced, at the same time, that it contains a large mixture of important truth, and that, although the author has sometimes been misled by too great a desire of generalizing his principles, he has had the

---

[18] (Ibid.)
* See Note (C.) below p. 119

merit of directing the attention of philosophers to a view of human nature which had formerly in a great measure escaped their notice. Of the great proportion of just and sound reasoning which the theory involves its striking plausibility is a sufficient proof; for, as the author himself has remarked, no system in morals can well gain our assent, if it does not border, in some respects, upon the truth. 'A system of natural philosophy (he observes) may appear very plausible, and be for a long time very generally received in the world, and yet have no foundation in nature; but the author who should assign as the cause of any natural sentiment, some principle which neither had any connection with it, nor resembled any other principle which had some connection, would appear absurd and ridiculous to the most injudicious and inexperienced reader.'[19] The merit, however, of Mr Smith's performance does not rest here. No work, undoubtedly, can be mentioned, ancient or modern, which exhibits so complete a view of those facts with respect to our moral perceptions, which it is one great object of this branch of science to refer to their general laws; and upon this account, it well deserves the careful study of all whose taste leads them to prosecute similar inquiries. These facts are indeed frequently expressed in a language which involves the author's peculiar theories: But they are always presented in the most happy and beautiful lights; and it is easy for an attentive reader, by stripping them of hypothetical terms, to state them to himself with that logical precision, which, in such very difficult disquisitions, can alone conduct us with certainty to the truth.

42 It is proper to observe farther, that with the theoretical doctrines of the book, there are everywhere interwoven, with singular taste and address, the purest and most elevated maxims concerning the practical conduct of life; and that it abounds throughout with interesting and instructive delineations of characters and manners. A considerable part of it too is employed in collateral inquiries, which, upon every hypothesis that can be formed concerning the foundation of morals, are of equal importance. Of this

[19] [The quotation runs together passages from the second and concluding sentences of TMS VII.ii.4.14, and does not follow the punctuation or spelling of the printed text exactly.]

kind is the speculation formerly mentioned, with respect to the influence of fortune on our moral sentiments, and another speculation, no less valuable, with respect to the influence of custom and fashion on the same part of our constitution.

43   The style in which Mr Smith has conveyed the fundamental principles on which his theory rests, does not seem to me to be so perfectly suited to the subject as that which he employs on most other occasions. In communicating ideas which are extremely abstract and subtile, and about which it is hardly possible to reason correctly, without the scrupulous use of appropriated terms, he sometimes presents to us a choice of words, by no means strictly synonymous, so as to divert the attention from a precise and steady conception of his proposition: and a similar effect is, in other instances, produced by that diversity of forms which, in the course of his copious and seducing composition, the same truth insensibly assumes. When the subject of his work leads him to address the imagination and the heart, the variety and felicity of his illustrations; the richness and fluency of his eloquence; and the skill with which he wins the attention and commands the passions of his readers, leave him, among our English moralists, without a rival.

OF SYMPATHY*
Dugald Stewart

That there is an exquisite pleasure annexed by the constitution of our nature to the sympathy or fellow-feeling of other men with our joys and sorrows, and even with our opinions, tastes, and humours, is a fact obvious to vulgar observation. It is no less evident that we feel a disposition to accommodate the state of our own minds to that of our companions, wherever we feel a benevolent affection towards them, and that this accommodating temper is in proportion to the strength of our affection. In such cases sympathy would appear to be grafted on benevolence; and perhaps it might be found, on an accurate examination, that the greater part of the pleasure which sympathy yields is resolvable into that which arises from the exercise of kindness, and from the consciousness of being beloved.

The phenomena generally referred to *sympathy* have appeared to Mr. Smith so important, and so curiously connected, that he has been led to attempt an explanation from this single principle of all the phenomena of moral perception. In this attempt, however, (abstracting entirely from the vague use which he occasionally makes of the word,) he has plainly been misled, like many eminent philosophers before him, by an excessive love of simplicity; and has mistaken a very subordinate principle in our moral constitution (or rather a principle *super-added* to our moral constitution as an auxiliary to the sense of duty) for that faculty which distinguishes right from wrong, and which (by what name soever we may choose to call it) recurs on us constantly in all our ethical disquisitions, as an ultimate fact in the nature of man.

I shall take this opportunity of offering a few remarks on

* 'Of Sympathy' and 'Note C. Smith's Moral Theory', from *The Philosophy of the Active and Moral Powers of Man* (1828), in *The Collected Works of Dugald Stewart* (Edinburgh, 1854–60), edited by Sir William Hamilton, vol. 6, pp. 328–33 and pp. 407–14. The footnotes without brackets are those of Dugald Stewart. Those within brackets were added by his editor, Sir William Hamilton.

this most ingenious and beautiful theory, in the course of which I shall have occasion to state all that I think necessary to observe concerning the place which *sympathy* seems to me really to occupy in our moral constitution. In stating these remarks, I would be understood to express myself with all the respect and veneration due to the talents and virtues of a writer, whose friendship I regard as one of the most fortunate incidents of my life, but, at the same time, with that entire freedom which the importance of the subject demands, and which I know that his candid and liberal mind would have approved.

In addition to the incidental strictures which I have already hazarded on Mr. Smith's theory, I have yet to state two objections of a more general nature, to which it appears to me to be obviously liable. But before I proceed to these objections, it is necessary for me to premise (which I shall do in Mr. Smith's words) a remark which I have not hitherto had occasion to mention, and which may be justly regarded as one of the most characteristical principles of his system.

'Were it possible,' says he, 'that a human creature could grow up to manhood in some solitary place, without any communication with his own species, he could no more think of his own character, of the propriety or demerit of his own sentiments and conduct, of the beauty or deformity of his own mind, than of the beauty or deformity of his own face. All these are objects which he cannot easily see, which naturally he does not look at, and with regard to which he is provided with no mirror which can present them to his view. Bring him into society, and he is immediately provided with the mirror which he wanted before. It is placed in the countenance and behaviour of those he lives with, which always mark when they enter into, and when they disapprove of his sentiments, and it is here that he first views the propriety and impropriety of his own passions, the beauty and deformity of his own mind.'[1]

To this account of the origin of our moral sentiments it may be objected, 1*st*, That granting the proposition to be true, 'that a human creature who should grow up to manhood without any communication with his own species, could no more think of the propriety or demerit of his own sentiments, than of the

---

[1] [*Theory of Moral Sentiments*, Part III. chap i. *sub initio*.]

beauty or deformity of his own face,' it would by no means authorize the conclusion which is here deduced from it. The necessity of social intercourse as an indispensable condition implied in the generation and growth of our moral sentiments, does not arise merely from its effect in holding up a mirror for the examination of our own character, but from the impossibility of finding, in a solitary state, any field for the exercise of our most important moral duties. In such a state the moral faculty would inevitably remain dormant and useless, for the same reason that the organ of sight would remain useless and unknown to a person who should pass his whole life in the darkness of a dungeon.

2*d*, It may be objected to Mr. Smith's theory, that it confounds the *means* or *expedients* by which nature enables us to correct our moral judgments, with the principles in our constitution to which our moral judgments owe their origin. These means or expedients he has indeed described with singular penetration and sagacity, and by doing so, has thrown new and most important lights on *practical* morality; but, after all his reasonings on the subject, the metaphysical problem concerning the primary sources of our moral ideas and emotions, will be found involved in the same obscurity as before. The intention of such expedients, it is perfectly obvious, is merely to obtain a just and fair view of circumstances; and after this view has been obtained, the question still remains, what constitutes the obligation upon me to act in a particular manner? In answer to this question it is said, that, from recollecting my own judgments in similar cases in which I was concerned, I infer in what light my conduct will appear to society; that there is an exquisite satisfaction annexed to mutual sympathy; and that, in order to obtain this satisfaction, I accommodate my conduct, not to my own feelings, but to those of my fellow-creatures. Now, I acknowledge, that this may account for a man's assuming the appearance of virtue, and I believe that something of this sort is the real foundation of the rules of good breeding in polished society;[2] but in the

---

[2] This remark I borrow from Dr. Beattie, who, in his *Essay on Truth*, observes, that 'the foundation of good breeding is that kind of sensibility or sympathy by which we suppose ourselves in the situation of others, adopt their sentiments, and in a manner perceive their very thoughts.' (P. 38, 2d edit. Edin. 1771.) The observation well deserves to be prosecuted.

important concerns of life, I apprehend there is something more, – for when I have once satisfied myself with respect to the conduct which an impartial judge would approve of, I feel that this conduct is *right* for me, and that I am under a moral obligation to put it in practice. If I had had recourse to no expedient for correcting my first judgment, I would, nevertheless, have formed some judgment or other of a particular conduct as right, wrong, or indifferent, and the only difference would have been, that I should probably have decided improperly, from an erroneous or a partial view of the case.

From these observations I conclude, that the words *right* and *wrong*,[3] *ought* and *ought not*, express simple ideas or notions, of which no explanation can be given. They are to be found in all languages, and it is impossible to carry on any ethical speculation without them. Of this Mr. Smith himself furnishes a remarkable proof in the statement of his theory, not only by the occasional use which he makes of these and other synonymous expressions, but by his explicit and repeated acknowledgments, that the propriety of action cannot be always determined by the *actual* judgments of society, and that, in such cases, we must act according to the judgments which other men *ought* to have formed of our conduct. Is not this to admit, that we have a standard of right and wrong in our own minds, of superior authority to any instinctive propensity we may feel to obtain the sympathy of our fellow-creatures?

It was in order to reconcile this acknowledgment with the general language of his system, that Mr. Smith was forced to have recourse to the supposition of '*an abstract man* within the breast, the representative of mankind and substitute of the Deity, whom nature has constituted the supreme judge of all our actions.'[4] Of this very ingenious fiction he has availed himself in various passages of the *first* edition [in fact, in the

---

[3]   Dr. Hutcheson, in his *Illustrations on the Moral Sense*, calls *ought* a *confused word*: 'As to that confused word *ought*,' &c. &c. (end of Section I.) But for this he seems to have had no better reason than the impossibility of defining it logically. And may not the same remark be applied to the words *time, space, motion*? Was there ever a language in which these words, together with those of *ought* and *ought not*, were not to be found? *Ought* corresponds with the δει of the Greeks, and the *oportet* and *decet* of the Latins.

[4]   Page 208, [3d and] 5th edit. [Part III. chap. ii.]

first five editions,[5]] of his book; but he has laid much greater stress upon it in the *last* [or *sixth*] edition, published a short time before his death.[6] An idea somewhat similar occurs in Lord Shaftesbury's *Advice to an Author*, where he observes, with that quaintness of phraseology which so often deforms his otherwise beautiful style, that 'when the wise ancients spoke of a demon, genius, or angel, to whom we are committed from the moment of our birth, they meant no more than enigmatically to declare, "That we have each of us a *patient* in ourselves: that we are properly our own subjects of practice: and that we then become due practitioners, when, by virtue of an intimate recess, we can discover a certain duplicity of soul, and divide ourselves into two parties.' ' He afterwards tells us, that, 'according as this recess was deep and intimate, and the dual number practically formed in us, we were supposed by the ancients to advance in morals and true wisdom.'[7]

By means of this fiction Mr. Smith has rendered his theory (contrary to what might have been expected from its first aspect) perfectly coincident in its practical tendency with that cardinal principle of the Stoical philosophy which exhorts us to search for the rules of life, not *without* ourselves, but *within:* 'Nec te quæsiveris extra.' [8] Indeed Butler himself has not asserted the authority and supremacy of conscience in stronger terms than Mr. Smith, who represents this as a manifest and unquestionable principle, whatever particular theory we may adopt concerning the origin of our moral ideas. It is only to be regretted, that, instead of the metaphorical expression of '*the man within the breast*, to whose opinions and feelings we find it of more consequence to conform our conduct than to those of the whole world,' he had not made use of the simpler and more familiar words *reason* and *conscience*. This mode of speaking was indeed suggested to him, or rather obtruded on him by the theory of sympathy, and nothing can exceed the

---

[5] [*Editor.*]

[6] See, in particular, Vol. I. p. 321, *et seq.*, 6th edit. [The paragraph beginning, 'But though man,' &c., Part III. chap. ii. *Of Duty.* Compare, indeed, that whole chapter, in the sixth or subsequent, with that in the fifth or previous editions. *Ed.*]

[7] [Sect. ii., near the beginning.]

[8] [Persius, *Sat.* i. 7.]

skill and the taste with which he has availed himself of its assistance in perfecting his system; but it has the effect, with many readers, of keeping out of view the real state of the question, and (like Plato's *Commonwealth of the Soul, and Council of State*) to encourage among inferior writers a figurative or allegorical style in treating of subjects which, more than any other, require all the simplicity, precision, and logical consistency of which language is susceptible.[9]

Note C, (Book II. p. 333.) *Smith's Moral Theory*

I shall throw together in this note, without much regard to order or connexion, a few slight observations on detached passages of Mr. Smith's theory. Some of these observations may, I hope, be useful in illustrating more fully certain phenomena referred by him, rather too exclusively, to the principle of sympathy or fellow-feeling.

In proof of the pleasure annexed to mutual sympathy, Mr. Smith remarks, – 'that a man is mortified when, after having endeavoured to divert the company, he looks around and sees that nobody laughs at his jest but himself.'[10] It may be doubted, however, if in this case a disappointed sympathy be the chief cause of his uneasiness. Various other circumstances undoubtedly conspire, particularly the censure which the silence of the company conveys of his taste and judgment, together with the proof it exhibits of their sullenness and want of good humour.

'The pleasure, too, which,' according to Mr. Smith, (Ibid.) 'we receive from reading to a stranger a poem whose effect on ourselves has been destroyed by repetition,' may be explained without any refinement about *sympathy*, by the satisfaction we always feel in communicating pleasure to another, combined with the flattering though indirect testimony paid to the justness of our taste, by its coincidence with that of an individual whose judgment we respect. The sympathy of an acknowledged fool would certainly be in the same circumstances a source of mortification.

In mentioning these considerations, I do not mean to dispute

---

[9]   See Note C.
[10]   [*Theory of Moral Sentiments*, Part I. sect. i. chap. 2] – Vol. I. p. 16, sixth edition.

that there is an exquisite pleasure arising from mutual sympathy; but only to suggest, that Mr. Smith has ascribed to this principle solely, various phenomena, in accounting for which other causes appear to be no less deserving of attention.

The versatile and accommodating manners which Mr. Smith has so beautifully described in various passages of his *Theory*, may be assumed from different motives: – In some men from a desire to promote the happiness of those around them; and where this is the case, it is unquestionably one of the most amiable and meritorious forms in which benevolence can appear, and contributes more by its daily and constant operation to increase the comfort of human life, than those splendid exertions of virtue which we are so seldom called upon to make. In other men, in whom the benevolent affections are not so strong, it may proceed chiefly from a view to their own tranquillity and amusement, and may render them agreeable and harmless companions, without giving them any claim to the appellation of *virtuous*. In many it arises from views of self-interest and ambition; and in such men, whatever pleasure we may have derived from their society, these qualities never fail to inspire universal distrust and dislike, as soon as they are known to be the real motives of that pliancy and versatility with which we were at first captivated. It would appear, therefore, that the accommodating temper, where it is approved as morally *right*, is not approved on its own account, but as an expression of a *benevolent* disposition.

From the combined efforts of the actor and of the spectator towards a mutual sympathy, Mr. Smith endeavours to trace the origin of two different sets of virtues. 'Upon the effort of the spectator to enter into the situation of the person principally concerned, and to raise his sympathetic emotions to a level with the emotions of the actor, are founded the gentle, the amiable virtues, the virtues of candid condescension and indulgent humanity. Upon the effort of the person principally concerned to lower his own emotions, so as to correspond as nearly as possible with those of the spectator, are founded the great, the awful, and respectable virtues, the virtues of self-denial, of self-government, of that command of the passions which subjects all the movements of our nature to what our own dignity and honour, and the propriety of our own conduct require.'[11] If the word *qualities* were substituted for *virtues*, I agree in general with this doctrine. The mode of expression, however, certainly requires correction. 'Candid condescension' and 'indulgent humanity' are always amiable; and when they really proceed from a disposition habitually benevolent, are with great propriety called *virtues*. 'Self-denial and self-government' are always *respectable*, and sometimes *awful* qualities; because they indicate a force of mind which few men possess; but it depends on the *motives* from which they are exercised, whether they indicate a virtuous or a vicious character.

As a farther illustration of the foregoing doctrine, Mr. Smith considers particularly the degrees of the different passions which are consistent with propriety, and endeavours to show, that in every case it is decent or indecent to express a passion strongly, according as mankind are disposed or not disposed to sympathize with it. 'It is unbecoming, for example, to express strongly any of those passions which arise from a certain condition of the body; because other men who are not in the same condition cannot be expected to sympathize with them. It is unbecoming to cry out with bodily pain, because the sympathy felt by the spectator bears no proportion to the acuteness of what is felt by the sufferer. The case is somewhat similar with those passions which take their origin from a particular turn or habit of the imagination.'[12]

All violent expressions of such passions are undoubtedly offensive, and good breeding dictates that they should be restrained; but *not* because the spectator finds it difficult to enter into the situation of the person principally concerned; perhaps the opposite reason would be nearer the truth. To eat voraciously in the presence of a company who have already dined, would be obviously indecent; but, I apprehend, not so much so as to eat even moderately in presence of one whom we knew to be hungry, and who was not permitted to share in the repast. With respect to *bodily pain*, it appears to me that there is no calamity whatever which so completely interests the spectator, or with which has sympathy is so acute and lively. It is on this account that a steady composure under it, while it indicates the manly quality of self-command, has something

---

[11] [Compare Part I. sect. i. chap. 5.]

[12] [Compare Part I. sect. ii. chap. 1.]

in it peculiarly amiable, when we suppose that it proceeds in any degree from a tenderness for the feelings of others. In many surgical operations it is probable that the imagination of the pain exceeds the reality; and there cannot be a doubt, that where the patient is the object of our love, the sufferings which *he* feels require less fortitude than ours.

'In the case of the unsocial passions of hatred and resentment, the sympathy of the spectator is divided between the person who feels the passion and the person who is the object of it. We are concerned for both, and our fear for what the one may suffer damps our resentment for what the other has suffered. Hence the imperfect degree in which we sympathize with such passions; and the propriety, when under their influence, of moderating their expression to a much greater degree than in the case of any other emotions.'[13]

Abstracting from all considerations of this kind, satisfactory reasons may be given for our listening with caution to the dictates of *resentment* when we ourselves are the sufferers. Experience must soon satisfy us how apt this passion is to blind the judgment, and to exaggerate in our estimation the injury we have received; and how certainly we lay in matter for future remorse for our cooler hours, if we obey its first suggestions. A wise man, therefore, learns to delay forming his resolutions till his passion has in some degree subsided; – *not* in order to obtain the sympathy of other men, but in order to secure the approbation of his own conscience. If he conceives to himself what conduct the impartial spectator will approve of, it is merely as an expedient to divest himself of the partialities of self-love; and when he acts agreeably to what he supposes to be, on this occasion, the unbiassed judgment of spectators, his satisfaction arises *not* from the possession of their sympathy, but from a consciousness that he has done his best to ascertain what was *right*, and has regulated his conduct accordingly.

'Where there is no envy in the case, our propensity to sympathize with joy is much stronger than our propensity to sympathize with sorrow.

'It is on account of this dull sensibility to the afflictions of

[13] [Compare Part I. sect. ii. chap. 3.]

others that magnanimity, amidst great distress, always appears so divinely graceful.'[14]

If this were true, would it not follow that the admiration of heroic magnanimity would be in proportion to the insensibility of the spectator?

'It is because mankind are more disposed to court the favour, to comply with the humours, and to judge with indulgence of the actions of the prosperous, than with those of the unfortunate, that we make parade of our riches, and conceal our poverty.' – 'It is the misfortunes of kings alone,' Mr. Smith adds, 'which afford the proper subjects for tragedy.'[15]

Of this last proposition I confess I have some doubts, at least to the extent in which it is here stated; and I am inclined to think that in those cases where it holds, it may be easily accounted for on more obvious principles. By far the greater number of tragedies are founded on historical facts; and history records only the transactions of men in elevated stations. But even in *these* tragedies, the most interesting personages are frequently domestics or captives. The old shepherd in *Douglas* is surely a more interesting character than Lord Randolph. And for my own part, I am not ashamed to confess that I have shed more tears at some *Tragédies bourgeoises* and *Comédies larmoyantes* of very inferior merit, than were ever extorted from me by the exquisite poetry of Corneille, Racine, or Voltaire.

The fortunes of the great, indeed, interest us more than those of men in inferior stations. But for this there are various causes, independent of that assigned by Mr. Smith. 1. Their destiny involves the fortunes of many, and frequently affects the public interest. 2. Their situation points them out to public attention, and renders them subjects of general and daily conversation; and, accordingly, we may remark a curiosity perfectly analogous to that which the history of the great excites, with respect to the biography of all men who have been long and constantly in the view of the world. The trifling anecdotes in the life of *Quin* or *Garrick* find as many readers as the important events connected with the History of Frederick the Great.

---

[14] [Part I. sect. iii. chap. 1.]

[15] [Part I. sect. iii. chap. 2.]

In my *Account of the Life and Writings of Mr Smith*,[16] I observed, that, according to the learned translator of Aristotle's *Ethics and Policies*, 'the general idea which runs through Mr. Smith's *Theory of Moral Sentiments* was obviously borrowed from the following passage of Polybius. "From the union of the two sexes, to which all are naturally inclined, children are born. When any of these, therefore, being arrived at perfect age, instead of yielding suitable returns of gratitude and assistance to those by whom they have been bred, on the contrary, attempt to injure them by words or actions, it is manifest that those who behold the wrong, after having also seen the sufferings and the anxious cares that were sustained by the parents in the nourishment and education of their children, must be greatly offended and displeased at such proceeding. For man, who, among all the various kinds of animals, is alone endowed with the faculty of reason, cannot, like the rest, pass over such actions but will make reflection on what he sees; and, comparing likewise the future with the present, will not fail to express his indignation at this injurious treatment; to which, as he foresees, he may also at some time be exposed. Thus again, when any one who has been succoured by another in the time of danger, instead of showing the like kindness to this benefactor, endeavours at any time to destroy or hurt him, it is certain that all men must be shocked by such ingratitude, through sympathy with the resentment of their neighbour, and from an apprehension also that the case may be their own. And from hence arises in the mind of every man, a certain *notion* of the nature and force of duty, in which consists both the beginning and the end of justice. In like manner, the man who, in defence of others, is seen to throw himself the foremost into every danger, and even to sustain the fury of the fiercest animals, never fails to obtain the loudest acclamations of applause and veneration from all the multitude, while he who shows a different conduct is pursued with censure and reproach. And thus it is that the people begin to discern the nature of things honourable and base, and in what consists the difference between them; and to perceive that the former, on account of the advantage that attends them, are fit to

---

[16] [*Works*, Vol. IX.]

be admired and imitated, and the latter to be detested and avoided." '

'The doctrine,' says Dr. Gillies, 'contained in this passage, is expanded by Dr. Smith into a theory of Moral Sentiments. But he departs from *his author* in placing the perception of right and wrong in sentiment or feeling, ultimately and simply. Polybius, on the contrary, maintains with Aristotle, that these notions arise from reason or intellect operating on affection or appetite; or, in other words, that the moral faculty is a compound, and may be resolved into two simpler principles of the mind.' – Gillies's *Aristotle's Ethics and Politics*, Vol. I. p. 302. 2d edit.

The only expression I object to in the preceding sentences, is the phrase *his author*, which has the appearance of insinuating a charge of plagiarism against Mr. Smith; a charge which, I am confident, he did not deserve, and to which the above extract does not in my opinion afford any plausible colour. It exhibits, indeed, an instance of a curious coincidence between two philosophers in their views of the same subject, and as such I have no doubt that Mr. Smith himself would have remarked, had it occurred to his memory when he was writing his book. Of such accidental coincidences between different minds, examples present themselves every day to those, who, after having drawn from their internal resources all the lights they could supply on a particular question, have the curiosity to compare their own conclusions with those of their predecessors. And it is extremely worthy of observation, that, in proportion as any conclusion approaches to the truth, the number of previous approximations to it may be reasonably expected to be multiplied.

In the instance before us, however, the question about originality is of little or no moment, for the peculiar merit of Mr. Smith's work does not lie in his general principle, but in the skilful use he has made of it to give a systematical arrangement to the most important discussions and doctrines of Ethics. In this point of view, the *Theory of Moral Sentiments* may be justly regarded as one of the most original efforts of the human mind in that branch of science to which it relates; and even if we were to suppose that it was first suggested to the author by a remark of which the world was in possession for two thousand years before, this very circumstance would only reflect a stronger lustre on the novelty of his design, and on the invention and taste displayed in its execution.

In the same work I have observed, that, 'in studying the connexion and filiation of successive theories, when we are at a loss in any instance for a link to complete the continuity of philosophical speculation, it seems much more reasonable to search for it in the systems of the immediately preceding period, and in the inquiries which *then* occupied the public attention, than in detached sentences, or accidental expressions gleaned from the relics of distant ages. It is thus only that we can hope to seize the precise point of view in which an author's subject first presented itself to his attention, and to account to our own satisfaction, from the particular aspect under which he saw it, for the subsequent direction which was given to his curiosity. In following such a plan, our object is not to detect plagiarisms, which we suppose men of genius to have intentionally concealed, but to fill up an apparent chasm in the history of science, by laying hold of the thread which insensibly guided the mind from one station to another.' Upon these principles our attention is naturally directed on the present occasion to the inquiries of Dr. Butler, in preference to those of any other author, ancient or modern. At the time when Mr. Smith began his literary career, Butler unquestionably stood highest among the ethical writers of England; and his works appear to have produced a still deeper and more lasting impression in Scotland than in the other part of the island. Of the esteem in which they were held by Lord Kames and Mr. Hume, satisfactory documents remain in their published letters; nor were his writings less likely to attract the notice of Mr. Smith, in consequence of the pointed and unanswerable objections which they contain to some of the favourite opinions of his predecessor Dr. Hutcheson.

The probability of this conjecture is confirmed by the obvious and easy transition which connects the theory of sympathy with Butler's train of thinking in his Sermon *On Self-Deceit.* In order to free the mind from the influence of its artifices, experience gradually teaches us (as Butler has excellently shown) either to recollect the judgments we have formerly passed in similar circumstances on the conduct of others, or to state cases to ourselves, in which we and all our personal concerns are left entirely out of the question. Hence it was not an unnatural inference, on the first aspect of the fact, that our only ideas of right and wrong, with respect to our own conduct, are derived from our sentiments with respect to the conduct of others. This accordingly (as we have already seen) is the distinguishing principle of Mr. Smith's theory.[17]

I have formerly referred to a note in Butler's fifth *Sermon*, in which he has exposed the futility of Hobbes's definition of Pity.[18] In the same note, it is remarked farther by the very acute and profound author, that Hobbes's premises, if admitted to be sound, so far from establishing his favourite doctrine concerning the selfish nature of man, would afford an additional illustration of the provision made in his constitution for the establishment and maintenance of the social union. 'If there be really any such thing as the fiction or imagination of danger to ourselves from sight of the miseries of others, which Hobbes speaks of, and which he has absurdly mistaken for the whole of compassion; if there be anything of this sort common to mankind distinct from the reflection of reason, it would be a most remarkable instance of what was furthest from his thoughts, namely, of a mutual sympathy between each particular of the species, – a fellow-feeling common to mankind. It would not indeed be an instance of our substituting others for ourselves, but it would be an example of our substituting ourselves for others.' To those who are at all acquainted with Mr. Smith's book, it is unnecessary for me to observe how very precisely Butler has here touched on the general fact which is assumed as the basis of the *Theory of Moral Sentiments*.

In various other parts of Butler's writings, there are manifest anticipations of Mr. Smith's ethical speculations. In his Sermon, for example, *On Forgiveness of Injuries*, he expresses himself thus: 'Without knowing particulars, I take upon me to assure all persons who think they have received indignities or injurious treatment, that they may depend upon it, as in a manner certain, that the offence is not so great as they themselves imagine. We are in such a peculiar situation, with respect to injuries done to ourselves, that we can scarce any more see them as they really are than our eye can see itself. If we could place ourselves at a due distance, (that is, be really unprejudiced,) we should frequently discern *that* to be in reality

---

[17] See pp. 329, 330 of this volume.

[18] Ibid., p. 193.

inadvertence and mistake in our enemy, which we now fancy we see to be malice or scorn. From this proper point of view we should likewise, in all probability, see something of these latter in ourselves, and most certainly a great deal of the former. Thus the indignity or injury would almost infinitely lessen, and perhaps at last come out to be nothing at all. Self-love is a medium of a peculiar kind; in these cases it magnifies everything which is amiss in others, at the same time that it lessens everything amiss in ourselves.'

The following passage in Butler's Sermon *On Self-Deceit*, is still more explicit. 'It would very much prevent our being misled by this self-partiality, to reduce that practical rule of our Saviour – *whatsoever ye would that men should do to you, even so do unto them*, – to our judgment or way of thinking. This rule, you see, consists of two parts. One is to substitute another for yourself when you take a survey of any part of your behaviour, or consider what is proper and fit and reasonable for you to do upon any occasion: The other part is, that you substitute yourself in the room of another; consider yourself as the person affected by such a behaviour, or towards whom such an action is done, and then you would not only see, but likewise feel the reasonableness or unreasonableness of such an action or behaviour.'

The same idea is stated with great clearness and conciseness by Hobbes. 'There is an easy rule to know upon a sudden, whether the action I be to do be against the law of nature or not. And it is but this, *That a man imagine himself in the place of the party with whom he hath to do, and reciprocally him in his.* Which is no more but changing (as it were) of the scales; for every man's passion weigheth heavy in his own scale, but not in the scale of his neighbour. And this rule is very well known and expressed in the old dictate, *Quod tibi fieri non vis, alteri ne feceris.*'[19]

It is observed by Gibbon that this *golden rule* is to be found in a moral treatise of Isocrates:[20]–"Α πάσχοντες ὑφ' ἑτέρων ὀργίζεσδε, ταῦτα τοῖς ἄλλοις μὴ ποιεῖτε. See *History of the Decline*, &c. – Vol. X. p. 191.

[19] *Moral and Political Works of Thomas Hobbes*, folio edition, London, 1750, p. 46.

[20] In *Nicocle. Opera*, Tom. I. p. 93, ed. Battie. [Tom. I. p. 147, ed. Auger. – Parts iv. c 14.]

Later Critical
Assessments

ON DR SMITH'S SYSTEM*
Thomas Brown

The system, to which I allude, is that which is delivered by Dr Smith, in his *Theory of Moral Sentiments*, – a work, unquestionably of the first rank, in a science, which I cannot but regard, as to man, the most interesting of sciences. Profound in thought, it exhibits, even when it is *most* profound, an example of the graces with which a sage imagination knows how to adorn the simple and majestic form of science, that is severe and cold, only to those who are themselves cold and severe, – as in those very graces, it exhibits, in like manner, an example of the reciprocal embellishment which imagination receives from the sober dignity of truth. In its minor details and illustrations, indeed, it may be considered as presenting a model of philosophical beauty, of which all must acknowledge the power, who are not disqualified by their very nature for the admiration and enjoyment of intellectual excellence, – so dull of understanding, as to shrink with a painful consciousness of incapacity at the very appearance of refined analysis – or so dull and cold of heart, as to feel no charm in the delightful varieties of an eloquence, that, in the illustration and embellishment of the noblest truths, seems itself to live and harmonize with those noble sentiments which it adorns.

It is chiefly in its minor analyses, however, that I conceive the excellence of this admirable work to consist. Its leading doctrine I am far from admitting. Indeed, it seems to me as manifestly false, as the greater number of its secondary and minute delineations appear to me faithful, to the fine lights and faint and flying shades, of that moral nature which they represent.

According to Dr Smith, we do not, *immediately*, approve of certain actions, or disapprove of certain other actions, when we have become aquainted with the intention of the agent, and the consequences, beneficial or injurious, of what he has done. All these we might know thoroughly, without a feeling

* From *Lectures on the Philosophy of the Human Mind* (Edinburgh, 1820), vol. 4, pp. 113–45.

of the slightest approbation or disapprobation. It is necessary, before any moral sentiment arise, that the mind should go through another process, – that by which we seem, for the time, to enter into the feelings of the agent, and of those to whom his actions have related, in its consequences, or intended consequences, beneficial or injurious. If, by a process of this kind, – on considering all the circumstances in which the agent was placed, we feel a complete sympathy with the passions or calmer emotions that actuated him, and with the gratitude of him who was the object of the action, – we approve of the *action* itself as *right*, and feel the *merit* of the *agent;* – our sense of the propriety of the action depending on our sympathy with the agent; our sense of the merit of the agent on our sympathy with the object of the action. If our sympathies be of an opposite kind, we disapprove of the action itself as improper, that is to say, unsuitable to the circumstances, and ascribe, not merit but demerit, to the agent. In sympathizing with the gratitude of others, we should have regarded the agent as worthy of *reward;* in sympathizing with the resentment of others, we regard him as worthy of *punishment.*

Such is the supposed process in estimating the *actions of others.* When we regard our *own conduct,* we in some measure reverse this process; or rather, by a process still more refined, we imagine others sympathizing with us, and sympathize with their sympathy. We consider how our conduct would appear to an impartial spectator. We approve of it, if it be that of which we feel that *he* would approve; – we disapprove of it, if it be that which, we feel by the experience of our own former emotions, when we have ourselves, in similar circumstances estimated the actions of others, would excite his disapprobation. We are able to form a judgment as to our own conduct, therefore, because we have previously judged of the moral conduct of others, – that is to say, have previously sympathized with the feelings of others; – and but for the presence, or supposed presence, of some impartial spectator, as a mirror to represent to ourselves, we should as little have known the beauty or deformity of our own moral character, as we should have known the beauty or ugliness of our external features, without some mirror to reflect them to our eye.

In this brief outline of Dr Smith's system, I have, of course, confined myself to the leading doctrine, of which his theory is the developement. If this doctrine of the necessary antecedence of sympathy to our moral approbation or disapprobation be just, the *system* may be admitted, even though many of his minor illustrations should appear to be false. If this primary doctrine be *not just*, the system, however ingenious and just in its explanation of many phenomena of the mind, must fail as a *theory of our moral sentiments*.

To derive our moral sentiments, – which are as universal as the actions of mankind that come under our review, – from the occasional sympathies, that warm or sadden us with joys and griefs and sentiments which are not our own, seems to me, I confess, very nearly the same sort of error, as it would be to derive the waters of an ever-flowing stream from the sunshine or shade which may occasionally gleam over it. That we have a principle of social feeling, which, in its rapid participation of the vivid emotions of others, seems to identify us, in many cases, with the happy or the sorrowful, the grateful or the indignant, it is impossible to deny. But this sympathy, quick as it truly is to arise, in cases in which the primary feelings are *vivid* and *strongly marked*, is not a perpetual accompaniment of every action of every one around us. There must be *some vividness* of *feeling* in others, or the *display of vividness of feeling*, – or at least such a situation as usually excites vivid feeling of some sort, in those who are placed in it, to call the sympathy itself into action. In the number of petty affairs which are hourly before our eyes, what sympathy is felt, either with those who are actively or those who are passively concerned, – when the agent himself performs his little offices with emotions as slight as those which the objects of his actions reciprocally feel; yet, in these cases, we are as capable of judging, and approve or disapprove, – not with the same liveliness of emotion, indeed, but with as accurate estimation of merit or demerit, – as when we consider the most heroic sacrifices which the virtuous can make, or the most atrocious crimes of which the sordid and the cruel can be guilty. It is not the absolute vividness of our emotion, however, but its mere correspondence in degree with the emotion of others, which affects our estimates of the propriety of their actions; and it must be remembered, that it is not any greater or less vividness of our sympathetic feeling, but the accuracy of our estimation of merit and demerit, whether great or slight, by the sympathetic feelings supposed, which is the only point in question. There is *no* theory of our moral distinctions, which supposes that we are to approve equally of *all* actions that are right, and to disapprove equally of all actions which are wrong; but it is essential to *our* theory – that theory which we are considering – that there should be *no feeling of right or wrong, merit or demerit,* – and, consequently, *no moral estimation whatever,* where there is no *previous sympathy in that particular case.* The humblest action, therefore, which we denominate right, must have awakened our sympathy, as much as those glorious actions which we are never weary of extolling, – in the very commendation of which we think not of the individual only with thankfulness, but with a sort of proud delight of ourselves, of our country, of the common nature of man, as ennobled by the virtue, that, instead of receiving dignity from the homage of our praises, confers dignity on the very gratitude and reverence which offer them. If we were to think only those actions *right,* in which our *sympathy* is excited, the class of *indifferent actions* would comprehend the whole life, or nearly the whole life, of almost all the multitude of those around us, and, indeed, of almost all mankind. A few great virtues and great iniquities would still remain in our system of practical ethics, to be applauded or censured; but the morality of the common transactions of life, which, though less important in each particular case, is, upon the whole, more important, from its extensive diffusion, would disappear altogether, *as morality* – as that which it is *right* to *observe,* and *wrong* to *omit,* – and though it might still be counted *useful,* would admit of no higher denomination of praise. The supposed necessary universality then, in our moral sentiments, of that, which, however frequent, is surely far from universal, would of itself seem to me a sufficient objection to the theory of Dr Smith.

Even if the sympathy for which he contends were *as universal,* as it is absolutely necessary for the truth of his theory that it should be, it must still be admitted that our sympathy is, in degree at least, one of the most irregular and seemingly capricious of principles in the constitution of the mind; and on this very account, therefore, not very likely to be the commensurable test or standard of feelings, so regular upon the whole, as our general estimates of right and wrong. But though it would be very easy to show the force of this objection, I hasten from it, and from all objections of this kind, to that which seems to me to be the essential error of the system.

This essential error, the greatest of all possible systematic errors, is no less than the assumption, in every case, of those very moral feelings, which are supposed to flow from sympathy, – the assumption of them as necessarily existing before that very sympathy in which they are said to originate.

Let us allow, then, every thing which we can suppose it possible for the author of the theory to have claimed, – let us admit, that the sympathy of which he speaks, instead of being limited to a few cases of vivid feeling, is as universal as he contends, – that it is as little variable in kind, or in degree, as our notions of right and wrong, – and, in short, that it is in perfect accordance with our moral sentiments; – even though, with all these admissions, we were to admit also the very process which Dr Smith supposes to take place exactly in the manner which he supposes, – it would be very evident, that still, after so many important concessions, the moral sentiments could not be regarded as having their source in the sympathy, but as *preceding* it; or, if no moral sentiments of any kind preceded it, the sympathy itself could not afford them – more than a mirror, which reflects to us, from the opposite landscape, the sunny hill, the rock, and the trees, gleaming through the spray of the waterfall, could of itself, without any external light, produce all that beautiful variety of colour with which it delights our vision, as if it were the very scene on which we have loved to gaze.

Let us consider, then, with a little nicer analysis, the process of which Dr Smith speaks, – admitting the sympathy for which he contends, and admitting it in the fullest extent which can be conceived necessary to his theory.

In this theory, as you have seen, he has separated our feeling of the propriety or impropriety of the action from our feeling of the merit or demerit of the agent, – ascribing the one to our sympathy with the emotions of the agent in the circumstances in which he was placed – the other to our sympathy with the gratitude or resentment of those who have been affected by the action. I have already endeavoured to show you, that we have only one feeling of *approvableness*, arising on the contemplation of an action, which, as variously referred – to the agent, or to the action considered abstractly – is at once the felt propriety of the action and the felt merit of the agent. Indeed, it seems to me as absurd to suppose that we can conceive an action to be wrong, in the moral sense of that word, without any notion of the demerit of the voluntary agent – or conceive the demerit of the voluntary agent, without any notion of the impropriety of his action, as it would be to suppose that we can imagine a circle without a centre, or a centre without a circle. But let us adopt, without objection, the supposed analysis which Dr Smith has made of our moral sentiments; and admit, that, in the constitution of these, there are two distinct feelings, that give occasion to corresponding moral notions of *propriety* and *merit*, – which one of these feelings alone could not have produced; – in short, let us admit, that we might have conceived an action to be morally *wrong*, without any demerit on the part of the agent, or have conceived the *greatest demerit on his part*, without any *moral impropriety in his action*.

The first supposed sympathy which we have to consider, is that which is said to give occasion to our moral estimates of actions as *proper* or *improper*, without regard to the merit or demerit of the agent, that are felt by us only through the medium of another sympathy.

This notion of moral propriety or impropriety, we are told, could not have been produced in us by the most attentive consideration of the action, and of all its circumstances; another process must intervene. We feel the propriety of the action, only because we sympathize with the agent. We make his circumstances our own, and, our passion being in unison with his, we regard it as suitable to the circumstances, and, therefore, as morally proper.

If we have, indeed, previous notions of moral right and wrong, or some other source in which they may be found, this belief of the propriety of certain feelings that accord with ours, might be sufficiently intelligible; but the most complete sympathy of feelings, the most exact accordancy, is not sufficient to constitute or give rise to the *moral* sentiments of which we are treating, – when there is nothing more than a sympathy of feelings, without that previous moral sentiment, which, in Dr Smith's system, we must always tacitly presuppose. In the very striking emotions of taste, for example, we may feel, on the perusal of the same poem, the performance of the same musical air, the sight of the same picture, or statue, a rapture or disgust, accordant with the rapture or disgust expressed by another reader, or listener, or spectator; – a sympathy far more complete than takes place in our consideration of the circumstances in which he may have had to regulate his conduct in any of the common affairs of life, – in which our secondary emotion, if it be at all excited, is excited but faintly. If mere accordance of emotion, then, imply the feeling of moral excellence of any sort, we should certainly feel moral regard for all whose taste coincides with ours; yet, however gratifying the sympathy in such a case may be, we do not feel, in consequence of this sympathy, any morality in the taste that is most exactly accordant with our own. There is an agreement of emotions, – a sort of *physical* suitableness, that is felt by us of the *emotions* as *effects*, to the *works of art as causes*, but nothing more; and, if we had not a principle of moral approbation, by which, independently of sympathy, and previously to it, we regard actions as *right*; the most exact sympathy of passions would, in like manner, have been a proof to us of an agreement of feelings, but of nothing more. It proves to us more, because the emotions, which we compare with our own, are recognized by us as *moral feelings*, independently of the mere agreement. We do not merely share the sentiments of the agent, but we share his *moral* sentiments, the recognition of which, as moral sentiments, has preceded our very sympathy.

Why is it that we regard emotions which do not harmonize with our own, not merely as unlike to ours, which is one view of them, – but as morally *improper*, which is a very different view of them? It must surely be, because we regard our own emotions which differ from them as morally *proper;* and, if we regard our own emotions as proper, before we can judge the emotions, which do not harmonize with them, to be *improper on that account*, what influence can the supposed sympathy and comparison have had, in giving birth to that moral sentiment which preceded the comparison? They show us only feelings that differ from ours, and that are improper because ours are proper. The sympathy, therefore, on which the feeling of propriety is said to depend, assumes the previous belief of that very propriety; – or if there be no previous belief of the moral suitableness of our own emotions, there can be no reason, from the mere dissonance of other emotions with ours, to regard these dissonant emotions as morally unsuitable to the circumstances in which they have arisen. We may, perhaps, conceive them to be *physically* unsuitable, in the same manner as we regard the taste as erroneous, which approves of poetry as sublime that to us appears bombastic or mean; but we can as little feel any moral regard in the one case as in the other, unless we have *previously* distinguished the one set of emotions as *moral* emotions, the other set as emotions of taste.

With respect to the former of the two sympathies, then, which Dr Smith regards as essential to our moral sentiments, the sympathy from which he supposes us to derive our notions of actions, as right or wrong, proper or improper, – that is to say, as morally suitable or unsuitable to the circumstances in which the action takes place, – we have seen that it assumes, as independent of the sympathy, the very feelings, to which the sympathy is said to give rise.

Let us next consider the latter of the two sympathies, to which we are said to own our notion of *merit or demerit in the agent*, as distinct from the *propriety or impropriety of his action*.

These sentiments of merit or demerit arise, we are told, not from any direct consideration of the agent, and of the circumstances of his action, but from our sympathy with the gratitude or resentment of those who have derived benefit or injury; or at least whom he is supposed to have wished to derive benefit or injury, from that good or evil which he proposed. If, on considering the circumstances of the case, we feel that our emotions of this sort would in a similar situation, harmonize with theirs; we regard the agent in the same light in which they regard him, as worthy of reward in the one case, or of punishment in the other, that is to say, as having *moral merit* or *demerit*.

If our sense of merit were confined to cases in which the action had a direct relation to others, with whose gratitude we might be supposed to sympathize, this theory of merit would at least be more distinctly conceivable. But what are we to think of cases, in which the action begins and terminates, without a thought of the happiness of others, in the amelioration of the individual himself, – of sacrifices resolutely but silently made to the mere sense of duty, – the voluntary relinquishment of luxurious indulgencies, – the struggle, and at last the victory over appetites and passions that are felt to be inconsistent with the sanctity of virtue, – and over *habits*, still more difficult to be subdued, than the very appetites or passions which may have given them their power. In such cases, our sense of the merit of the victor in this noble strife, – when we do not think of the gratitude of a single individual, because there is in truth no gratitude of which to think, – is, notwithstanding, as vivid, as if we had around us whole families and tribes of the grateful to excite our sympathy, and to continue to harmonize with it. The world, indeed, the great community of individuals, it may be said, is truly benefited by every increase of virtue, in any one of the individuals who compose it; and it may be possible, in this way, to *invent* some species of gratitude of the whole multitude of mankind, that may be supposed to awake our sympathy, and thus to make us feel a merit even in such cases, which otherwise we should not have felt. But, though it may be possible for us, with due care and effort of thought, to invent this abstract or remote gratitude with which ours may be supposed to harmonize; can it be imagined by any one, but the most obstinate defender of a system, that this strange sympathy, of which no one, perhaps, has been conscious in any case, truly and constantly takes place whenever we thus approve, – that we do not feel any merit whatever in the voluntary privations which virtue makes, till we have previously excited ourselves to admire them, by reflecting on a grateful world? Such a reflex thankfulness, if it occur at all, does not occur to one of many thousands, who require, for their instant perceptions of the merit, only the knowledge of the sacrifices of present enjoyment which have been made, and of the pure emotions which led to the sacrifices. It is not only the Hercules who freed the world from robbers and monsters that we admire. We admire, at least, as much, in the beautiful ancient allegory, the same moral hero when he resisted the charms and the solicitations of Pleasure herself. The choice of Hercules, indeed, is fabulous. But the choice which he is fabled to have made, has been the choice of the virtuous of every age; and, in every age, the sacrifices internally and silently made to duty and conscience, have been ranked in merit with the sacrifices which had for their direct object the happiness of others, and, for their immediate reward, the gratitude of the happy. Why is it that we look with so much honour on the martyr in those early ages of persecution, which, collecting around the victim every instrument of torture, required of him only a few grains of incense to be thrown before a statue, – more noble, indeed, than the imperial murderer whom it represented, but still only a statue, – the effigy of a being of human form, who, under the purple which clothed him, with the diadem and the sceptre, and the altar, – far from being a god, was himself one of the lowest of the things which God had made! When, placed thus between idolatry and every form of bodily anguish, – with life and guilt before him, and death and innocence, – the hero of a pure faith looked fearlessly on the cross or on the stake, and calmly, and without wrath, on the statue which he refused to worship, and on all the ready ministers of cruelty, that were rejoicing in the new work which they had to perform, and the new amusement which they were to give to the impatient crowd, – do we feel that there was no merit in the magnanimity, because we cannot readily discover some *gratitude* which we may participate? – or, if we do feel any merit, is it only on account of some gratitude which we have at last *succeeded* in discovering? We do not think of any thankfulness of man. We think only of God and virtue, – and of the heroic sufferer, to whom God and virtue were *all*, and the suffering of such a moment *nothing*.

That our feeling of merit, then, is not a reflected gratitude, but arises from the direct contemplation of the meritorious action, might, if any proof were necessary, appear sufficiently evident from the equal readiness of this feeling to arise in cases in which it would be difficult to discover any gratitude with which we can be supposed to sympathize, and in which the individual himself, and the circumstances of his action, are all that is before us. But though this, and every other objection to Dr Smith's theory of our feeling of merit were to be abandoned, there would still remain the great objection, – that the sympathy which he supposes in this case, as in that formerly examined by us, proceeds on the existence of that very moral sentiment which it is stated by him to produce.

We discover the merit of the agent, in any case, it is said, by that sympathetic tendency of our nature, in consequence of which, on considering any particular action, we place ourselves in the situation of those who are benefited by the action, when, if we feel an emotion of gratitude like theirs, we of course consider the agent himself as *meritorious*, – worthy of the reward of which *they* consider him to be worthy; and in like manner, on considering any action of injustice or malevolence, we feel the demerit of the agent, by sympathizing with the resentment of those whom the action has injured.

Such is the process asserted. But what is it that is truly supposed in this process, as distinguishing the sympathetic and secondary feelings, from the primary feelings of those who were directly concerned?

We place ourselves in the situation of others – or, rather, without willing it, or knowing the charge till it is produced, we feel ourselves, by some sudden illusion, as if placed in their situation. In this imaginary sameness of circumstances, we have feelings similar to theirs. They view their benefactor as worthy of reward. We, therefore, considering for the moment the benefit as if conferred on us, regard him likewise as worthy of reward: – or if they consider him worthy of punishment, we too consider him worthy of punishment. Their gratitude or resentment is founded on real benefit received, or real injury. Our gratitude or resentment is founded on the illusive momentary belief of benefit or injury. But this difference of reality and illusion in the circumstances which give occasion to them, is the only difference of the feelings; unless indeed, that, as the illusion cannot be of very long continuance, and is, probably, even while it lasts, less powerful than the reality, our sympathetic feelings, however *similar* in *kind*, may be supposed to be *weaker* in *degree*.

The effect of the sympathy, then, being only to transfuse into our breasts the gratitude or resentment of those who have been immediately benefited or injured, by any generous or malevolent action; – if the original gratitude imply belief of merit in the object of the gratitude, and the original resentment imply belief of demerit in its object, *we may*, by our sympathy with these direct original feelings, be impressed with similar belief of merit or demerit. But, in this case, it is equally evident, that, if *our reflex* gratitude and resentment involve notions of merit and demerit, the original gratitude and resentment which we feel by reflection, must in like manner have involved them; and must even have involved them with more vivid feeling, since the difference of vividness was the chief or only circumstance of difference in the direct and the sympathetic emotions. The sympathy, then, to which we are supposed to owe our moral sentiments of merit and demerit, presupposes those very sentiments; since the feelings which arise in us by sympathy, only from the illusion by which we place ourselves in the situation of others, must, in those who were truly in that very situation, have arisen directly with at least equal power.

It is some previous gratitude with which we sympathize; it is some previous resentment with which we sympathize; and merit is said to be only that *worthiness of reward* which the gratitude itself implies, – and demerit that worthiness of punishment which is implied in the primary resentment. If the feeling of gratitude implied no notions of any relation of worthiness, which our benefactor's generosity bears to the reward which we wish that we were capable of bestowing on him, – and our resentment, in like manner, implied no notion of a similar relation of the injustice or cruelty of him who has injured us, to that punishment of his offence which we wish and anticipate, – we might then, indeed, be obliged to seek some other source of these felt relations. But if the actual gratitude or resentment of those who have profited or suffered, imply no feelings of merit or demerit, we may be certain, at least, that in whatever source we are to strive to discover these feelings, it is not in the mere reflection of a fainter gratitude or resentment, that we can hope to find them.

After admitting to Dr Smith, then, every thing which he could be supposed to claim, or even to wish to claim, with respect to the universality, the steadiness, and the vividness of our sympathetic feelings, we have seen, that in both the sympathies which he supposes to take place, – that from which we are said to derive our moral sentiments of the propriety or impropriety of actions, and that from which we are said, in like manner, to derive our moral sentiments of merit or demerit in the agent, – the process to which he ascribes the origin of these moral sentiments cannot even be understood, without the belief of their previous existence. The feelings with which we sympathize, are themselves moral feelings or sentiments; or, if they are not moral feelings, the reflection of them from a thousand breasts cannot alter their nature.

EXAMINATION OF DR SMITH'S SYSTEM CONCLUDED;
RECAPITULATION OF THE DOCTRINES OF MORAL
APPROBATION

My last Lecture, Gentlemen, was chiefly employed in considering a theory of our moral sentiments which has been stated and defended with great eloquence, by one of the profoundest philosophers, whom our country and our science can boast –

a theory which founds our moral sentiments, not on the direct contemplation of the actions which we term virtuous; but on a sympathy, which it is impossible for us not to feel, with the emotions of the agent, in the circumstances in which he has been placed, and with the emotions, also, of those to whom his actions have been productive of benefit or injury; – our direct sympathy with the agent, giving rise to our notion of the propriety of his actions, – our indirect sympathy with those whom his actions have benefited or injured, giving rise to our notions of merit or demerit in the agent himself. Both these supposed sympathies I examined with a more minute review, than that to which they have usually been submitted; and, in both cases, we found that, even though many other strong objections to which the theory is liable were abandoned; and though the process for which the theorist contends were allowed to take place, to the fullest extent to which he contends for it; his system would still be liable to the insuperable objection, that the moral sentiments which he ascribes to our secondary feelings, of mere sympathy, are assumed as previously existing, in those original emotions with which the secondary feelings are said to be in unison. If those to whom an action has directly related, are incapable of discovering, by the longest and minutest examination of it – however much they may have been benefited by it, or injured, and intentionally benefited or injured – any *traces* of *right* or *wrong*, merit or demerit, in the performer of the action; those whose sympathy consists merely in an illustory participation of the same interest, cannot surely derive, from the fainter reflex feelings, that moral knowledge which even the more vivid primary emotions were incapable of affording, – anymore than we can be supposed to acquire from the most faithful echo, important truths that were never uttered by the voices which it reflects. The utmost influence of the liveliest sympathy, can be only to render the momentary feelings the same, as if the identity of situation with the object of the sympathy were not illusive, but real; and what it would be impossible for the mind to feel, if really existing, in the circumstances supposed, it must be impossible for it also to feel, when it believes itself to exist in them, and is affected in the same manner, as if truly that very mind, with whose emotions it sympathizes.

If, indeed, we had *previously* any moral notions of actions as right or wrong, we might very easily judge of the propriety or impropriety of the sentiments of others, according as our own do or do not sympathize with them; and it is this *previous* feeling of propriety or impropriety which Dr Smith tacitly assumes, even in contending for the exclusive influence of the *sympathy*, as itself the original source of every moral sentiment. The sentiments of others could not fail, indeed, in that case, to appear to us *proper*, if they coincided with sentiments which we had before, in our own mind, recognized as *proper, or morally suitable to the circumstances – improper* if they differed from *these*. But, if we have no previous moral notions whatever, the *most exact sympathy* of feelings can tell us only that *our* feelings are *similar* to the feelings of some other person, – which they may be, as much when they are vicious as when they are virtuous, or when they are neither virtuous nor vicious; – the *most complete dissonance*, in like manner, can tell us only that our feelings are *not* similar to those of some other person. When another calls *scarlet* or *green* what we have previously felt to be *scarlet* or *green*, we think that *his* vision and *ours agree*; but we presuppose, in him as in ourselves, that visual sensibility which distinguished the colours; and we do not consider him an object of moral regard, because his vision coincides with ours. When he is affected with a delightful emotion, similar to ours, on the contemplation of a work of art, we acknowledge mentally, and are pleased, perhaps, with this coincidence of taste. But the coincidence does not seem to us to be that which constitutes the emotions of taste. On the contrary, it presupposes, in both, an independent susceptibility of these emotions, by which we should, individually, have admired what is beautiful, and distinguished from it what is ugly, though no one had been present with us to participate our sentiments. When, in like manner, we admire, with vivid approbation, some generous action, – that is to say, according to Dr Smith's language, when we sympathize with the feelings of any one in the circumstances in which he has been placed, – we have a coincidence of feelings, indeed, as exact, though probably not more exact, than in a case of simple vision, or admiration of some work of art, in which no moral sentiment was felt; – and this very coincidence, in like manner, presupposes a capacity of distinguishing and admiring what is *right*, – without which, there would have been a similarity of feelings, and nothing more, precisely as in the other cases. It is not a mere coincidence of feeling, however, which we recognize in our moral sentiments, like that which we recognize in the most exact coincidence of taste. We feel, not merely that another has acted as we should have done, and that his motives, in similar circumstances, have been similar to ours. We feel, that, in acting as he has done, he has acted properly; – because, independently of the sympathy which merely gives us feelings to measure with our own, as we might measure with our own any other species of feelings, we are impressed with the *propriety* of the sentiments, according to which we trust that we should ourselves have acted; – so thoroughly impressed with these *previous* distinctions of right and wrong, that, in the opposite case of some act of atrocious delinquency, no sympathy in vice of one villain with another, can make the *common crime* seem a *virtue* in the eyes of his accomplice, – who is actuated by similar motives and therefore by similar feelings, in a sympathy of the finest unison, – when he adds his arm to the rapine, and afterwards to the murder, which is to conceal and to consummate the guilt.

The moral sentiments which we have as yet considered, are those which relate to the *conduct and feelings of others*. The same inconsistencies which are found, on the theory of *these*, is to be found, as might be supposed, in the application of the principle to other species of supposed sympathy which we have still to consider, – in the sentiments which we form of *our own moral conduct*. That we should be capable indeed, of forming a moral estimate of our *own actions*, from the direct contemplation of the circumstances in which we may have been placed, and of the good or evil which we may have intentionally produced, would evidently be subversive of the whole theory of sympathy; since, with the same knowledge of circumstances, and of intention, if we could form any moral judgment of our *own* actions, we might be equally capable of forming some moral judgment of the actions of *others*. It was absolutely necessary, therefore, for Dr Smith to maintain, that we have no power of judging of our own actions directly, – that, knowing the choice which we have made, and all the circumstances which led to our choice, and all the consequences of benefit or injury to individuals, and to the world, which our choice may have produced, – it is yet absolutely impossible for us to distinguish, *without the aid of the real or supposed sentiments of others*, any difference of propriety or impropriety, right or wrong, merit or demerit, or whatever other

names we may use to express the differences of vice and virtue;
– though our vice had been the atrocious fury of plunging a
dagger in the heart of her who had been our happiness in
many connubial years, and who was slumbering beside us on
the same pillow in the calmness of unsuspecting love; or our
virtue, the clemency of drawing back from the bosom of the
assassin whom we had laid at our feet, the dagger which we
had wrenched from his murderous hand. Even of actions so
different as these, it would be absolutely impossible for us, we
are told, to form any moral distinction, if we were to look on
them only with our own eyes, and measure them by the feelings
of our own heart. Before the one can appear to us less virtuous
than the other, we must imagine some witnesses, or hearers,
of what has been done, and sympathize with their sympathy.
Such is the process which Dr Smith believes to take place. But,
surely, if our original feelings, on the consideration of all the
circumstances of an action, involve no notion of right or
wrong, – the sympathy with our feelings, or our sympathy
with that sympathy, or even an infinite series of reciprocal
sympathies, if these should be thought necessary, cannot afford
the moral notions of which the original feelings, themselves
more vivid, afforded no elements. If the impartial spectator be
able to discover merit or demerit, by making our case his own,
and becoming conscious as it were of *our* feelings; our feelings,
which he thus makes his own, must speak to *us* with the same
voice of moral instruction, with which, during his temporary
illusion, they speak to *him*. If, considering our action and all
its consequences, we cannot discover any merit or demerit,
they, considering our action in all its circumstances as theirs,
must be alike insensible of any merit or demerit: – or, if they
have feelings essentially different from ours, they have *not*
made our case their own; – and what is misnamed *sympathy*
has not been *sympathy*. Unless we presuppose, as I before said,
on their part some moral notions of what is right or wrong,
meritorious or worthy of punishment, by which they may
measure our conduct and feelings, – all the knowledge which
the most complete system can afford, is merely that they have
certain feelings, that we have had certain feelings, and that
these feelings are similar to each other; as our feelings have
coincided before in various other emotions, perceptions, judgments that involved or suggested no moral notion whatever.
 We have now then considered, both in its relation to our

sentiments of our own moral conduct, and in its relation to our sentiments of the conduct of others, the very celebrated theory of Dr Smith, – a theory, which I cannot but regard as involving, in morals, the same error that would be involved in a theory of the source of light, if an optician, after showing us many ingenious contrivances, by which an image of some beautiful form may be made to pass from one visible place to another, were to contend, that all the magnificent radiations of that more than etherial splendour which does not merely adorn the day, but constitutes the day, had their primary origin in *reflection*, – when reflection itself implies, and cannot be understood but as implying the previous incidence, and, therefore, the previous existence, of the light which is reflected. A mirror presents to us a fainter copy of external things; but it is a copy which it presents. We are, in like manner, to each other, mirrors, that reflect from breast to breast joy, sorrow, indignation, and all the vivid emotions of which the individual mind is susceptible; but though, as mirrors, we mutually give and receive emotions, these emotions must have been *felt* before they could be communicated. To ascribe original moral feelings to this mental reflection, is truly, then, as much an error, in the theory of morality, as the doctrine of the production of light by reflection without the previous incidence of light, would be an error in the theory of catoptrics.

The argument, after the fuller views of it which I have given, may be recapitulated in very brief compass.

There are only two senses in which sympathy can be understood; *one* having immediate relation to the *feelings*, the other to the *situation*, of him with whom we are said to sympathize. We partake his emotions *directly*, as if by instant contagion; or we partake them indirectly, by first imagining ourselves in the circumstances in which he is placed; the emotion, in this latter case, being similar, merely because the situation, in which we imagine ourselves for the moment, is similar, and arising in us when the situation is imagined to be ours, precisely in the same manner, and according to the same principles, as it arose in the mind of *him* who truly existed in the circumstances in which our imagination has placed *us*. In either case, it is equally evident, that sympathy cannot be the *source* of any *additional knowledge*: – it only gives a wider diffusion, to feelings, that previously exist, or that might have previously existed. If it *reflect* to us the very emotions of others, as if by contagion, without any intervening influence of imagination on our part; it reflects feelings that have been *directly excited* in *them*, the primary subjects of the feelings, by their real situation; and which *they* would not the less have had, though no one had been present to sympathize with them, or even though the tendency to sympathy had not formed a part of the mental constitution. If, on the other hand, sympathy do not reflect to us the very emotions of others, but make us first enter, by a sort of spiritual transmigration, into *their* situation, and thus, indirectly, impress us with their feelings; it still, in making their situation ours, while the illusion lasts, excites in us only the feelings, which we should have had, if the situation had been really ours; and which the same tendencies to emotion that produce them *now*, would *then* have produced, though no sympathy whatever had been concerned in the process. All which is peculiar to the sympathy is, that, instead of one mind only, affected with certain feelings, there are two minds affected with certain feelings, and a recognition of the similarity of these feelings – a similarity which, far from being confined to our moral emotions, may occur as readily, and as frequently, in every other feeling of which the mind is suscep-tible. What produces the moral notions, therefore, must evidently be something more than a recognition of similarity of feeling, which is thus common to feelings of every class. There must be an independent capacity of moral emotion, in consequence of which we judge those sentiments of conduct to be right, which coincide with sentiments of conduct previously recognized as right – or the sentiments of others to be improper, because they are not in unison with those which we have previously distinguished as proper. Sympathy, then, may be the *diffuser* of moral sentiments, as of various other feelings; but, if no moral sentiments exist previously to our sympathy, our sympathy itself cannot give rise to them.

Such, in outline, is the great objection to Dr Smith's theory, as a theory of our moral sentiments. It professes to explain, by the intervention of sympathy, feelings, which must have existed previously to the sympathy; – or at least, without the capacity of which, as original feelings, in the real circumstances supposed, the illusive reality, which sympathy produces, would have been incapable of developing them. It is on a mere assumption, then, – or rather on an inconsistency, still more illogical than a mere assumption, – that the great doctrine of his system is founded; yet, notwithstanding this essential defect, which might seem to you inconsistent with the praise that was given when I entered on the examination of it, the work of Dr Smith is, without all question, one of the most interesting works – perhaps I should have said the most interesting work, – in moral science. It is valuable, however, as I before remarked, not for the leading doctrine of which we have seen the futility; but for the minor theories which are adduced in illustration of it, – for the refined analysis which it exhibits in many of these details, – and for an eloquence which, adapting itself to all the temporary varieties of its subject, – familiar with a sort of majestic grace, and simple even in its magnificence, – can play amid the little decencies and proprieties of common life, or rise to all the dignity of that sublime and celestial virtue which it seems to bring from heaven, indeed, but to bring down, gently and humbly, to the humble bosom of man.

That his own penetrating mind should not have discovered the inconsistencies that are involved in his theory, and that these should not have readily occurred to the many philosophic readers and admirers of his work, may, in part, have arisen, – as many other seeming wonders of the kind have arisen, – from the ambiguities of language. The meaning of the important word *sympathy*, is not sufficiently definite, so as to present always one clear notion to the mind. It is generally employed, indeed, to signify a mere participation of the feelings of others; but it is also frequently used as significant of *approbation* itself. To say that we sympathize with any one in what he has felt or done, means often that we thoroughly approve of his feelings; and, in consequence of this occasional use of the term as synonymous with approbation, the theory, which would identify all our moral approbation with sympathy, was, I cannot but think, more readily admitted, both by its author, and by those who have followed him; since what was not true of *sympathy*, in its strict philosophic sense, was yet true of it in its mixed popular sense. Indeed, if the word had been always strictly confined to its two accurate meanings, – as significant either of the mere direct participation of feelings previously existing, or of the indirect participation of them in consequence of the illusive belief of similarity of circumstances, – it seems to me as little possible that any one should have thought of ascribing to sympathy original feelings, as, in the analogous cases which I before mentioned, of ascribing to an echo the original utterance of the voices which it sends to our ear, – or the production of the colours which it sends to our eye, to the mirror which has only *received* and *reflected* them.

Of all the principles of our mixed nature, sympathy is one of the most irregular, – varying not in different individuals only, but even in the same individual in different hours or different minutes of the same day; and varying, not with slight differences, but with differences of promptness and liveliness, with which only feelings the most capricious could be commensurable. If ever virtue and vice, therefore, or our views of actions as right and wrong, varied with our sympathy, we might be virtuous at morning, vicious at noon, and virtuous again at night, without any change in the circumstances of our action, except in our greater or less tendency to vividness of sympathy, or to the expectation of more or less vivid sympathies in others. How absurd and impertinent seems to us, in our serious hours, the mirth that, in more careless moments, would have won from us, not our smile only, but our full sympathy of equal laughter; and how dull, when our mind is sportive, seems to us the gravity of the sad and serious, – of the venerable moralizers on years that are long past, and years that are present, – to whose chair, under the influence of any sorrow that depressed us, we loved to draw our own, while we felt a sort of comfort as we listened to them, in the slow and tranquil tone, and the gentle solemnity of their fixed but placid features. What is true of our sympathy with mere mirth, or sadness, is true of every other species of sympathy; original temperament, habit, the slightest accident of good or bad fortune, may modify, in no slight degree, the readiness, or, at least, the liveliness of moral sympathy with which we should have entered into the feelings of others, – into their gratitude, or anger, or common love or hate; and if, therefore, our estimate of the propriety or impropriety of actions had been altogether dependent on the force of our mere sympathetic emotion, it would not have been very wonderful, if the greater number of mankind had regarded the very propriety or impropriety, as not less accidental than the sympathies from which they flowed.

ADAM SMITH*[1]
James Mackintosh

The great name of Adam Smith rests upon the *Inquiry into the nature and Causes of the Wealth of Nations;* perhaps the only book which produced an immediate, general, and irrevocable change in some of the most important parts of the legislation of all civilized states. The works of Grotius, of Locke, and of Montesquieu, which bear a resemblance to it in character, and had no inconsiderable analogy to it in the extent of their popular influence, were productive only of a general amendment, not so conspicuous in particular instances, as discoverable, after a time, in the improved condition of human affairs. The work of Smith, as it touched those matters which may be numbered, and measured, and weighed, bore more visible and palpable fruit. In a few years it began to alter laws and treaties, and has made its way, throughout the convulsions of revolution and conquest, to a due ascendant over the minds of men, with far less than the average obstructions of prejudice and clamour, which choke the channels through which truth flows into practice. The most eminent of those who have since cultivated and improved the science will be the foremost to address their immortal master:

Tenebris tantis *tam clarum extollere lumen*
Qui primus potuisti, ILLUSTRANS COMMODA VITÆ.
Te sequor!–*fw*(Lucret. lib. iii.)

In a science more difficult, because both ascending to more simple general principles, and running down through more minute applications, though the success of Smith has been less complete, his genius is not less conspicuous. Perhaps there is no ethical work since Cicero's *Offices*, of which an abridgment enables the reader so inadequately to estimate the merit, as the *Theory of Moral Sentiments.* This is not chiefly owing to

---

* From *Dissertation on the Progress of Ethical Philosophy*, 2nd ed. (Edinburgh, 1836), pp. 232–42.

[1] Born in 1723; died in 1790.

the beauty of diction, as in the case of Cicero; but to the variety of explanations of life and manners which embellish the book often more than they illuminate the theory. Yet, on the other hand, it must be owned that, for purely philosophical purposes, few books more need abridgment: for the most careful reader frequently loses sight of principles buried under illustrations. The naturally copious and flowing style of the author is generally redundant, and the repetition of certain formularies of the system is, in the later editions, so frequent as to be wearisome, and sometimes ludicrous. Perhaps Smith and Hobbes may be considered as forming the two extremes of good style in our philosophy; the first of graceful fulness falling into flaccidity; while the masterly concision of the second is oftener tainted by dictatorial dryness. Hume and Berkeley, though they are nearer the extreme of abundance,[2] are probably the least distant from perfection.

That mankind are so constituted as to sympathize with each other's feelings, and to feel pleasure in the accordance of these feelings, are the only facts required by Dr Smith, and they certainly must be granted to him. To adopt the feelings of another, is to *approve* them. When the sentiments of another are such as would be excited in us by the same objects, we approve them as *morally proper*. To obtain this accord, it becomes necessary for him who enjoys or suffers, to lower his expression of feeling to the point to which the bystander can raise his fellow-feelings; on which are founded all the high virtues of self-denial and self-command; and it is equally necessary for the bystander to raise his sympathy as near as he can to the level of the original feeling. In all unsocial passions, such as anger, we have a *divided sympathy* between him who feels them and those who are the objects of them. Hence the propriety of extremely moderating them. Pure malice is always to be concealed or disguised, because all *sympathy* is arrayed against it. In the private passions, where there is only a *simple sympathy* – that with the original passion – the expression has more liberty. The benevolent affections, where there is a *double sympathy* – with those who feel them, and those who are their objects – are the most agreeable, and may be indulged with

---

[2] This remark is chiefly applicable to Hume's *Essays*. His *Treatise of Human Nature* is more Hobbian in its general tenor, though it has Ciceronian passages.

the least apprehension of finding no echo in other breasts. Sympathy with the gratitude of those who are benefited by good actions, prompts us to consider them as deserving of reward, and forms the *sense of merit;* as fellow-feeling with the resentment of those who are injured by crimes leads us to look on them as worthy of punishment, and constitutes the *sense of demerit.* These sentiments require not only beneficial actions, but benevolent motives for them; being compounded, in the case of merit, of a direct sympathy with the good disposition of the benefactor, and an indirect sympathy with the persons benefited; in the opposite case, with precisely opposite sympathies. He who does an act of wrong to another to gratify his own passions, must not expect that the spectators, who have none of his undue partiality to his own interest, will enter into his feelings. In such a case, he knows that they will pity the person wronged, and be full of indignation against him. When he is cooled, he adopts the sentiments of others on his own crime, feels *shame* at the *impropriety* of his former passion, pity for those who have suffered by him, and a dread of punishment from general and just resentment. Such are the constituent parts of remorse.

Our moral sentiments respecting *ourselves* arise from those which others feel concerning us. We feel a self-approbation whenever we believe that the general feeling of mankind coincides with that state of mind in which we ourselves were at a given time. 'We suppose ourselves the spectators of our own behaviour, and endeavour to imagine what effect it would in this light produce in us.' We must view our own conduct with the eyes of others before we can judge it. The sense of duty arises from putting ourselves in the place of others, and adopting their sentiments respecting our own conduct. In utter solitude there could have been no self-approbation. The *rules* of morality are a summary of those sentiments; and often beneficially stand in their stead when the self-delusions of passion would otherwise hide from us the non-conformity of our state of mind with that which, in the circumstances, can be entered into and approved by impartial bystanders. It is hence that we learn to raise our mind above local or temporary clamour, and to fix our eyes on the surest indications of the general and lasting sentiments of human nature. 'When we approve of any character or action, our sentiments are derived from four sources; *first*, we sympathize with the motives of the agent; *secondly*, we enter into the gratitude of those who have been benefited by his actions; *thirdly*, we observe that his conduct has been agreeable to the general rules by which those two sympathies generally act; and, last of all, when we consider such actions as forming part of a system of behaviour which tends to promote the happiness either of the individual or of society, they appear to derive a beauty from this utility, not unlike that which we ascribe to any well-contrived machine.'[3]

REMARKS

That Smith is the first who has drawn the attention of philosophers to one of the most curious and important parts of human nature – who has looked closely and steadily into the workings of *Sympathy*, its sudden action and reaction, its instantaneous conflicts and its emotions, its minute play and varied illusions – is sufficient to place him high among the cultivators of mental philosophy.

He is very original in applications; and explanations; though, for his principle, he is somewhat indebted to Butler, more to Hutcheson, and most of all to Hume. These writers, except Hume in his original work, had derived sympathy, or great part of it, from benevolence.[4] Smith, with deeper insight, inverted the order. The great part performed by various sympathies in moral approbation was first unfolded by him; and besides its intrinsic importance, it strengthened the proofs against those theories which ascribe that great function to Reason. Another great merit of the theory of sympathy is, that it brings into the strongest light that most important characteristic of the moral sentiments which consists in their being the only principles leading to action, and dependent on emotion or sensibility, with respect to the objects of which,

---

[3] *Theory of Moral Sentiments*, ii. 304. Edinb. 1801.

[4] There is some confusion regarding this point in Butler's first sermon on Compassion.

it is not only possible but natural for all mankind to agree.[5]

The main defects of this theory seem to be the following:

1. Though it is not to be condemned for declining inquiry into the origin of our fellow-feeling, which, being one of the most certain of all facts, might well be assumed as ultimate in speculations of this nature, it is evident that the circumstances to which some speculators ascribe the formation of sympathy at least contribute to strengthen or impair, to contract or expand it. It will appear, more conveniently, in the next article, that the theory of sympathy has suffered from the omission of these circumstances. For the present, it is enough to observe how much our compassion for various sorts of animals, and our fellow-feeling with various races of men, are proportioned to the resemblance which they bear to ourselves, to the frequency of our intercourse with them, and to other causes which, in the opinion of some, afford evidence that sympathy itself is dependent on a more general law.

2. Had Smith extended his view beyond the mere play of sympathy itself, and taken into account all its preliminaries, and accompaniments, and consequences, it seems improbable that he should have fallen into the great error of representing the sympathies in their primitive state, without undergoing any transformation, as continuing exclusively to constitute the moral sentiments. He is not content with teaching that they are the roots out of which these sentiments grow, the stocks on which they are grafted, the elements of which they are compounded; – doctrines to which nothing could be objected but their unlimited extent. He tacitly assumes, that if a sympathy in the beginning caused or formed a moral approbation, so it must ever continue to do. He proceeds like a geologist who should tell us that the layers of this planet had always been in the same state, shutting his eyes to transition states and secondary formations; or like a chemist who should inform us that no compound substance can possess new qualities entirely different from those which belong to its materials. His

---

[5] The feelings of beauty, grandeur, and whatever else is comprehended under the name of Taste, form no exception, for *they do not lead to action*, but terminate in delightful contemplation; which constitutes the essential distinction between them and the moral sentiments, to which, in some points of view, they may doubtless be likened.

acquiescence in this old and still general error is the more remarkable, because Mr Hume's beautiful *Dissertation on the Passions*[6] had just before opened a striking view of some of the compositions and decompositions which render the mind of a formed man as different from its original state, as the organization of a complete animal is from the condition of the first dim speck of vitality. It is from this oversight (ill supplied by moral rules, a loose stone in his building) that he has exposed himself to objections founded on experience, to which it is impossible to attempt any answer. For it is certain that in many, nay in most cases of moral approbation, the adult man approves the action or disposition merely *as right*, and with a distinct consciousness that no process of sympathy intervenes between the approval and its object. It is certain that an unbiassed person would call it *moral approbation*, only as far as it excluded the interposition of any reflection between the conscience and the mental state approved. Upon the supposition of an unchanged state of our active principles, it would follow that sympathy never had any share in the greater part of them. Had he admitted the sympathies to be only elements entering into the *formation of Conscience*, their disappearance, or their appearance only as auxiliaries, after the mind is mature, would have been no more an objection to his system, than the conversion of a substance from a transitional to a permanent state is a perplexity to the geologist. It would perfectly resemble the destruction of qualities, which is the ordinary effect of chemical composition.

3. The same error has involved him in another difficulty perhaps still more fatal. The sympathies have nothing more of an *imperative* character than any other emotions. They attract or repel like other feelings, according to their intensity. If, then, the sympathies continue in mature minds to constitute the whole of conscience, it becomes utterly impossible to explain the character of command and supremacy, which is attested by the unanimous voice of mankind to belong to that faculty, and to form its essential distinction. Had he adopted the other representation, it would be possible to conceive, perhaps easy to explain, that conscience should possess a quality which belonged to none of its elements.

---

[6] *Essays and Treatises*, vol. ii.

4. It is to this representation that Smith's theory owes that unhappy appearance of rendering the rule of our conduct dependent on the notions and passions of those who surround us, of which the utmost efforts of the most refined ingenuity have not been able to divest it. This objection or topic is often ignorantly urged; the answers are frequently solid; but to most men they must always appear to be an ingenious and intricate contrivance of cycles and epi-cycles, which perplex the mind too much to satisfy it, and seem devised to evade difficulties which cannot be solved. All theories which treat conscience as built up by circumstances inevitably acting on all human minds, are, indeed, liable to somewhat of the same misconception; unless they place in the strongest light (what Smith's theory excludes) the total destruction of the scaffolding which was necessary only to the erection of the building, after the mind is adult and mature, and warn the hastiest reader, that it then rests on its own foundation alone.

5. The constant reference of our own dispositions and actions to the point of view from which they are estimated by others, seems to be rather an excellent expedient for preserving our impartiality, than a fundamental principle of Ethics. But impartiality, which is no more than a removal of some hinderance to right judgment, supplies no materials for its exercise, and no rule, or even principle, for its guidance. It nearly coincides with the Christian precept of doing unto others as we would they should do unto us; an admirable practical maxim, but as Leibnitz has said truly intended only as a correction of self-partiality.

6. Lastly, this ingenious system renders all morality *relative*, – by referring it to the pleasure of an agreement of our feelings with those of others, by confining itself entirely to the question of moral approbation, and by providing no place for the consideration of that quality which distinguishes all good from all bad actions; a defect which will appear in the sequel to be more immediately fatal to a theorist of the *sentimental*, than to one of the *intellectual* school. Smith shrinks from considering utility in that light as soon as it presents itself, or very strangely ascribes its power over our moral feelings to admiration of the mere adaptation of means to ends – which might surely be as well felt for the production of wide-spread misery, by a consistent system of wicked conduct, – instead of ascribing it to benevolence, with Hutcheson and Hume, or to

an extension of that very sympathy which is his own first principle.

[FROM] INTRODUCTION TO ETHICS, INCLUDING A CRITICAL SURVEY OF MORAL SYSTEMS*

Theodore Jouffroy

LECTURE XVI
THE SENTIMENTAL SYSTEM – SMITH

GENTLEMEN,

I have endeavored, in preceding lectures, to give you an idea of the systems which find in the love of self the principle of morality. They form the first class of systems which, in their examination of human nature, either overlook or mutilate the moral principle. To-day I pass to another class.

The radical error of the systems now to be discussed is a far less important one than that of the systems already considered. These latter, by placing the principle of morality in the pursuit of personal good, do nothing less, in fact, than deny the existence, in human nature, of any disinterested motive – than which a grosser error cannot be committed. The systems which now come under our attention are guilty of no such wrong as this: they admit the existence of a motive distinct from self-love; they recognize the fact of disinterestedness, and find in this the principle of morality: their mistake is, that they overlook the real fact, or misapprehend its nature. To-day, then, gentlemen, we are to enter upon the examination of systems which teach that man does often act disinterestedly, but which, in their attempt to ascend to the source of this disinterestedness, miss the way, or see it but dimly, and thus misrepresent the true principle of morality.

Disinterested systems, if I may call them so, have originated in modern times, as they have in all the great philosophical eras with which history makes us acquainted. When the spirit of philosophy first awakes in any country, no inquiry is made as to the principle of morality; for the human mind meets

---

* Translated from the French by William H. Channing (Boston, 1840), vol. 2, pp. 98–176.

with questions of more pressing importance, which it is long occupied in solving. But the time comes, when philosophy finally begins to discuss the moral problem, and seeks to learn the destiny of man, and, from a knowledge of it, to deduce rules for conduct; and, in all cases, the first solution adopted is the doctrine of happiness, or the selfish system. The reason for this is plain. Good sense suggests that, in our attempt to solve the moral problem, we should look for the determining motives of human volitions; and, among these motives, none is so apparent at once to the eye of the observer as the love of pleasure and the dread of pain. In every philosophical movement, therefore, when the human mind has commenced its search for the principle of conduct and the motive of action, has the selfish system first appeared. In most cases, the doctrine has been taught without a perception of its consequences; but, whether its discoverer and promulgator has recognized them or not, sooner or later they practically display themselves; for never in the world can a principle be introduced without a development of its natural fruits: in the course of events, earlier or later, are they all necessarily revealed. Now, the consequences of self-love are odious in their effects on human nature; and they are so, not only because they mutilate it, but because it is the noblest part which they reject. Universal sympathy accompanies disinterested purposes and acts, while antipathy is oftener felt for interested ones. The true consequences of self-love cannot be seen, then, without exciting against them a general indignation and disgust, in time extended to the system in which they originate. Observe, the doctrine contained in the fundamental maxim, that the pursuit of happiness is the end of man, has nothing in itself which shocks our minds; on the contrary, we may say, that, understood in a large and comprehensive manner, it is true; so that the system, regarded merely in its principle and its superficial influence, has nothing to excite alarm, and has often been received by the noblest minds without a scruple or a doubt; as, for instance, in the seventeenth century, it was adopted by Leibnitz on the one side, and by Bossuet on the other, though nothing could seem more opposed than the doctrine of interest to the Christian spirit of the latter, and to the gigantic and severe intellect of the first. As soon, however, as a more thorough analysis has brought to light the strict and necessary consequences of the system, and revealed its real tendencies, conscience becomes alarmed, good sense raises its voice, and a philosophical reaction follows, the first object of which is to prove that there is something disinterested in the human soul, and consequently another motive than the pursuit of selfish good. Then follows a more philosophical and rigorous analysis of the different motives which influence the will – an analysis whose object is to find the sources of disinterestedness in human nature, and in them the spring of all virtue and devotion. To discover this disinterested principle demands a far more attentive study of psychological facts than to see the principle of self-interest. For this plays on the surface, if I may say so, while the operation of the other is profound; and it may therefore with truth be said, that the philosophy of self-love is the philosophy of children. To find this solution of the moral problem demands no reflection, no study of man. But the principle of disinterestedness is apprehended with more difficulty – so deep in our inmost nature does it act; so that, in the reaction to which I have alluded, many errors and half-truths are advanced, before the true principle of morality is conceived with precision. Therefore it is, that, in modern times, we have seen such a multitude of systems, which – all proclaiming the fact of disinterestedness, and pretending to indicate its real source – have given, nevertheless, such different explanations. A like diversity characterized, in ancient times, the disinterested school, although it was then more limited, because human opinions, in those ages, were moulded into simpler forms than in modern days, and because, as analysis extends further to shades of ideas, and multiplied systems are invented to represent them, these systems blend and assimilate more together, and are less marked by distinctive traits.

The systems which profess to base morality upon the foundation of a disinterested principle, are of two kinds. The distinction of the first is, that it finds the origin of disinterested volitions in an intellectual perception of moral good and evil. In other words, the first class of these systems explains the existence of our ideas of moral good and evil by an operation of reason, which judges acts to be good and bad in themselves, and absolutely. According to this doctrine, therefore, the perception of moral good and evil is a rational fact – a phenomenon, not of the sensibility, but of the intellect.

The second class of disinterested systems, on the contrary, explains the distinction between good and evil in the soul, and the disinterested volitions thence resulting, by facts which belong to the sensibility, and not to the reason; so that disinterestedness, according to this doctrine, is not the result of a judgment, but of an instinctive impulse.

Sentimentalism and rationalism are, therefore, the two characteristics, by which systems professing to be disinterested, and, under some form or other, opposing the selfish system, may be distinguished and classified.

My desire is, gentlemen, by an exposition of a few of the systems embraced under these two categories, to give you an idea of all which either one class or the other may include. I cannot attempt to describe each of these various doctrines, for the task would be endless; and it will be quite sufficient, if I show you, by a few examples, how some, by seeking the disinterested element in the sensibility, and others in reason, have disfigured the true principle. These systems are all worthy of our highest regard; the intentions of their authors were generous and noble; and, though they have erred in their search of the disinterested motive of volition, they yet have put faith in disinterestedness, and some have caught glimpses of it, and approached it nearly.

I will begin with an exposition of the sentimental systems; and from them I will select the one which, of all others, is the most ingenious and original – I mean that of Adam Smith, as it is exhibited in his work entitled 'The Theory of Moral Sentiments.' In the present lecture, it will be my purpose to give you some idea of the principles of this most remarkable system.

Smith is the most original writer that Scotland has produced for a hundred and fifty years. With his great work on political economy you must already be somewhat acquainted. Of that science he was truly the father – establishing it, as he did, upon a foundation of such facts as would have escaped the attention of any mind less penetrating than his own. With him, philosophy was, comparatively, a secondary interest; and the principal results of his inquiries upon such subjects may be found in his work on the moral sentiments. The views which this work contains, however, are characterized by all the originality and richness of his mind; and, deceived as he undoubtedly was as to the principle of morality, it may yet with truth be said, that the facts of human nature, by him brought to light and analyzed, make this book one of the most precious and useful that can be consulted in studying the science of human nature. I will limit myself to a description of the chief facts upon which his system is based; they are perfectly true in themselves, and his error was only in deducing from them consequences which they do not justify.

Whenever we see a man deeply affected with any sentiment or passion, our nature, without the intervention of either reason or will, tends to reproduce the sentiment or passion; in other words, our nature is disposed to place itself in the situation of the person who is the object of our regard. This phenomenon, though obscure in certain cases, is perfectly clear and apparent in others. When we gaze upon a mother, whose whole look and air manifest warm love for the child upon her knee, we cannot but feel a similar disposition springing up in our own hearts; and, in a thousand instances which it is not worth our while particularly to notice, the same thing might be observed, as every one will testify. Yet more; this natural inclination to feel in ourselves the emotions which we witness in another human being goes so far, that we even experience it in regard to beings of other species, when they are to any considerable degree animated, and bear affinity to ourselves. We cannot see, for instance, a dog manifesting deep inward pain, without feeling a similar emotion; and the joyfulness and vivacity of a bird, as it skips singing from bough to bough, awakens in our minds also joyful emotions. And this instinct acts even when the object that excites it is repugnant to our taste. The sight of a serpent creeping with undulating movement on the ground inspires us with some disposition to imitate him. And, in general, whenever a sensible phenomenon, of which we ourselves are capable, is observed in any being whose nature is at all similar to our own, there springs up a desire to feel and do the same. This property of human nature is sympathy, or, at least, the root and germ of that to which we give this name.

That our agreeable or disagreeable sentiments acquire new force and acuteness when shared by a fellow-being, is a fact demonstrated by innumerable circumstances. When we are in a theatre, where but few are assembled to behold the representation, we experience infinitely less pleasure than when the room is crowded, and we are conscious that all around us are minds affected like our own; this is notorious. The mere thought that our souls are in unison with other souls – that the sentiments which they experience are similar to ours in nature and degree – this mere thought is in itself a source of pleasure; in this mere sense of harmony we deeply rejoice.

To these two facts a third may be added. So strong and instinctive is our desire for this agreement of feeling between ourselves and those around us, that, whenever we experience an emotion, and express it where any person is present who is not similarly affected, involuntarily and unconsciously we lower our tone and soften down the utterance of our feeling, that we may thus be brought more nearly into harmony with his calmness; while, on the other hand, the unexcited person is quickened by the sight of our emotion, till, by an instinctive complaisance, his sympathetic feeling rises as high as our original feeling. This fact is one of such constant occurrence, that all must have observed it. When you are strongly moved by any passion, I ask, do you manifest it in its full force in the presence of indifferent spectators? Certainly not. You temper its expression, from a regard for their feelings. And they, on their part, being conscious that you are under the influence of a certain impulse, and that you are partially concealing it from a desire of being in harmony with them, not only share your feeling through sympathy, but, by an effort, seek to be animated with equal strength of passion, that the state of their sensibility may correspond with yours. These three facts, which have now been noticed, are purely instinctive; neither reason nor will concur to produce them.

There are various laws governing this principle of sympathy, which the acute mind of Smith succeeded in discovering and establishing. I wish to give you an idea of them, before proceeding to describe the moral consequences which were deduced from them by this philosopher. But, first, let me present a single observation upon one point where I differ from Smith. Smith thinks that this natural propensity is not one which, in every case, takes the form of sympathy, but that often, far from feeling a desire to imitate, we are conscious, instead, of an antipathy. For instance, when we see a man impelled by some malevolent passion, our nature, Smith thinks, experiences a repugnance, rather than any wish to be inspired with a similar feeling. This fact I am, of course, not disposed to deny; but I explain it quite differently. I believe that the first impulse of every human being, without exception, where signs of any emotion in a fellow-being are manifested, is to be similarly affected; but this impulse, it appears to me, is, in many instances, restrained and modified, either by reflection or by a sympathy yet more powerful for emotions experienced by other beings. This, however, is a point which is of importance only as a matter of science. It is perfectly true that there are cases in which sympathy is simple, while in others it is divided among two, three, or more objects, according as more or fewer persons are affected by the passion manifested. And it is to the laws which govern sympathy in such cases that I now wish to direct your attention.

Let us suppose that we see a man who is excited with the passion of anger, and not without adequate cause; instantly two facts of sympathy appear. On the one side, I sympathize with the anger which is manifested; on the other, I sympathize with him who is the object of this rage, because I see that he is threatened with a danger. Whether the individual is conscious or ignorant of his danger, imagination still represents him to me as exposed to it, and I feel as a human being should who is the object of another's hate. Sympathy places me at once, then, in the situation of the angry man, and of the person against whom his indignation is directed; my sympathies, therefore, become divided; part attach themselves to him who is in a passion, part to him who is the object of aversion. From this it follows, that if I myself am excited with anger, and experience the desire felt by all men, in different degrees, of being in harmony with their fellow-creatures, I must moderate the expression of my passion; for in proportion as I control myself will their sympathy with the object of my anger lessen, and their sympathy with me increase. This guarded exhibition of passion, in the presence of fellow-men, is instructive in all, especially if the persons around are strangers. A man alone in his chamber gives way to the full violence of his rage; in the presence of his wife and children, he restrains, in some degree, the utterance of his passion; but in the presence of one whom he holds in high esteem, and whose respect he desires to gain, his excitement at once and instinctively disappears. This fact is an additional proof of that need of sympathy, which, as we have seen, all human beings feel. Sympathy demands that the expression of any passion should be moderated, and instinctively it is done; sympathy requires that the least manifestation of them should be repressed, and they are repressed at once. Suppose – although the supposition is incredible – that I am animated by a purely malevolent affection; or, in other words, that unjustly, and without cause, I am filled with a desire to do some one an injury; in such a case, according to Smith, this malevolent feeling would excite no sympathy; according to my idea, it would, although the sympathy would be controlled by that felt for the object of my malevolence: in either view, the result is the same. In a case where such malevolence is exhibited, sympathy tends to attach itself exclusively to the being who is threatened. The man, then, who feels it, is naturally inclined, not only to express it with moderation, but not to manifest it at all; it is the bad, therefore, who are hypocrites; and hypocrisy is instinctive in them, and not the result of reflection only; reason, indeed, may give new force to the instinct, and the love of esteem may lead to dissimulation; but the feeling precedes the act of reasoning, and this instinctive impulse, according to Smith, is only one form in which is manifested the desire of being in harmony of feeling with our kind.

Thus have I shown you some instances in which sympathy is composed of several and of opposite elements; there are others, where it is simple, and, consequently, of a uniform character. Sympathy of this sort may be seen in cases where our emotions have no reference to the well-being of others; for example, in the love of truth: however strong this feeling may be, it cannot affect the happiness of our fellow-beings; the disposition, therefore, can excite in other men only emotions of pure sympathy; and there is no motive of instinct or reason why we should conceal them at all, or prevent the expression of our whole feeling. However much I may love beauty or truth, I see not why I should moderate the utterance of my pleasure in the presence of others; for I have no ground for supposing that they are animated by any opposing sentiment.

Finally, there are inward emotions which may excite sympathies of various, though not opposing kinds. Thus, when I see a man full of emotions of pity, charity, love, friendship, a twofold sympathy arises; I sympathize with the benevolence of the one party, and the gratitude of the other – with the object of the benevolent feeling, and the object of the grateful feeling. Now, as you will see, these two kinds of sympathy, so far from being opposed, tend to strengthen each other: it follows, therefore, that the benevolent affections are, of all others, those which inspire most sympathy, and which, consequently, contribute most to produce among men that harmony of feeling which all instinctively desire; and finally, it follows, that there can be no necessity for dissimulation, by restraining ourselves in giving them expression.

From this short exposition, you may see, that the analysis of the phenomenon of sympathy has furnished Smith with an explanation of a vast variety of the facts of human nature – an explanation which is as ingenious as its fundamental idea is simple. How he employs it to account for moral facts, properly so called, I will now proceed to show.

What, asks Smith, is the approbation or disapprobation of another's sentiments? In what cases do we approve – in what disapprove them? On reflection, we shall see, that we approve when we share them, and disapprove them when we do not; that we approve them entirely when we share them entirely, and partially when we share them partially; in a word, that approbation and disapprobation are not only in our reason an effect of the purely sensible phenomena of sympathy and antipathy, but in every case are an exact representation of these feelings. If this is true, the origin of approbation or disapprobation, in reference to others, is perfectly explained; they spring from sensibility – from the instinctive phenomenon of sympathy. Our judgments upon the sentiments and acts of our fellow-beings are really only the expression of the degree of our sympathy or antipathy for these sentiments and acts. But we thus account for only a part of our moral judgments; it remains to be seen, how those arise which are directed to our own sentiments and acts.

Smith asserts, that if a man should live alone, he would never judge of his actions as being good or bad; for the only means by which he could determine the quality of actions would be wanting. This singular opinion of his is founded on the idea that sympathy is the principle from which is deduced the rule by which we estimate the moral qualities of all acts, whether of ourselves or others, and distinguish the good from the bad. Now, as it is absolutely necessary that two human beings at least should exist, before the sentiment of sympathy can be developed, it is impossible that the solitary man should conceive this rule, and thus judge of the morality of actions. But how does sympathy enable him to conceive this rule? Let us see.

Smith states, as a fact, that we have the power, whenever we are animated by any disposition, or perform any act, or follow any course of conduct, of looking upon this sentiment, act, or conduct, as an indifferent spectator, and of experiencing, in some degree, such a sentiment of sympathy as we should at seeing such sentiments, acts, and conduct in another person. Now, is this fact upon which Smith rests his explanation exactly true? Have we really the power of making ourselves spectators of our own dispositions and acts, and of feeling at the sight such sentiments as the dispositions and acts of other beings excite? For my part, gentlemen, I am ready to say that we do, undoubtedly, possess this power; and, with a few exceptions, I am ready to recognize the effects which he ascribes to it.

Smith declares that when we are carried away by a violent passion, this passion still continues to act, though in so feeble a manner that its influence is scarcely to be traced; and, further, that when the passion is abated and calmed, it reappears in full energy with all its consequences; and this is true; for then do we represent vividly to ourselves the appearance which we have exhibited, and feel, in all their distinctness, the sentiments of sympathy or antipathy which our acts are fitted to awake. It is of little consequence, in Smith's opinion, whether these feelings of sympathy or antipathy are more or less acute, or whether they are manifested earlier or later: the important fact is, that we do really experience them: he asks us only to grant that we have the capacity of being thus impressed, and his system, he thinks, is justified.

If, says he, we have an urgent natural desire to be, in our dispositions and sentiments, in harmony with our fellow-beings, it is only necessary for us to feel that a particular disposition would excite their antipathy, to make us consider it bad; and if, on the contrary, we are conscious of a disposition which would excite their sympathy, we shall think it good; and, finally, should we be aware that our state of feeling is one which would excite their mingled sympathy and antipathy, we should judge it to be neither perfectly good nor perfectly bad. Hence a principle by which we judge of our own sentiments and acts, by sympathy, as we should those of our fellow-beings; so that, just as we should estimate the acts of others, by the sympathy or antipathy which they excite in us, do we estimate our own, by the sympathy or antipathy which they are fitted to excite in others, – a sympathy and antipathy, for which, in both cases, we are indebted to our power of placing ourselves in the situation of other persons, and thus entering into their feelings.

From these two principles, for the moral estimation of the sentiments and acts of ourselves and others, results a more general principle, by which to judge of all dispositions and modes of conduct: it is by means of these that we ascend to the general maxim, which, according to Smith, is the fundamental principle of morality – that the goodness of an act is in direct ratio to the approbation which it receives from others, and that the best acts are those which are fitted to excite pure and universal sympathy, – a sympathy unmingled with antipathy, – the sympathy not of a few, but of every individual of the human race. Hence, gentlemen, a scale of the moral good and evil of acts, graduated by this universal standard, and a code of rules for conduct.

In proportion as experience teaches us to recognize the acts which are fitted to awaken pure sympathy or antipathy, or mingled sympathy and antipathy, do we learn to estimate their value, and impress on the memory their moral quality. Hence the maxims and rules which we find in the minds of the mature. When once discovered by experience and stored in memory, we become able to form judgments immediately, by means of these ascertained and established rules; and thus the labor of making estimates of our own and others' acts is abridged, and self-command strengthened, in cases where passion is so violent as to deprive us of our power of judging by sympathy. At such times, I may rely for direction on the rule which pronounces the emotion good or bad, and yield to or restrain it, without fear of feeling remorse when my calmness is restored. The same is true of those instances in which the perplexities and cares of life prevent me from freely entering into the inmost feelings of others, and subjecting their dispositions to the test of my sympathy or antipathy: the test by which I must then judge is the rule that pronounces what sentiments and acts are proper in any given situation. Hence we may appreciate the utility of the rules which result from experience, and are the fruits of repeated applications of the principle of sympathy or antipathy.

Such is the manner in which Smith explains, by sympathy, the fundamental phenomenon of moral distinctions. And of course he finds no difficulty in accounting for secondary moral phenomena. But, as time will not permit me to follow him into all these details, I will select, as a specimen, the origin, which, with entire fidelity to his main principle, he assigns to the sentiment of merit or demerit.

You are already well informed as to the nature of this phenomenon; you are aware, that, when we contemplate a good or bad action, a judgment of reason accompanies our sensation of pleasure or pain, and that, in the one case, we consider the agent worthy of reward, in the other, of punishment, and are thus inclined to wish them happiness or suffering. This phenomenon admits of a very simple explanation in the system of Smith. When I witness an act of benevolence, I experience not only a feeling of sympathy for the state of mind of the benevolent person, but also for that of the object of his kindness. What is this? It is gratitude. And what is gratitude, except a desire of benefiting him who has done us a favor, and because he has done it? Participating as a spectator in this feeling, I wish well to the author of the act; I feel, in other words, that he merits happiness as a reward for his conduct. What happens, on the contrary, when I see a man animated with malevolence? I feel no sympathy for him; but all my feelings are directed towards him who is the object of hated, into whose situation and state of mind I fully enter. Now, what are your emotions when you perceive yourself to be regarded with aversion? Instinctively, you desire to return ill for ill; a spectator, then, who sympathizes with your feelings, must judge your enemy to be worthy of punishment; that is to say, deserving of the pain, which, in his malevolence, he seeks to inflict on you. Such, in Smith's view, is the natural explanation of the judgment of merit and demerit.

With apparently equal facility, he explains the pleasure that we experience when we have done well, and the remorse which accompanies wrong doing. By my power of becoming a spectator of my own dispositions and acts, I feel for myself, when I have acted right, a sentiment of sympathy; and this emotion makes me conclude that others, who behold the act, feel for me a similar sentiment. I am conscious, therefore, of a profound accordance between my conduct and their feelings, and between their emotions and my own; and we have before seen how delightful in this sense of harmony. In this, then, consists the pleasure of doing well. Yet more; having established the rule by which to determine the moral quality of acts, I feel authorized to pronounce my conduct right, because I have learned that all conduct is right which secures the sympathy of others. In this consists the approbation which I feel for myself, and which blends with the sensation of pleasure. For the opposite reason, I feel, when I have done wrong, the peculiar pain which is called *remorse*, and disapprove and blame myself.

Thus have I exhibited the general elements of Smith's system; and you can readily imagine how it may be carried out and completed. In his work, however, the applications of it are innumerable, and their ingenuity and delicacy are infinite.

As soon as a man's nature is developed, and the principle of moral estimation and the rules of experience are established in his mind, he possesses all necessary elements for the approbation of my benevolent act which he may behold. He experiences a twofold sympathy; first, for the motives of the agent; secondly, for the happiness and gratitude of the object. Again, he perceives the conformity of the act done with the rule of morality communicated by experience; so that, independently of the instinctive judgment, there is also a judgment of reason upon its goodness. A mature man, then, feels, in the contemplation of a good action, not only a sentiment of sympathy, and a kind emotion for the agent, but to these is added a rational judgment of approbation. In children, and often in men of vulgar minds, this third element, indeed, is wanting; for, before it can exist, reason must have created, or experience introduced, the general rules of morality whose formation we have explained; and approbation, as a judgment of reason, is only the recognition of an act as conformable to these rules; it necessarily, therefore, presupposes them. But this is not all; the action appears to us fitted, by its nature, to promote such a general system of conduct as will tend to bring the sentiments of all men into harmony. Now, this universal harmony is felt to be eminently beautiful, or, rather, as we might say, to be moral beauty itself; and we pronounce the act, therefore, not only good, but beautiful. It is here that Smith finds the principle of moral beauty, which he esteems the source of all beauty.

As this latter point may seem less clear than those already mentioned, let us dwell a little longer upon its consideration.

If all men should conduct themselves in such a way as to secure for their acts the sympathy of their fellow-beings, it is plain that there would ensue an entire accordance of feeling, and consequently a state of perfect harmony. It is this harmony that is beautiful; and Smith compares the pleasure, which the prospect of it affords, to that which we experience when gazing upon a complicated piece of mechanism, whose various movements resolve themselves into one. This gratification of taste is felt, to some degree, in the contemplation of every action that is morally good.

Smith has not overlooked nor concealed the fact, that, in many instances, a good act, far from securing the kind affections of men, subjects us, on the contrary, to their hate; and he explains this anomaly, by saying that men are often animated by passions and prejudices which are themselves discordant with the universal laws of morality. He acknowledges, therefore, that there are circumstances, in which a good man is called upon to brave the antipathy of his immediate associates, that he may win the sympathy of mankind at large. And it is here that the application of the principle of sympathy becomes peculiarly delicate and difficult, and its insufficiency displayed. But it must be fully granted, that Smith has not hesitated to bring his system to this test; he has admitted, that the virtuous man must often, in doing what he ought, – and precisely because he does what he ought, – place himself in opposition to the spirit of his country and of his age, and thus bring upon himself the antipathy of his contemporaries. Smith might have passed by in silence this case, which it is so embarrassing, by his principles, to explain; and, therefore, although his attempted explanation does but little credit to the logical powers of the philosopher, yet the candor, with which he has stated the difficulty, secures our respect for the probity of the man.

Such, then, gentlemen, are the fundamental ideas of Smith. In my next lecture, I will present some critical remarks upon this ethical system.

LECTURE XVII
THE SAME SUBJECT CONTINUED

Gentlemen,

Ethical systems are characterized and distinguished by the nature of their answers to certain questions, which every ethical system must attempt to solve. The destiny of man on earth – that is to say, the end to which his efforts should be directed

– the test by which good is distinguished from evil in conduct – or, in other words, the rule by which the moral quality of acts may be determined – and, lastly, the motive which impels us to act conformably to this rule, and insures its supreme control over our wills – such are the fundamental points, which it is the object of every ethical system to determine, and which different systems determine differently. A system, which should give no answer to either of these questions, would not be an ethical system. In answering any one, however, it answers all; for, so closely connected are the end of life, the rule of moral estimation, and the legitimate motive for action, that, when one is determined, the answer to the other two naturally follows; and, consequently, if we know the opinion of a philosopher upon either of these points, we are acquainted with his entire ethical system.

These considerations indicate the proper method of discovering the true character of an ethical system. If we desire to ascertain definitely the character of a system, and to obtain an expression of it, precisely as it is, the true way is to seek a reply to these three questions, or to some one of the three; when its answer is given, we shall know all that can be known about it, and can classify it.

Answers to these several questions are not given with equal readiness by all systems; the replies of some are immediate and direct; but those of others are so subtle and equivocal, so inconsistent with themselves, and contradictory to the common sense of men, that we cannot, without difficulty, disengage the thought which they express, and strip the disguise from their real meaning.

Selfish systems give the clearest answer to the three questions which we have suggested. And hence arises the simplicity of their solution of the moral problem, derived as it is from an order of phenomena of which every individual has a distinct and vivid consciousness. A system, which teaches that pleasure is the end of life, is comprehended at once; and, if the pursuit of pleasure is the end, it is evident that the motive must be the desire of happiness, and, consequently, that the test of goodness in conduct is the tendency of acts to promote our welfare. Nothing, then, can be simpler or clearer than the selfish systems; and the only difficulty in regard to them is to detect the shades of difference which distinguish them.

This is far from being the case with systems which seek in

instinct for an explanation of the moral facts of human nature; these are as obscure as the instinct itself. Obliged, in establishing their foundation, to describe, in their primitive aspect and subsequent transformations, numerous facts, – which, as they belong to the spontaneous part of our nature, are most subtle and transient, – these systems do not present that appearance of simplicity, by which the selfish systems are characterized; and it is necessary, therefore, if we would understand exactly their answers to the fundamental questions of morality, to analyze them with care, and follow the various windings by which they attempt to evade them. And, true as this is of the instinctive systems in general, it is peculiarly so of the system of Smith, whose mind was so ingenious and fruitful, that it sacrificed willingly, to the pleasure of describing facts and of displaying their various relations and consequences, the rapid and methodical order that never loses sight of the thread of its inductions, but proceeds, with clearness of reasoning, from the phenomena by which it professes to explain moral questions, to the precise conclusions fairly involved.

I have studied Smith's system with all the attention which it demands, that I might be able to give a thorough and exact idea of it; and I feel prepared to describe its precise answers to the three great questions which every ethical system is bound to solve. It is necessary, if we would judge of the truth of this complicated system, that we should see its exact nature; and we can do this only by bringing it to the test of these three questions, and determining precisely its answer to each. This, then, I shall attempt to do; I shall successively present to the doctrine of sympathy these questions, state its answers, examine each of these answers in itself and in comparison with human nature, and thus endeavor to determine the adequateness and truth of the system. It may seem as if such an examination must be unnecessarily long; but, besides the consideration that it is absolutely required by the obscurity of the system, it may be said that we shall really gain time in pursuing this course; for, if we can but discover the error of Smith's system, we shall have equally detected the mistakes of all other systems which seek, in the spontaneous impulses of human nature, a solution of the moral problem. And be assured, that the instinctive system will lose nothing in being judged by the system of sympathy; its defence was never in better hands.

Smith was a profound observer, an ingenious dialectician, and a fine writer; no other philosopher has ever surrounded the system with such an air of plausibility, nor brought to its support so many facts, nor strengthened it by so many analogies, nor applied it in such a variety of specious ways. And, in addition, this system has the merit of being founded upon the very instinct which seems most entitled to respect. I do not hesitate to say, that, if Smith cannot maintain the system of instinct, its defence must be hopeless.

To resume, then; the method by which I shall be governed in this examination of Smith's system, is as follows: – I shall inquire, first, what rule or principle it recognizes for moral estimation; secondly, what motive it supposes us to be impelled by, when we act conformably to this rule; thirdly, and lastly, what end it assigns to human conduct in the present life. I shall then take up its various answers on these different points, determine whether they are consistent and admissible in themselves, and then compare them with the real facts. Let us now proceed to the first point proposed.

Our moral judgments extend to two classes of actions – those performed by other beings, those performed by ourselves. We determine the character of these acts, and pronounce them good or bad, by means of some principle. What, in Smith's opinion, is this principle?

Our judgments upon acts, according to this philosopher, are only the consequence of those passed upon the affections and sensible emotions which produce them. Sensible affections are, in his opinion, the peculiar and direct objects of moral estimation, which is limited to these affections when they issue in no acts, and extends to acts when the affections are followed out. Now, before we can estimate the moral worth of an affection, we must contemplate it under two points of view; first, with reference to its exciting cause; next, to the effects which it is fitted to produce. Considered in relation to its cause, it may be proper or improper; considered in relation to its tendency, it may have merit or demerit. Propriety, then, and impropriety, merit and demerit, are the moral properties by which affections, and consequently acts, may be estimated. By what principle or rule do we judge whether an affection is proper or improper on the one side, and has merit or demerit on the other? Such is the question to be determined. If we can discover this principle, from which, according to Smith, this twofold judgment is derived, we shall have discovered the principle given by his system for the moral estimation of actions; because, to determine the moral quality of affections, or of acts, is, in his opinion, the same thing. Let us inquire, then, what this principle is, by which we judge our own acts and the acts of others.

Our manner of judging of the propriety or impropriety of the emotions of others is as follows: – To a certain degree, the impartial spectator experiences, through sympathy, the emotion he beholds; and, as he can approve only so far as he shares an emotion, the degree of his sympathy determines how far he will consider and pronounce it proper; in proportion as it is manifested by the person who feels it, in a stronger or weaker degree than this sympathy, will it be considered too weak or too strong, and consequently, disapproved as improper. For instance, a man receives a blow, and gives signs of pain: I, as witness of his sufferings, am aroused to sympathy, and partake his feeling; but, in me, this sympathetic emotion rises only to a certain height; if the original subject of the emotion manifests it in a stronger degree than this, it seems to me improper; but if in a similar degree, then it seems to me proper. This common example will serve to indicate the principle of all our judgments of propriety and impropriety, both of the dispositions and acts of others.

Affections will differ from each other in regard to their propriety or impropriety; in the benevolent affections, for example, the spectator may participate in the highest possible degree, while there are others in which he cannot share at all, such as envy, and other malevolent feelings. These latter, therefore, are radically improper, as well as all acts which emanate from them; the expression of them must be entirely suppressed, and on no account must they be allowed to influence our conduct. Between these two extremes may be ranked the various emotions of which our sensibility is susceptible.

Such is the rule by which we judge of the propriety or impropriety of the affections of other beings; and, as you see, it is nothing else than the sympathetic emotion of an impartial spectator. The degree of the sympathy determines the degree of the propriety or impropriety of all affections, and, consequently, of all acts, in which they issue. Let us pass now to the consideration of merit and demerit.

The tendency of emotions may be beneficial or injurious. In

the first case, they excite in their object gratitude; in the second, resentment. I, as an impartial spectator, am impelled to share in the feelings which I see exhibited. I am animated, therefore, at once, by the benevolent or malevolent disposition of the agent, and by the gratitude or resentment of the object. Well: according to Smith, when the impartial spectator sympathizes entirely and unreservedly with the feelings of the object of these dispositions, he participates in them, and approves them, and therefore adopts them altogether. His judgment is, then, that the affection of the agent is deserving of recompense in the one case, and of punishment of the other; for what is gratitude except the desire of rendering good for good? or resentment, except the desire of rendering evil for evil? Such, then, is the origin and true nature of the judgment of merit and demerit.

But in what cases does the impartial spectator sympathize entirely with the gratitude or resentment of the object? He sympathizes entirely with the gratitude of the object, when he also sympathizes entirely with the affection of the agent – that is to say, when he judges it to be proper; and he sympathizes entirely with the resentment of the object, when he cannot sympathize at all with the affection of the agent – that is to say, when he judges it to be improper. On this twofold condition does the impartial spectator sympathize entirely with the gratitude or resentment of the one party, and, in consequence, judge that the dispositions of the other have merit or demerit.

Hence, gentlemen, you see that it is the sympathy of the spectator which determines the merit or demerit of emotions and acts, just as it determines their propriety or impropriety. When is an affection, and the action emanating from it, and the agent experiencing it, judged by me to be deserving of punishment or reward? It is when I partake entirely of the gratitude or resentment which the affection inspires in the person who is its object. And when is sympathy thus perfect? It is when I participate fully in the benevolent emotions of the agent, and feel nothing of his malevolence. It is sympathy, then, that instinctively determines for me, the impartial spectator, the merit and demerit, as it does the propriety and impropriety of sentiments, actions, and agents. Here, then, according to this system, is the principle of all our judgments of other beings.

And now let us inquire what is the principle by which we judge of ourselves.

With regard to our own emotions, and, consequently, our actions, and ourselves, we are capable of judging, as we judge in the case of others; that is to say, we form estimates of them, under the twofold aspect of propriety and impropriety, of merit and demerit. What is the nature of this phenomenon, and what is the principle of these judgments? Let us observe the explanation which the system gives.

Smith maintains that I can judge of my own affections and actions only by placing myself in the situation of an impartial spectator, and by regarding them from his point of view. Without this mental process, which would be impossible, of course, for a solitary man, we should never pass moral judgments upon ourselves. When I am animated, therefore, with any emotion, and wish to determine its propriety or impropriety, its merit or demerit, this is what I do – I place myself in the situation of an impartial spectator, and, with the power which I have of entering into the feeling of others, I feel, at sight of this sentiment, precisely as an impartial spectator would himself. I am able, therefore, to judge of its moral quality exactly as others would judge, and as I should myself judge, if the sentiment were displayed by another, only with greater precision, because my knowledge is more accurate, both of the sentiment itself, of its relation to its cause, and of its actual tendency.

Smith does not deny, that when emotions are strong, it is difficult, at the moment, to contemplate them impartially, and thus sympathize with them. But this only shows, that, in such cases, we judge amiss, and it still remains true, that this operation of mind is necessary for a correct judgment; and a strong proof of this is, that we never form as just an estimate of our affections, as in moments when we are not under their influence; or, in other words, when there is no obstacle to my thus placing myself in the situation of a spectator.

Thus, gentlemen, it appears, that the system is consistent with itself; and that the principle, by which we determine the moral quality of our own acts, is the same as that by which we judge of the acts of our fellow-beings. In both cases, it is the sympathetic emotion of the impartial spectator that decides. The only difference between the two cases is, that, in the first, the sympathy is felt immediately, while in the second, it is awakened only by an indirect operation of mind.

One other point remains to be mentioned, to complete a fair and full analysis of Smith's system. Smith asserts that an experience of the judgments passed upon others, and expressed by them, gradually teach us to know what affections are proper or improper, and have merit or demerit. Hence arise general rules, which impress themselves on our memories, and become those laws of morality which are so often considered primitive in our nature, but which really are only generalizations from particular judgments of the instinct of sympathy. Now, when these rules, resulting from experience, are once established in our minds, it often happens that we pass judgments without regard to sympathy; and thus our mode of moral estimation, originally instinctive, becomes reasonable. Such is the fact, and you can comprehend it perfectly. What, in such cases, is the principle of moral qualification? Is it altered? By no means; for these rules are only the expression of emotions experienced by the impartial spectator, and have no other authority than his sympathy. It is the emotion of the impartial spectator, which, in this case, as in all others, judges and decides.

In every possible application, then, the system is consistent, and its answer is always the same, whether we judge of our own affections or of the affections of other beings, – whether we judge instinctively or by rules, – whether we consider acts in the light of their propriety or impropriety, their merit or demerit; the mode of moral appreciation remains the same, the system reiterates its principle, and asserts that its rule of the sympathy of the impartial spectator is a sufficient test for moral judgments. Such is the exact answer of Smith's system to the first question proposed.

And now, gentlemen, this rule of moral qualification being fully determined and brought to light, we are prepared to judge of its correctness, and appreciate the truth of the system which is based in part upon it. This must be our next step.

The first difficulty presented by this rule is, that it cannot be easily comprehended. I perfectly understand that the supposed spectator may feel sympathy; but I cannot explain the impartiality, which Smith requires. What kind of impartiality is it that he speaks of? Evidently, it is not an impartiality of the judgment; for reason must not be allowed to enter into moral estimates, or they will no longer emanate when simple sympathy, and the system is destroyed. When I see a man moved by some affection, I feel for him, according to Smith, an instinctive sympathy, by which, and by which alone, I judge of his conduct; intellect has nothing to do with the forming of this decision. By the impartiality of the spectator, then, cannot be meant the impartiality of reason, for this has nothing to do with the moral estimation of the act. We are compelled, therefore, to understand the expression as applying solely to sympathy. And here the difficulty presents itself – How shall we comprehend this expression? What interpretation shall we put upon the word? What means the impartiality of an instinct? We speak of a man as impartial; but when is he so? Only then he exercises judgment. Suppose the faculty of judgment suppressed, and the word means nothing. Impartiality is possible only where there is judgment; and when we say that judgment is impartial, our idea is precisely this – that it is influenced by no passion. Why can I not be impartial in regard to a friend? Because sympathy biases my judgment in his favor. And I cannot be impartial in regard to an enemy, for an opposite reason. It becomes all the more difficult to comprehend what is meant by the impartiality of sympathy, because, in the common acceptation of words, it is the absence of sympathy that constitutes impartiality. And let no one suppose that this objection consists in a mere play upon words; this error in expression actually betrays the error of the principle. Undoubtedly we may make instinct our rule of moral judgment; but we cannot, without abjuring good sense, adopt, as the law for conduct, the impulses of any thing so essentially capricious; we must make choice, then, among these impulses, and admit the influence of some, while we reject that of others; in other words, we are compelled to regulate this rule. And it is in this attempt that we are led to conceive this idea of the impartiality of instinct, or some other similar idea, such as cannot be correctly expressed, for the reason that it seeks to represent what has really no existence. It is because this system does violence to the nature of things, that it cannot be described without doing violence to language.

But let us overlook this objection, and pass to an examination of Smith's rule for moral estimates. And I assert that this rule is one which is peculiarly fluctuating and unsettled, and, consequently, that it can be determined only with great difficulty.

Let me suppose myself in the presence of a great number of persons of different ages, sexes, and professions; and, to fulfil as far as possible the condition of impartiality required, let me suppose, in addition, that I am a perfect stranger to them, and that there is no connection whatever between us, of friendship, of interest, or of any other kind; and now let me manifest, in the presence of these spectators, some emotion; what will be the consequence? These various sensibilities will sympathize with me in very different degrees. Lively sensibilities will partake vividly of my emotions – cold ones but feebly; minds preoccupied will feel nothing, while others, which are attentive, may be profoundly touched; between the emotions of the men and women, of the young and old, of the man of the world and the peasant, of the merchant and the soldier, of one who has a sad and another a joyous temperament, there will inevitably be infinite shades of difference; in a word, circumstances whose number cannot be counted, nor whose influence estimated, will modify the sympathy which my emotion excites. Which of these kinds of sympathy shall be my rule, which shall I select as a test of the propriety or impropriety of my feeling? Shall I adopt the sympathy of this or that particular person? or shall I take the mean of all the sympathies? But why should I adopt this mean? or how shall I determine what it is, among so many which are unknown and not to be appreciated? And how, then, can I determine, according to the doctrine of Smith, whether my emotion is proper or improper?

But now let me change my position; let me in turn become spectator of another's emotions. This morning, I should have entered into his feelings more than I do now; this evening I shall share them less; if I am hungry, I shall be indifferent; if I have dined, I shall be complaisant; my mind is full, perhaps, of philosophy, or of business, and I pay no heed; I am in an imaginative mood, and I am affected even to tears. Which, now, of these feelings of sympathy, shall I select for my test of moral appreciation? Even should I be able to fix upon my rule, yet age, sickness, a thousand circumstances, may enter in to make me change my rule, and plunge me in uncertainty. And if I, a single spectator, and distinctly conscious of my own emotions, find it difficult, in my judgments of others, to decide upon the rule of impartial sympathy in my mind, how shall I, when called to judge myself, select such a rule from the infinitely diverse, impartial sympathies, not only of society around me, but, as Smith demands, of the human race at large? How can you expect that I should identify myself with the men of all places and times, and draw from feelings so various and mutable, and which often I cannot know, that rule of the *mean* of sympathies needed for the moral appreciation of my own sentiments and acts? Assuredly, to subject us to such conditions in acquiring a rule by which to judge and act, is to make morality impossible.

But yet more is to be said, gentlemen: not only is the rule a mutable one, and, therefore, hard to be determined, but, even supposing it known and fixed, it is still, as even Smith himself acknowledges, inadequate; for, as I have already said in my exposition of the system, cases will and must arise, in which an upright man will feel that in acting in a certain way he does right, and yet that, far from obtaining the sympathy of his fellow-beings, his conduct will excite their antipathy. If he is acting in some public capacity, he may, indeed, hope to receive from the justice of history the sympathy of after ages; but, as to his contemporaries, he is sure of losing the sympathy, not only of a few persons, but of his whole nation. Smith has the candor to acknowledge that such cases may arise, and the fairness to confess that a man is then bound to follow the right and despise public opinion. But how can he do this without denying his system, and abjuring his rule of moral appreciation? Much as we may admire the ingenuity with which he has attempted to escape from this dilemma, it is impossible not to see that his efforts are fruitless, and that his theory is wrecked upon this difficulty. You shall judge.

I have already told you, that when we are deliberating as to the conduct which it is right, under certain circumstances, to pursue, we have, in the opinion of Smith, but one means of deciding; and that is, to place ourselves in the situation of an impartial spectator, and allow our minds to be affected with his emotions; for his sentiment is not merely the true test, but it is the only one by which we can estimate our acts. Now, who is this impartial spectator? Is it John or Peter? No! but an abstract spectator, who has neither the prejudices of the one nor the weaknesses of the other, and who sees correctly and soundly, precisely because he is abstract. It is in the presence of this abstract spectator, who is another *me*, separate from the impassioned *me*, and its judge, that, in my deepest consciousness, I deliberate, decide, and act. Not only is this spectator no particular man, but he does not even represent any portion of society – no age nor sex, no village nor city, no nation nor era; he represents humanity – he represents God. The sentiments of this secret witness, whose impartiality is so perfect, give us the true principle of moral estimation, and the true rule for conduct.

Assuredly, gentlemen, this would be giving a most ingenious turn to his principle, were it nothing more; but it is, in fact, doing something very different; it is introducing an entirely new view, into which Smith has unconsciously entered, without perceiving that he was not led into it by setting out from his own principle, and that he cannot return from it to his principle again.

How, according to Smith's system, do I become acquainted with the moral worth of actions? By a knowledge of the sentiments of others; their approbation is my rule; and, as this depends upon their sympathy, their sympathy is my rule; to form a judgment, therefore, I must place myself in their situation, and strive to enter into their feelings; and so truly is this, according to Smith, the only rule for estimating sentiments and acts, that if I was alone in the world, or cast away on a desert island, I could not pass judgment upon my acts or sentiments, and they would have no moral character in my eyes. Such, unquestionably, is the doctrine of Smith; and all his illustrations confirm it. Now, what is it that I do, when, for the sentiments of actual spectators, I substitute those of an abstract spectator? Most evidently, gentlemen, I not only abandon the rule of sympathy, and adopt another in its place, but I even deny this rule, and pronounce it false, and condemn it; for this abstract spectator does not exist, and never existed; and his sentiments, therefore, have no reality, and are wholly fictitious. It is no longer by the sentiments of others that I judge, but by my own. The sentiments of others I reject wholly, and prefer my own; this abstract spectator is one of my own creation; he has no existence in the world without; he is neither a real individual, nor a combination of real individuals; he is an emanation from my own sentiments. I judge, then, by my own sentiments, which, according to this system, are incapable of judgment, the sentiments of others, which, as it teaches, are the only judge; I reverse the system so far as it can be reversed; I make supreme the rule which it pronounces false, and reject the rule which it approves; I enter into another world and another system – a world and system where sympathy is no longer regarded, and where the sentiments of others, so far from being the test for mine, are judged by mine.

In this fiction of an impartial spectator, then, Smith recognizes implicitly that there is a law, superior to that of sympathy; for, by the sentiments of this abstract spectator, which sympathy did not communicate, and which can only be my own, I form moral estimates of the sympathies of other beings, and condemn them, and look only to those eternal laws of right and wrong which conscience and reason reveal.

In truth, gentlemen, it is quite plain that this abstract spectator, imagined by Smith, is nothing else than reason, judging, in the name of order, and of the immutable nature of things, the mutable and blind decisions of men. It is a consciousness of the reality of this supreme faculty, that embarrasses Smith in the exposition of his system; and he has pictured to himself this faculty, which judges of our own and others' acts, and weighs, impartially, the decisions of others' sympathy for us, and our sympathy for them, under the image of an abstract spectator, because, of all symbols by which conscience can be represented, this is the one which seems most in harmony with his fundamental hypothesis, that we can judge of our own actions only by entering into the feelings of others towards us. Instead of the words *conscience*, or *reason*, therefore, he makes use of the expression *abstract spectator;* in his strong prepossession in favor of his system, he believes that it is by representing to ourselves the sentiments of this imaginary being, that we are able to pass judgment upon our acts; and he is quite unaware, that, in so doing, he contradicts his assertion that a solitary man would form no moral estimates; for, in the most desert island, this abstract spectator would still be our companion, and enable us to judge of our acts, our sentiments, ourselves.

Thus have I shown, as I believe, that the rule of sympathy is one which it is difficult to comprehend; that it is mutable; and, lastly, that it is an inadequate one. And now I will submit it to a yet severer test: let it be granted, for the moment, that it is clear, fixed, and applicable to every case; are these such qualities as are sufficient to secure for it our respect? By no means. These merits must pass for nothing, if it is not the real rule – the true rule of moral judgments. For what is it that we seek in ethical science? Not imaginary rules, which may explain our moral judgments, but those real rules which do actually determine them. Consciousness alone can decide this point. Smith has pretended to describe the manner by which we estimate our own and others' acts, and consciousness must decide whether this is the way in which we really judge. To consciousness, then, let us appeal.

Are we conscious, then, when we are to judge of the acts of others, that we first give loose to our sensibility, and observe how far it sympathizes with the sentiments by which they are animated, and then determine, from the nature and degree of our own emotions, taken as a rule, what judgments we shall pass? For my part, gentlemen, I say, that, so far from being conscious of such a process of mind, we are even conscious of an opposite one. When I wish to judge impartially of the conduct of my fellow-beings, I make it my first care, if I feel that it excites me, to stifle my emotions and forget them. And why? Because thus I secure the impartiality of my judgment. Singular proceeding indeed, if it is my sensibility which should be the judge! It is not at the moment when I behold some exhibition of strong passion, that I feel most capable of appreciating its propriety or justice; for then my sensibility overpowers me; emotions of sympathy or antipathy possess my mind; and I am perfectly aware that the feeling disturbs my judgment, and destroys its proper freedom and clearness of view. And why should it not be so in regard to moral judgments, when we know that it is in regard to judgments of taste? When an accomplished reader recites a piece of poetry, if I wish to judge of its beauty, I must not yield to the impression produced by the reading, or I shall be a prey to the emotion which the skilful declamation has awakened; I must await the publication of the piece, and peruse it coolly; and then shall I be competent to form an impartial judgment. Far, then, from being conscious of the facts described by Smith, when I judge of the acts of my fellow-beings, I have a distinct consciousness of quite opposite facts, which make known a wholly different rule of moral appreciation.

His description is equally wanting in fidelity, in relation to judgments on our own acts; although, in this case, I do recognize a phenomenon which may explain, though it cannot justify, his opinion. When I am animated with some emotion, and desire, before yielding to its influence, to determine its character, I often distrust my own judgment; and, if the emotion is very strong, I feel distinctly that my judgment is not in a condition to be impartial. It is fully capable in itself of appreciating the moral good or evil of an affection, and of distinguishing a right from a wrong action; this I am perfectly aware of, and am not anxious on that account; my only fear is, that, in the present instance, it is not in a condition to be impartial. What shall I do, then? I appeal to the sentiments of other men; I place myself in the situation of an indifferent person, and strive to imagine what his opinion would be of the emotion which I experience, and the act to which it impels me. But why this appeal to the sentiments of a fellow-being, and this effort to enter into them? It is because I believe that, as regards this emotion and act, the judgment of another is freer than mine from the influence of such sentiments as may prevent a correct moral estimate. It is from a regard to that impartiality of which his judgment is capable, while mine is not, that I wish to consult his opinion; and not at all because I consider his sympathy as the true and only rule of the morality of my affections and conduct; for I feel, all the while, that this rule, which I believe him to possess, exists also in my own mind, and it is not this, therefore, which I seek; I seek only an impartial application of this rule.

Such, according to my understanding of our sentiments and acts, is the only fact that has any analogy with Smith's ideas, and from this, perhaps, his system took its origin; but Smith has altered the real nature of the fact, by transforming into the rule of our judgments of ourselves what is merely a means of controlling them. And the proof that this recourse to the sympathy of others is nothing more, is the fact, that, in numerous cases, there is no such recourse; and that, even when it does take place, we often do not follow the opinions of other men, but prefer our own, as Smith himself acknowledges.

Consciousness, therefore, contradicts Smith's system, and does not recognize, in his pretended rule of moral appreciation, the rule which actually dictates our judgments. It is not true that we seek in our own sensibility the judgments which we pass upon others; and neither is it true that we seek in the opinions of others the principle of moral estimation for our own sentiments and conduct. As to the former point, the rules of moral appreciation are to be found in ourselves; and, as to the second, they consist not in emotions of sympathy, but in conceptions of reason. It is true that Smith may say, in answer, that he recognizes these inward laws, and gives a perfectly clear explanation of their origin. But consciousness cannot confound the rules which he acknowledges with those of morality, nor the decisions of sympathy, of which they are the generalization, with the true moral judgments given by reason. Consciousness does not admit that the true laws of morality emanate from the successive decisions of sympathy upon the acts and sentiments of ourselves and others reciprocally; and it perceives that, if there is any thing in the code of sympathy which is more than a generalization of the opinions of those about us, it can still be a rule of conduct for vain and ambitious men only, but never for a good man.

I must ask your attention for a moment longer, while I examine Smith's principle of moral qualification under another point of view, and inquire what is its authority.

The ethical philosopher has something more to do than to point out a rule of moral estimation; this rule must be shown also to have a moral authority over the will – an authority which is undeniable, and such as can explain the moral facts of human nature, and the moral ideas which we find in human intelligence; and as among these ideas are duty, right, obligation, all of which imply the idea of law, this principle must have the character of a law, and impose obligations, and thus give obedience the character, not of propriety merely, but of duty. Let us see whether Smith's principle fulfils these conditions.

When I examine the authority of Smith's moral rule, I find that it represents only the general law of an instinct. In all possible cases, if you generalize and reduce to distinct decisions what the sympathy of an impartial spectator declares, you will have, according to this system, the laws of moral conduct. And these moral laws have no other authority than that of an instinct of sympathy. What is this instinct of sympathy? Is it our only instinct? No: it is one only of several. This system elevates, then, the impulses of one particular instinct into being the laws of morality. But whence does this instinct derive its marvellous power of communicating to its impulses the character of a law, with all its peculiar authority and supremacy? If I ask Smith, he gives me no reply. If I examine human nature, I find no explanation of this wonderful prerogative. I have an instinct of sympathy, as I distinctly recognize; I agree that this instinct is developed according to certain laws;

I do not deny that it influences my will as a motive; but I have a multitude of other instincts also – instincts which are purely personal – the instinct of love, the instinct of imitation, the instinct of knowing, the instinct of acting – all of which are phenomena of a similar nature. Whence comes, then, the peculiar right and power of sympathy? Whence does it derive its title? By what process do its impulses become rules by which are to be judged, approved, condemned, the impulses of all other instincts? and not only these, but the acts of all our faculties – even those of intellect and reason? If this mysterious privilege of sympathy cannot be explained, at least I ask whether it is one which we feel and are conscious of – whether these rules of sympathy do speak to us with the tone of command – whether in a word, although ignorant of the source of their power, we are yet aware that they do exert this right of obligation.

It is wonderful to observe, gentlemen, by what gradual substitutions of equivalent expressions, and by what insensible transitions, Smith attempts to elevate the impulses of sympathy into the condition of rules, and by which he finally succeeds in communicating to them some appearance of this character. We must follow the series of these ingenious sophisms, if we would comprehend his system, and lay bare all its imperfections.

Smith's mode of reasoning is as follows: – How am I affected by the exhibition of another's emotions? Sympathy is awakened, and either I participate in them, or I do not. When do I approve a sentiment? When I participate in it. Approbation, then, is a consequence of sympathy; and, in all its degrees, is only a faithful transcript of the emotions of sympathy. To say that I approve a sentiment, is to say that I participate in it; and to say that I participate in it, is to say that I approve it; and reciprocally to say that I do not approve it, is to say that I do not participate in it. What can be simpler or more proper than to substitute the word *approve*, therefore, for that of *participate?* Well, then, says Smith, what is morally good? Is it not that which we approve? And what ought we to do? Surely that which is good. Can any thing be more plain, more natural? Will any one deny, that to *approve* and to *pronounce good* are the same things, or that that *ought* to be done which is *good?* How plausible are such propositions! Observe now the conclusion; that which *ought* to be done is precisely what impartial sympathy approves; the instinctive emotions of sympathy, therefore, are the laws of human conduct, and the rules of morality; such is the strict consequence of the preceding reasonings.

I trust that you already perceive the sophistry of such an induction; it consists in pronouncing things to be equivalent which are not so. Let us expose, successively, these false equations; the system itself must bear the blame.

To participate in the sentiment of another being, is simply, according to Smith's system, to feel an emotion equal to that which he experiences: the phenomenon is purely a sensible one. To approve this sentiment, is, in the language of ethics, to consider it proper, good, lawful: this is a purely intellectual fact. Are these two things identical? Not at all. A judgment is a judgment; an emotion is an emotion; but an emotion is no more a judgment than a sensation is an idea. There is no more reason for identifying these two things than there is for declaring them equal. Is the emotion, then, of such a nature, that, when presented to the view of reason, the judgment is an immediate consequence? In other words, do I approve every emotion which I feel to be equal to yours? Whence comes the necessity of any such consequence? I can see none, and facts contradict it. I share a thousand emotions, without morally approving or disapproving them; I condemn many emotions which I share; and, on the other hand, I approve many things which are neither emotions nor the result of emotions; and I even approve emotions which I not only do not participate in, but which are absolutely displeasing to me. There is no reason whatever, therefore, for pronouncing the sensible fact of sympathy to be equal to the rational fact of approbation. Any equality which there is between them, is only in appearance, and the appearance consists wholly in words. So much for the first sophism.

Our author proceeds to say, that, when I approve an emotion, I feel it to be good; to which I answer, This is not the way in which the human mind reasons; from the goodness of the act we are led to approve it, but not from our approbation to pronounce it good. For what is it that merits approbation? It is that which is good; but that is not necessarily good which is approved. Before we can infer the goodness of an act, as a conclusion, from the fact of its being approved, it must be proved that the approbation is merited, which is saying, in other words, that it is good; this shows that the approbation is a consequence of an antecedent perception of goodness. Smith reverses this order of nature, for he makes the approbation the sign and proof of the goodness. Instead of the true equation between that which is good and that which merits approbation, he substitutes a false equation between that which is approved and that which is good. This is the second sophism.

Once possessed of the word *good*, Smith dashes on with full sails, and without difficulty arrives at the idea of obligation; for what is more evident to reason than that that which is good ought to be done, and that which is evil avoided? But what mean such words as these, in a system which preserves nothing of moral good but its name, while it destroys the reality? Obligation is attached, not to words, however, but to things; and the word, which is but an appearance, can produce only an apparent obligation. Such is the third sophism.

And now, gentlemen, our conclusion is, that, in establishing as the principle and rule of moral approbation the emotions of an impartial spectator, Smith has elevated into a law of conduct a fact that is purely sensible and instinctive – a fact possessing no more authority than every other instinctive and sensible fact – and, consequently, possessing none at all. Under whatever disguise, therefore, this fact may be enveloped, and through whatever ingenious transformations it may be made to pass, it is still impossible to communicate to it the character which it wants: there is not, therefore, in the system of Smith, any such thing as a moral law; and it is incompetent to explain our ideas of duty, or right, and all other such ideas as imply the fact of obligation; and if it attempts to do so, it must, necessarily, fall into sophisms, and come to empty conclusions, which vanish when we approach to examine them.

Thus, gentlemen, – and with the consideration of this point I shall close my lecture, – Smith himself is conscious, that, after all his efforts, his principle of moral qualification is still wanting in the character of obligation; and he has been compelled, therefore, to employ one further mode of evasion, which it is well you should be acquainted with, if only to convince you of the power of truth, and to show you what embarrassment systematic minds must feel, and to what sophistries the loftiest genius must descend, in its attempt to endue error with a character which it cannot justly claim.

It is the strict consequence of the system of Smith, that whatever others approve and praise will appear to me good, and whatever they blame and disapprove will appear to me bad; and that the rule of conduct, therefore, is to be sought in the approbation and praise of our fellow-men.

Now, conscience revolts instinctively at this idea of finding a rule for conduct in the opinions of others. There are so many occasions when the opinion of the world must be wrong; the principle subjects our conduct to such a dependence upon the caprices and mutations of opinion; and, finally, it is so often assigned as a motive for conduct, by men who are wholly governed by vanity or ambition, – that a doctrine professing this principle is much better calculated to repel than attract us. Smith himself, indeed, has too much good sense to allow himself to believe or teach that the desire of praise and the fear of censure is the only motive for good men. He is driven, therefore, into finding some means of escaping from this consequence of his system; and you shall see how he has attempted to do so.

We cannot, he says, desire to be praised, or fear to be blamed, without desiring to be the legitimate object of praise, and fearing to be the legitimate object of blame. The desire of praise and the fear of blame is succeeded by the desire of being praiseworthy and the fear of being blameworthy; and this latter sentiment soon becomes, in all sensible minds, infinitely the stronger of the two; the other remaining prevalent only in vain and frivolous natures.

You see, gentlemen, the transition by which Smith endeavors to substitute for the love of praise the love of that which may merit it, and for the fear of blame the fear of that which may deserve it. If the transition was legitimate, the true end and the true rule for good men would be found; for what we should seek or shun is not the praise and blame, which the world so blindly distributes, but the qualities which make us worthy to receive them; and Smith, being a good man, feels and allows it. But he does so by availing himself to the most sophistical and false equivalent expressions.

We can comprehend, as I readily acknowledge, that the desire of praise may create a desire of being the object of praise; but why? It is because these two desires are really only different forms of the same desire; to love praise and to love to be its object are the same thing. The motive of the good man is not to be found in either one or the other; the motive of the good man is the desire of being the *legitimate* object of praise, whether he obtains it or not. Between this and the desire of praise there is as wide a difference as possible; for, to have the latter, we need only to know what praise is, and we can gratify it by performing, in any case, the acts which are necessary to obtain it; while, to have the former, we must know what conditions are necessary to make us legitimate objects of praise; and, to gratify it, we must fulfil these conditions. Now, the system of sympathy cannot make us acquainted with these conditions, because it has no other sign or measure of what is worthy and good, than the praise itself. The desire of being the legitimate object of praise is impossible, then, in such a system; and Smith really admits a new principle of moral appreciation, perfectly distinct from that which sympathy gives, and which is the only one that it can give, when he substitutes for the desire of praise the desire of being worthy of it. He saves his system from absurdity only by abandoning its principle, and his pretended equation of the desire of praise and the desire of deserving it is only a sophism.

And now let me recapitulate what has been said in this lecture. Smith's rule for moral judgment is one, then, which, in my opinion, it is difficult to comprehend; supposing it to be comprehended, it is so fluctuating a one that we cannot settle it; even if it were settled, it would yet be inadequate, because there are cases to which it does not apply; but allowing that it is adequate, it is not the true rule which we are conscious of obeying; and this last idea is confirmed by the fact that it has no authority and no character of a law, and thus cannot explain the moral facts and ideas of human nature.

Such are the observations which I have felt bound to submit to your attention, in relation to the answer given by the system of sympathy to the first question proposed as a test. They have led me so far, that I am obliged to postpone until the next lecture a consideration of its answers to the other two questions. This is giving a great deal of time to the discussion of a particular system, to be sure; but you will find the criticism so interesting, I trust, as not to complain of its length. And, in my view, the remarks suggested by Smith's system extend to all others which seek in instinct for the laws of morality; and I feel, therefore, that time thus employed is really gained, not lost.

LECTURE XVIII
THE SAME SUBJECT CONTINUED

GENTLEMEN,

In my last lecture, I examined Smith's system, for the purpose of determining what answer it gives to the first of the three questions, which every ethical system is bound to solve; and I described and discussed this answer. I proceed to-day to test this system by the two remaining questions, and to criticise the solution of them.

The first of these two questions is this: What is the motive to which we yield when we act right? Let us first inquire, then, how Smith answers it; and, having determined the motive to which he ascribes the legitimate decisions of will, let us examine its authority, and see how far it explains our moral ideas.

We act well, according to any system, when we practise the different virtues which it recognizes. By inquiring, then, what Smith considers the principal virtues, and seeking to know the motive that impels us to perform them, we shall determine the motive to which we yield in doing right, according to the doctrine of sympathy.

You know that, in Smith's opinion, we judge of acts by the affections which lead to them; and that we judge of the affections themselves under a double point of view; first, in relation to the object calling them forth, in which case they are pronounced proper or improper; and next, in relation to their tendency, in which they are considered as having merit or demerit. Propriety and merit are the two moral qualities, of which affections, and consequently actions, are susceptible; such, in other words, are the two elements of moral good.

To the first of these two qualities of affections correspond, as Smith teaches, two virtues. The effort to restrain within proper limits the manifestation of our affections, constitutes the first of them, which is self-command, the source of all honorable virtues. The opposite effort of elevating our sympathetic emotions as nearly as possible to a level with the original affections of other persons constitutes the second, which is benevolence, the source of all amiable virtues. Both have a common end, which is a harmony of affection. In tempering the violence of our original affections in the first instance, and elevating the tone of our sympathetic affections in the second, we seek the same result, which is to bring our sensibility into unison with that of our fellow-beings; in both cases, we anticipate their emotions, and, in this mutual drawing near of affection, meet them half-way. Self-command and benevolence – such are the two virtues, by the practice of which, in our double capacity of spectator and actor, we impress upon our affections and acts the character of propriety, and realize the greatest possible degree of harmony between the sentiments of our fellow-beings and our own.

To the second moral quality of affections, merit, two virtues also belong – charity and justice. The repressing of all affections which could produce the ill of others, indignation alone excepted, constitutes justice; the development of affections which tend to increase the good of others, constitutes charity. Charity is the source of all meritorious virtues; justice of all estimable ones; for, as the only end of justice is to prevent wrong, it cannot produce merit, while charity, by multiplying good, makes us the proper object of the gratitude of others, and, consequently, meritorious.

Such, gentlemen, according to Smith, are the four cardinal virtues, into which all others may be resolved. From the practice of these four virtues, results, as this philosopher teaches, all the morality of human conduct. And now, let us inquire, to what motive we, in his opinion, yield, in practising these several virtues.

Virtuous acts, Smith says, are sometimes instinctive, sometimes reasonable. They are instinctive when they spring from the direct impulse of sympathy; they are reasonable when they flow from the rules, which, as we have seen, are the generalizations of these impulses. Let us consider these cases separately.

To what motive do we yield, when we confine, within the bounds of propriety, the expression of an original affection, and when we elevate our sympathetic emotions to a level with the affection of another? To the instinct of sympathy, answers Smith; that is to say, to the desire which every human being feels of harmonizing, in his affections, sentiments, and dispositions, with those of his fellow-beings. Sympathy is delightful to him who experiences it, and to him who is its object; we are instinctively impelled to give and to seek it; and from this results the instinctive effort which constitutes self-command on the one side, and benevolence on the other.

We yield to the same motive, says Smith, in the instinctive

exercise of justice and of charity; but, in this case, it assumes a peculiar form. When I am charitable, I seek not so much the sympathy of others as their gratitude; and when I am just, I seek rather to avoid their resentment than their antipathy. But is not gratitude the strongest sympathy, and resentment the strongest antipathy? In seeking gratitude and avoiding resentment, then, we really are only striving to gain, and dreading to lose, their sympathy. The spontaneous practice of charity and of justice is determined, therefore, by the same motive which produces the other two virtues; that is to say, by the sympathetic instinct, which impels us to seek a harmony between our own sentiments and those of our fellow-beings. The practice of all virtue, then, emanates from this one motive.

You will please to remark one thing, gentlemen; which is, that, according to Smith, this motive is an instinct, and not a result of calculation. We can desire the love, benevolence, and esteem of our kind, from a prospect of the agreeable or useful consequences of such sentiments. Smith denies, however, that it is from such considerations that sympathy makes us desire them. Sympathy seeks them, Smith declares, for their own sake, because they are its proper objects, as food is the object of hunger. In adopting the sympathetic instinct as the motive of virtue, Smith thinks, therefore, that he refers virtue to a disinterested motive; and it is thus that he pretends to establish the fact of disinterestedness in human nature. Without doubt, Smith has good reasons for saying that the sympathetic instinct is not interested; but whether he is justified, therefore, in calling the volitions produced by it disinterested, and in finding in them the type of true disinterestedness, is an altogether different question, to be considered hereafter.

When, instead of being instinctive, the practice of these virtues is reasonable, to what motive do we yield, in the opinion of Smith? To the authority of rules. Whence comes the authority of these rules? From the fact that they represent the conduct by which we may merit the sympathy of our fellow-beings, and avoid their antipathy. These rules are the generalization of particular judgments of the sympathetic instinct; their only merit in our eyes, and sole title to obedience, is, that they indicate the true course of action to be pursued in the satisfaction of our desire for sympathy. This desire, therefore, is the true motive of obedience to these rules. And it is to this we yield in the reasonable, as in the instinctive, practice of virtue.

The result to which we come, then, is, that the instinctive desire of sympathy is the motive of all virtue, and, consequently, of all right conduct – a motive that influences the will sometimes directly, sometimes indirectly, by rules, but always exclusive of other motives. Not only is this the result naturally given by the principle of sympathy, but I now say, in addition, that this result is not altered by the two expedients which, as I showed in my last lecture, Smith has employed to give to his principle an extent to which it has no claim, and to deduce from it consequences which have no connection with it. A few words will suffice to show that this is true.

The first of these expedients is the notion of an abstract spectator. This is the means by which Smith hopes to prove that sympathy is not limited to a knowledge of the conditions necessary for obtaining the sympathy of our countrymen and contemporaries, but that it is competent to make known the conditions upon which we may merit the sympathy of the human race, of present and of future generations, of men enlightened with perfect wisdom and reason. That this hope is futile, and that it is impossible to deduce logically such infallible moral judgments from any generalization of particular estimates of instinctive sympathy, I have, as I think, unanswerably demonstrated in my last lecture. But, whether the instinct of sympathy has a wider or a narrower range, Smith's idea as to the motive of virtue remains unchanged either he believes that the conditions for obtaining the sympathy of the human race are made known by the instinct of sympathy, or that they are not. In the first case, he is consistent in his belief that the motive of our volitions in fulfilling these conditions is the desire of sympathy; in the second, he manifests a consciousness that his system is false, and that it is not adequate to explain the rules of morality; and then it is unimportant to inquire what the motive is to which he attributes our obedience; for it is one foreign to the system of sympathy, and it is only the motive to virtue presented by this system that we seek.

The same must be said of Smith's second expedient, by which he endeavors to show that the love of praise, directly emanating from the instinct of sympathy, immediately begets the desire of being praiseworthy; which desire no sooner becomes supreme, than we endeavor to act in such a way as may make us the legitimate objects of approval, even should this conduct awaken their displeasure. Smith has unquestionably failed in this attempt, as well as in the first; but, whether he has or has not proved the justness of attributing this influence to sympathy, the motive assigned remains the same; and again he is exposed to the dilemma, either of sincerely and thoroughly believing that the principle of his system really produces this desire of being praiseworthy, or that it does not. If he allows that sympathy cannot explain this desire, then he is conscious that his principle cannot account for all our acts of will, and he is forced to admit another and independent principle; and thus he destroys his system, acknowledges that it is false, and there is no further need of asking what motive for virtue he adopts. If, on the contrary, he considers that the desire of praise and the desire of being praiseworthy are equivalent, then, although he may be deceived, he is still consistent in believing that the desire of sympathy is the single motive of all virtuous acts.

Thus, gentlemen, it appears that Smith has not altered, by either of these attempts, the conclusion legitimately to be drawn from his principles; and, therefore, the only motive of all legitimate actions, acknowledged in his system, is seen to be the instinct of sympathy. And now let us inquire what is the authority of this motive, and how far it is adequate to explain our moral ideas.

In absolute truth, the reason why we ought to do good is so included in the very idea of good, that there is no difference between the moral law and the motive which makes obedience to it our duty. But when we substitute a false law of morality for the true one, the authority is no longer recognized in the law itself, and we are obliged to seek it in the motive to which we yield in obeying it. This is precisely what becomes necessary in the system of sympathy. Good, in this system, is that which is conformable to the emotions of an impartial spectator. Such a rule has, as we have already seen, no authority; it remains, then, to be seen whether the authority, which does not reside in the rule, may be found in the motive which influences us when we act in accordance with it. Let us inquire.

What is the desire of sympathy? An instinct. Is this instinct the only one active in human nature? Far from it: I have many other instincts. Are the instincts the only motives by which I am impelled? No; for I do not always act instinctively: sometimes I am governed by views of interest, sometimes by a sense of order, by a love of truth, or by some other conception of reason. To judge, then, of the authority of the motive of sympathy, I must compare it with these other motives, which also influence my will, and see what is the nature of its superiority. We will begin with the instincts.

In comparing the action of the instinct of sympathy with that of any other personal instinct, I find that, whenever these are brought into opposition, sometimes one, sometimes the other, triumphs; and that the determining cause of this superiority, unless some considerations of reason enter, is always the greater energy which either may at the moment possess. Experience proves, then, that, in its impulsive force, the instinct of sympathy is exactly equal to all other instincts. But what influence has an instinct over my will, except this power of impulse? and on what ground can it be considered entitled to supreme sway, except that of its energy – an energy of which the pleasure following its gratification must always be the essential element? This energy – which is the only claim of superiority, then, that the sympathetic instinct can possess – sympathy itself, then, cannot communicate.

Its superiority must come, then, from a judgment of reason, declaring its title to be better than that of any other instinct. But, if reason thus decides, it is by means of some rule foreign from, and higher than, instinct; and, therefore, if, governed by this judgment, we prefer the inspirations of instinctive sympathy to all other impulses, our motive is no longer derived from instinct, but from this higher rule; that is to say, from reason; but this the system of sympathy cannot admit. According to this system, then, the instinct of sympathy, both by right and in fact, is neither more nor less than equal to every other instinct, and can have no real title to superiority.

And now let us compare this sympathetic instinct with self-love. Is its superiority here manifest? Far from it. As a matter of fact, when the instincts of sympathy and of interest well understood come in conflict, the former yields at least as often as it triumphs, and, as a matter of right, the superiority of interest well understood is clear. Whenever these motives clash, one of two things happens: either self-love approves or disapproves the instinct of sympathy; approving when it sees that there will be a gain in yielding the will to the sympathetic impulse, and disapproving when it anticipates suffering as a consequence of so doing. In the first case, our volition is determined by two cooperating motives; and far from feeling that the motive of interest is secondary, we recognize it, on the contrary, as the principal one, at least so long as the instinct acts unaided, and derives no support from a motive of reason. In the second case, sometimes the instinct, sometimes the judgment triumphs; but, unless the instinct is directed by some rational motive, we always feel, in yielding to it, that we should act more wisely in obeying the dictate of self-interest. The instinct of sympathy, therefore, far from appearing to be superior to self-love, is acknowledged by us to be inferior; and this superiority of the motive of interest is owing to its character of being rational: on this ground, and on this ground alone, does it legitimately rule over the instinctive impulse; and if at any time the sympathetic tendencies of our nature appear to have the nobler character, it is communicated to them by a motive, also rational though yet higher – the moral motive.

Is there any need, now, of attempting to show, that a superiority of the instinct of sympathy over the disinterested motives of reason is a yet more chimerical supposition? Influenced by these motives, by the love of order, for example, reason sometimes approves, sometimes disapproves the impulses of sympathy; for it is an error to think that its approbation is uniform; there may be, and are, cases in which reason decides that we ought to resist our best sympathies, even that sweetest and most sacred of all, the love of a parent to a child. In cases where it approves, we obey two motives; and far from the instinct seeming to us to be the principal, it is the rational motive, which always appears to us to wear this character of superiority. The same is true of cases where reason condemns the instinct; for, then, whether we do or do not yield to the impulse, we still recognize that we ought to obey the judgment.

Whether we compare, therefore, the action of the instinct of sympathy with that of other instincts, or with that of either the selfish or disinterested motives of reason, we can find no signs of its superiority; it has no more authority than every other instinct, and it has far less than the rational motives. If, then, this is the motive to which we really ought to yield, no reason appears why we should do so; and the authority, which we could not find in the idea of good as given by the system of sympathy, is no more to be found in the motive, which, according to this system, impels us to right conduct.

This Smith seems to have thought himself, and his efforts to establish the authority of the instinct of sympathy are manifest. Unfortunately, they led only to evident paralogisms. Instead of proving that the instinct of sympathy is the true moral motive, he describes the characteristics of this moral motive, and then gratuitously attributes them to the instinct of sympathy; thus proving, to be sure, that, if the instinct had these characteristics, it would be the moral motive, but forgetting altogether the evidence that it possesses them.

No one has better described than Smith the supreme sway of the moral motive over the appetites and instincts, and all the faculties of our nature; and the passages in which he establishes this point are perfectly true as well as beautiful. Whatever may be our idea of the moral faculty, to it always belongs, says Smith, the direction of our conduct, and, consequently, the superintendence of all our faculties, passions, and appetites. It is false, that the moral faculty is like our other faculties, having no more right than they to prescribe laws. No other faculty passes judgment upon its kindred faculties; love does not judge resentment, nor resentment love; these two faculties may be in opposition, but they neither approve nor disapprove each other; it is the special function of the moral faculty, on the contrary, to judge, approve, and censure the other faculties; it is a sense, of which all other principles of our nature are the appropriate object. Each sense is sovereign judge as to its object; there is no appeal, in a question of color, from the eye to the ear, nor from the ear to the eye, in a question of sound; that which is pleasing to the eye is beautiful, to the taste sweet, to the ear harmonious; and the peculiarity of the moral faculty is a power of judging of the degree in which the ear should be charmed, the eye delighted, the taste gratified – of the degree, in other words, in which it is proper, meritorious, good, that either of our faculties should be restrained. The words *good, bad, just, unjust, merit, demerit, propriety, impropriety,* express what is pleasing or displeasing to this faculty; it is, therefore, the governing power in our nature. Its laws are real laws, in the true acceptation of that word; for they regulate the right acts of free agents, and by their sanctions administer reward and punishment; and so far is this word *laws* from having a just application to our faculties of seeing, hearing, moving, and all our other faculties, that, when we speak of their laws of action, we mean to signify that they operate in a necessary way.

Unquestionably this is perfectly true. But, in the first place, Smith has not seen, that this subordination of all our faculties is not peculiar to the moral motive, but may equally belong to every motive and impulse. If we propose, as the supreme end of conduct, the sympathy of others, we shall regulate accordingly all our appetites, instincts, and faculties, and make them subordinate to this end. We shall do the same if we propose, as our end, self-interest, literary reputation, or any other end. It is not, then, the special character of the moral faculty, that it subjects to its rule, as supreme, the action of our other faculties; every other faculty may do this, and in an equal degree, whenever it is made the ruling motive of conduct. The special characteristic of the moral motive – and this is the second point which Smith has overlooked – is that, among all possible motives for action, it alone can be obligatory, and for this reason – that, though other motives may present different ends to be pursued, the moral motive alone presents, as an end, that which ought to be done, which is the true end of human life, and which is seen by us to be legitimate and sacred in itself. This is what distinguishes the moral motive from all others. Smith may prove, to be sure, that, in taking as a rule for conduct the inspirations of the instinct of sympathy, we obey a principle by which we may intelligently control the action of all our natural faculties; but the same thing might be proved of every other principle of conduct; and it by no means follows that this principle and the moral principle are identical. Smith does not prove exactly, what it was necessary he should prove to establish this identity, that this instinct is obligatory, and that the end to which it impels us is legitimate and sacred in itself. If he had proved this, the authority of the instinct of sympathy would have been no longer doubtful; but this cannot be proved of any faculty except the moral one, for it is true of this motive alone.

Smith believes that he recognizes the moral motive in the instinct of sympathy, for this additional reason, that it renders us impartial. If we should hear, he says, that the empire of China was swallowed up, we should be less affected than by the loss of a finger. How can the partiality of these judgments be remedied? By sympathy. When we place ourselves in the situation of an impartial spectator, each event assumes its relative value, and we learn to estimate it, not by the rule of self-love, but by that of justice. It would be easy to demonstrate, that sympathy, acting by itself, would be without power to prevent this preponderance of our selfishness. But even if I admit this, the reasoning of Smith would still be a paralogism. Interest, well understood, produces some of the effects of the moral motive. Does it follow from this that it is the moral motive? The point to be proved is not that the instinct of sympathy acts *like* the moral motive, but that it *is* the moral motive. Now, how can the moral motive be recognized? By its authority. Among all possible motives, the moral motive alone appears to us as one that *ought* to govern our conduct. It is when recognized by this sign, that we are able to judge of its tendencies; and it is because these tendencies are those of the moral motive, that they seem to us legitimate. But, first, to say that certain tendencies are legitimate, and, then, because a motive appears to have these tendencies, to conclude that it is the moral motive, is a pure paralogism.

Thus, as you see, gentlemen, we seek in vain for any right, possessed by the instinct of sympathy, of controlling our conduct; there is none to be found; and this is equally true of all other instincts. In refuting the system of Smith, I refute, therefore, every other moral system, which seeks in instinct for the regulating principle of volition; and this is my apology for such a lengthened discussion.

If the motive of sympathy has no authority, it is plain that it cannot explain our moral ideas, for each of them implies a motive of obligation. Smith's system, indeed, may employ, in a certain sense, the words which represent these ideas; but it can do so only by altering the meaning which they have in common acceptation. Your attention has already been directed to this change of signification, in relation to the words *merit* and *demerit*; and I know will proceed to show a similar misuse of the words *duty* and *right*.

Smith gives two definitions of *duty* – a fact which itself indicates that he felt an embarrassment in attempting to explain it. We are governed by *duty*, he says, when we obey the rules of conduct which emanate from sympathy, and by *sentiment* when we yield directly to the instinct of sympathy. But what are these rules? They are generalizations of particular judgments of instinctive sympathy: the authority of the rules, then, is derived from that of those judgments; and the motive which compels us to respect the one, is the same with that which leads us to yield to the other. If it is a duty, then, to obey the laws, it is because it is a duty to obey the instinct, on which supposition, the distinction of Smith is without foundation. But it cannot be a duty to obey an instinct; for neither the judgments of the instinct, nor the desire of sympathy impelling us to yield to it, are obligatory; it cannot, then, be a duty to obey these rules; and duty, as Smith understands it, is not duty as we understand it; for, in our idea, it has the character of obligation, which in his it has not; so that, in using the word with such a signification, Smith actually suppresses the idea which it has always represented in human intelligence.

Smith has the art of connecting his errors with a truth, and of thus rendering them specious. Thus, in the present instance, he founds his definition of duty upon a true distinction, recognized by every one, between acting from sentiment and acting from duty. The distinction is in perfect harmony with the true nature of man, which acts sometimes dutifully, sometimes instinctively. But when we convert instinct into duty, we commit an absurdity; for we thus destroy the distinction between these two moving springs of action; and, whether we obey instinct or the rules emanating from it, the motive remains the same, and the character of the volition is unchanged.

Smith inconsistently gives, however, another definition to the word *duty*. There is but one virtue, says he, whose omission causes positive injury; this virtue is justice; it is the only one, then, which others have a *right* to compel us to regard; and, therefore, it is the only one which it is a *duty* to practise, in the true acceptation of that word; such is the true meaning of the words *right* and *duty*. Doubtless, gentlemen, it is a duty to respect justice; and other men have a right to exact from us a respect for it, and even to constrain us to observe its dictates. But upon what are such a right and duty founded, in the system of sympathy? Follow closely this reasoning of Smith. Why is justice a duty? Because others have the right to compel us to observe it. Whence comes their right? From the fact that injustice would do them a positive wrong. My only *duty*, then, is not to injure others; my only *right* is to prevent their injuring me. I violate *duty* whenever I do evil to a fellow-being; he violates my *right* whenever he does an evil to me; I have fulfilled my whole *duty* when I avoid causing others pain; they have respected entirely my *right*, when they have caused me none. I ask, now, who would admit such propositions? Who would allow that they coincide with the true ideas of duty and right? But for the moment I will adopt these definitions, and then ask, whence, in the system of Smith, comes the obligation not to injure others, and why is it the only obligation? The emotions of the impartial spectator make me aware that he sympathizes with justice, indeed, but that he sympathizes with other virtues also; the desire of the sympathy of my fellow-beings will impel me to the practice of this virtue, but it will impel me equally to the practice of other virtues. In proportion as the antipathy resulting in injustice is stronger, justice may find in the desire of sympathy a more efficient aid; but this difference is one of degree merely. If instinct can enforce obligation to a certain degree, it can in all degrees; and, on the other hand, if it cannot enforce obligation to this degree, it cannot in any; so that neither the rule of moral appreciation, nor the motive recognized by this system, are sufficient to explain the difference between justice and all other virtues. The system, therefore, must be abandoned, and, at the expense of being inconsistent, some other explanation must be found. How does Smith attempt to explain this difference? By two considerations: first, that injustice inflicts pain; secondly, that we have a right to repel it by force. But, abstractly considered, it is not true that the specific characteristic of injustice is that it causes injury; and it is no more true that from this characteristic is derived the right of repelling it by force; for, on the one hand, justice often authorizes, and even commands, the infliction of pain; and, on the other, so far from injustice being recognized by the fact that it is something which we have a right to repel with force, it is precisely because it is recognized as injustice that we have this right of forcibly repelling it. Not only, therefore, is the system of sympathy incompetent to prove that justice is a duty, but all Smith's efforts to determine in which the duty consists, lead only to a mutilation of the idea; so perverted does even the justest mind become by a false system, and so impossible is it found, even at the cost of most palpable inconsistencies, to return again into the way of truth, when once led by system into error.

Nothing would be easier than to prove that what I have now said of *duty*, as explained by this system, applies with equal force to every other moral idea; but this would lead me into useless repetition; and I hasten, therefore, to test Smith's system by the third question, of which I have a right to ask a solution, and inquire what end it assigns for human conduct in the present life.

According to Smith, the supreme and final end of every human being is to contribute, with all his power, to the production of perfect harmony of sentiment among men. Such is the definitive result which all virtuous conduct tends to produce; such is the end to be sought in all our deliberations, purposes, and acts.

Unquestionably, gentlemen, a complete harmony of sentiments, and a perfect cooperation of will among all members of the human family, is one of the effects which a universal practice of the moral law would produce: every virtuous action has this tendency; every vicious act an opposite one. Yet more; I admit that, among the instincts of our nature, those which are called *sympathetic*, tend more directly, at least in appearance, (on which point I will hereafter explain my meaning,) to produce this result, than the so called *personal* instincts. But having made these concessions, we have still to inquire whether this universal harmony of sentiment and will is the true and legitimate end of the individual, which he should set before him as the true object of pursuit, and to which all thoughts and acts of life should incessantly be directed; for this is the point which every ethical system is bound to decide. This is a result, says Smith, which sympathy tends to produce. Well, let it be granted; and what then? The point which an ethical system is bound to determine is the *legitimate* end of human action: an ethical system ought, therefore, not only to assign an end to conduct, but to prove that this end is the legitimate one. This is what Smith, however, neglects to do. Of two courses of reasoning open to him, and which, though not strictly logical, would yet have given some appearance of foundation to his system, Smith has adopted neither: he has not attempted to prove the legitimacy of this universal harmony as a result, and thence inferred the legitimacy of sympathy as a motive; nor has he attempted to show the legitimacy of sympathy as a motive, and thence concluded that this universal harmony is a legitimate result. We have already seen that he has not established the authority of sympathy as a motive; and now I will proceed to show that he has been equally unsuccessful in proving that this universal harmony is the legitimate need for human conduct.

In what way does Smith attempt to prove that this harmony is man's true end in this world? First, he shows that it is beautiful. The spectacle of a number of men animated with similar sentiments has, he says, the character of beauty. The effect of such a sight is like that produced by the contemplation of a complicated piece of mechanism, whose wheels, notwithstanding their number and diversity, work together together to one grand result. What is the human race but an exceedingly complicated machine; and what can be more eminently beautiful than the harmony and perfect concurrence of so many hearts and wills? I am far from denying the magnificent effect of such a result; but I cannot but say, in reply to Smith, that this consideration of beauty is not to the purpose, and proves nothing; for, supposing that the conduct of a man whose end is self-interest, should, through long years, and under varied circumstances, be steadily directed to his end in every separate act, the conditions of beauty here mentioned would be fulfilled. But would it thence follow that this conduct was good? By no means; and for this reason, that beauty is a different thing from morality. Undoubtedly, whatever is moral is at the same time beautiful; and without doubt, if we may trust our weak reason, in God these two attributes coincide, and are but a twofold aspect of the same essence; but here, on earth, beauty is not goodness; there are beautiful things without number, which have, in our view, no moral character. To establish the morality of conduct, then, it is not enough that we should prove it to be beautiful, although it might be a sufficient proof of its beauty, to show that it is moral.

Secondly, Smith proves that a universal accordance among men would be useful; and asserts that men would be perfectly happy if this harmony could be produced. I have no wish to contradict this; although, certainly, this would appear to me to be only one element of happiness, and not complete happiness. But let this, too, be granted. Is utility, then, morality? If so, then self-love is a virtue; and it will be all in vain for Smith to prove the disinterestedness of sympathy. I have said, and I believe, that whatever is good is, for that reason, useful, and nothing can be so productive of utility as goodness. But from this it by no means follows, that the ideas of utility and of good are the same, and that the conception of the first is the acquisition of the latter. Between the utility and the legitimacy of an end there is the widest difference; and if Smith could produce a thousand proofs of the utility of this harmony, he would have done nothing to demonstrate its legitimacy.

Thus, then, gentlemen, Smith proves satisfactorily that a universal harmony of feeling among human beings is the final end of sympathy, and that this end is beautiful and useful; but he does not prove that it is man's true end; and for this reason, that he cannot prove it. His system assigns, indeed, a rule, a motive, and an end for human conduct, but they, one and all, emanate from instinct; and as the instinct is devoid of moral character, the rule can have no obligation, the motive no authority, the end no legitimacy. It is a rule to be followed, a motive to be obeyed, an end to be pursued, at our own option; in a word, it is morality deprived of its essential element of obligation. If a mind, under the direction of this system, then, does right, it must be attributed to the general coincidence between the impulses of sympathy and the requisitions of the moral law. But this coincidence is still greater between the dictates of the moral law and the counsels of interest well understood; for interest includes all instincts, while sympathy recognizes but a few. I have before said, and I repeat, that instinctive tendencies, self-interest, and the moral law, impel man equally to the pursuit of his true end; but they differ in the degree in which they enable him to comprehend what it is, and in the authority of the motives which they present for its pursuit; and *morality* depends upon the manner in which we pursue, and the view with which we regard our end. Hence the coincidences and differences which we observe among the various systems of ethics. God has not intrusted us to the single guidance of the law of duty; he has not committed exclusively to this austere motive the accomplishment of an end, whose consequences will extend to the human race and the whole creation; our nature would have been too weak to be governed by this sole motive; and therefore has he, with admirable wisdom, provided numberless secondary motives, all powerful and attractive, which tend to the same direction, and become the auxiliaries of the moral law. The agreement of these motives with the moral law has deceived many philosophers; they have overlooked the fact that these motives are all devoid of the character of obligation, and, consequently, that neither of them can be the moral law they seek. The failure of their attempts to explain our moral ideas, by means of a supposed law that is really not a law, should have undeceived them; but once lost on a false track, the mind no more returns. It follows out its principle, reconciling its errors with common sense by unconscious sophistry. Such is the spectacle which Smith, notwithstanding his clear intellect, presents; and this is one consideration that has led me to give so detailed an exposition of his views.

When reason, combining into the one general end of personal good the separate ends, to which our several passions impel us, rises to the idea that this personal good is the end of our nature, and that this end is but one element of a universal order, that every rational and free being is summoned to advance, then, and then only, is an end which ought to be pursued, a law which ought to be respected, a motive which ought to be obeyed, revealed. And here is the source of those various moral ideas, which neither instinct nor interest can account for, because interest and instinct do not give them birth. Traced back to their true principle, these ideas may be explained easily, without sophistry, and in a natural and common sense; but referred to self-love or to instinct, they remain inexplicable; and the combined resources of the most ingenious mind can account for them only by mutilating and deforming their real nature.

REVIEW OF THE PRINCIPAL CRITICISMS OF ADAM SMITH'S THEORY*

James Anson Farrer

The result of the preceding chapter, in which the relation of
Adam Smith's theory to other ethical theories has been defined,
is that it is a theory in which all that is true in the 'selfish'
system of Hobbes or Mandeville, in the 'benevolent' system of
Hutcheson, or in the 'utilitarian' system of Hume, is adopted
and made use of, to form a system quite distinct from any one
of them. It seeks to bridge over their differences, by avoiding
the one-sidedness of their several principles, and taking a wider
view of the facts of human nature. It is therefore, properly
speaking, an Eclectic theory, if by eclecticism be understood,
not a mere commixture of different systems, but a discriminate
selection of the elements of truth to be found in them severally.

The ethical writers who most influenced Adam Smith were
undoubtedly Hume and Hutcheson, in the way of agreement
and difference that has been already indicated. Dugald Stewart
has also drawn attention to his obligations to Butler.[1] It would
be interesting to know whether he ever read Hartley's *Observations on Man*, a work which, published in 1749 – that is,
some ten years before his own – would have materially assisted
his argument. For Adam Smith's account of the growth of
conscience – of a sense of duty, is in reality closely connected
with the theory which explains its origin by the working of
the laws of association. From our experience of the constant
association between the acts of others and pleasurable or
painful feelings of our own, according as we sympathize or not
with them, comes the desire of ourselves causing in others
similar pleasurable, and avoiding similar painful, emotions –
or in other words, that desire of praise and aversion to blame
which, refined and purified by reference to an imaginary and
ideal spectator of our conduct, grows to be a conscientious
and disinterested love of virtue and detestation of vice. The

---

* From *Adam Smith* (London, 1881), chap. 14, pp. 172–201.

[1] *Active and Moral Powers*, vol. i., p. 412.

rules of moral conduct, formed as they are by generalization from particular judgments of the sympathetic instinct, or from a number of particular associations of pleasurable and painful feelings with particular acts, are themselves directly associated with that love of praise or praiseworthiness which originates in our longing for the same sympathy from other men with regard to ourselves that we know to be pleasurable in the converse relation. The word 'association' is never once used by Adam Smith, but it is implied at every step of his theory, and forms really as fundamental a feature in his reasoning as it does in that of the philosopher who was the first to investigate its laws in their application to the facts of morality. This is, perhaps, internal evidence enough that Adam Smith never saw Hartley's work.[2]

But the writer who, perhaps, as much as any other contributed to the formation of Adam Smith's ideas, seems to have been Pope, who in his *Essay on Man* anticipated many of the leading thoughts in the *Theory of Moral Sentiments*. The points of resemblance between the poet and the philosopher are frequent and obvious. There is in both the same constant appeal to nature, and to the wisdom displayed in her laws; the same reference to self-love as the basis of the social virtues and benevolence; the same identification of virtue with happiness; and the same depreciation of greatness and ambition as conducive to human felicity.

Adam Smith's simple theory of happiness, for instance, reads like a commentary on the text supplied by Pope in the lines, –

'Reason's whole pleasure, all the joys of sense,
Lie in three words – Health, Peace, and Competence.'

Said in prose, the same teaching is conveyed by the philosopher: 'What can be added to the happiness of the man who is in health, who is out of debt, and has a clear conscience?'

Or, to take another instance. Adam Smith's account of the order in which individuals are recommended by nature to our care is precisely the same as that given by Pope. Says the

---

[2] Yet in his *Essay on the External Senses*, of which the date is uncertain, and in his *History of Astronomy*, which he certainly wrote before 1758, mention is made by Adam Smith of the association of ideas. It is probable, however, that he was acquainted with the doctrine, not from Hartley, but from Hume's statement of it in the *Inquiry concerning Human Understanding*.

former: 'Every man is first and principally recommended to his own care,' and, after himself, his friends, his country, or mankind become by degrees the object of his sympathies. So said Pope before him: –

> 'God loves from whole to parts: but human soul
> Must rise from individual to the whole.
> Self-love but serves the virtuous mind to wake,
> As the small pebble stirs the peaceful lake;
> The centre moved, a circle straight succeeds
> Another still, and still another spreads;
> Friend, parent, neighbour, first it will embrace;
> His country next; and next all human race.'

To turn now from the theory itself to the criticisms upon it: it may perhaps be said, that if the importance of an ethical theory in the history of moral philosophy may be measured by the amount of criticism expended upon it, Adam Smith's *Theory of Moral Sentiments* must take its place immediately after Hume's *Enquiry concerning the Principles of Morals*. The shorter observations on it by Lord Kames and Sir James Mackintosh bear witness to the great interest that attached to it, no less than the longer criticisms of Dr. Brown, Dugald Stewart, or Jouffroy, the French moral philosopher. The various objections raised by these writers, all of whom have approached it with that impartial acuteness so characteristic of philosophers in regard to theories not their own, will best serve to illustrate what have been considered the weak points in the general theory proposed by Adam Smith. But in following the main current of such criticism, it is only fair that we should try in some measure to hold the scales between the critics and their author, and to weigh the value of the arguments that have been actually advanced on the one side and that seem capable of being advanced on the other.

First of all, it is said that the resolution of all moral approbation into sympathy really makes morality dependent on the mental constitution of each individual, and so sets up a variable standard, at the mercy of personal influences and local custom. Adam Smith says expressly indeed, that there is no other measure of moral conduct than the sympathetic approbation of each individual. 'Every faculty in one man is the measure by which he judges of the like faculty in another;' and as he judges of other men's power of sight or hearing by reference to his own, so he judges of their love, resentment, or other moral states, by reference to his own consciousness of those several affections.

Is not this to destroy the fixed character of morality, and to deprive it – as Protagoras, the Greek sophist, deprived it long ago in his similar teaching that man was the measure of all things – of its most ennobling qualities, its eternity and immutability? Is it not to reduce the rules of morality to the level merely of the rules of etiquette? Is it not to make our standard of conduct dependent merely on the ideas and passions of those we happen to live with? Does it not justify Brown's chief objection to the system of sympathy, that it fixes morality 'on a basis not sufficiently firm'?

Adam Smith's answer to this might have been, that the consideration of the basis of morality lay beyond the scope of his inquiry, and that, if he explained the principle of moral approbation by the laws of sympathy he appealed to, the facts commanded acceptance, whatever the consequences might be. He would have reasserted confidently, that no case of approbation occurred without a tacit reference to the sympathy of the approver; and that the feeling of approbation or the contrary always varied exactly with the degree of sympathy or antipathy felt for the agent. Therefore, if as a matter of fact every case of such approbation implied a reference to the feelings of the individual person approving, then those feelings were the source of moral judgment, however variable or relative morality might thus be made to appear.

He would also have denied that the consequence of his theory did really in any way weaken the basis of morality, or deprive it of its obligatory power over our conduct. The assertion of such a consequence has been perhaps the most persistent objection raised against his system. Sir James Mackintosh, for instance, makes the criticism, that 'the sympathies have nothing more of an *imperative* character than any other emotions. They attract or repel, like other feelings, according to their intensity. If, then, the sympathies, continue in mature minds to constitute the whole of conscience, it becomes utterly impossible to explain the character of command and supremacy, which is attested by the unanimous voice of mankind to belong to that faculty, and to form its essential distinction.'[3] But as, of all Adam Smith's critics, Jouffroy has been the one who has urged this argument with the greatest force, it will be best to follow his reasoning, before considering the force of the objection.

According to him, no more moral authority can attach to the instinct of sympathy than can attach to any other instinct of our nature. The desire of sympathy, being simply an instinct, can have no claim to prevail over the impulses of our other instincts, whenever they happen to come into conflict, than such as is founded on its possible greater strength. For instance, the instinct of self-love often comes into conflict with, and often prevails over, the instinct of sympathy, the motive of self-interest well-understood being thus superior to our sympathetic impulses both in fact and by right. If then there is a superiority in the instinct of sympathy above all our other instincts, it must come from a judgment of reason, decisive of its title; but since such decision of reason implies a reference to some rule other and higher than instinct, our motive in preferring the inspirations of instinctive sympathy to all other impulses must be derived from this higher motive, or, in other words, from reason and not from instinct. Hence, since the sympathetic instinct bears no signs of an authority superior to that of other instincts, there is no real authority in the motive which, according to Adam Smith, impels us to right conduct. Instead of proving that the instinct of sympathy is the true moral motive, Adam Smith describes truly and beautifully the characteristics of the moral motive, and then gratuitously attributes them to the instinct of sympathy. But he fails to apply to rules of conduct founded upon such an instinct, that which is the special characteristic of the moral motive, namely, that it alone is obligatory – alone presents us, as an end to be pursued, an end which *ought* to be pursued, as distinct from other ends suggested by other motives, which may be pursued or not as we please. 'Among all possible motives, the moral motive alone appears to us as one that *ought* to govern our conduct.'

Jouffroy applies the same reasoning to Adam Smith's explanation of our moral ideas, those, for example, of *Right* and *Duty*. For if the motive of sympathy bears with it no authority,

[3] *Progress of Ethical Philosophy*, p. 240; compare also Dugald Stewart's *Active and Moral Powers*, vol. i., p. 331.

it is evident that it cannot explain ideas both of which imply and involve a motive of obligation. If duty is obedience to rules of conduct that have been produced by sympathy, and these rules are only generalizations of particular judgments of instinctive sympathy, it is plain that the authority of these rules can be no greater than that of the judgments which originally gave rise to them. If it is equally a duty to obey the instinct as to obey the rules it gives rise to, it is superfluous to explain duty as a sense of the authority of these rules, seeing that it is already involved in the process of their formation. And if again it can never be a duty to obey the instinct, because neither its direction nor the desire of sympathy which impels us to follow it can ever be obligatory, it can none the more be a duty to obey the rules which are founded upon the instinct. The authority of the moral rules or principles of conduct stands or falls with the authority of the instinct; for if the latter can enforce obligation to a certain degree, it can enforce it in all degrees; and if it cannot enforce it to this degree, then it cannot in any. It is therefore Jouffroy's conclusion, that 'there is not, in the system of Smith, any such thing as a moral law; and it is incompetent to explain our ideas of duty, of right, and of all other such ideas as imply the fact of obligation.'[4]

The question then is, How far is such criticism well-founded? How far is it relevant to the subject-matter of Adam Smith's treatise?

Adam Smith might have replied to Jouffroy's objections by asking whether, putting aside the question of the soundness of his theory of the origin of moral approbation, any theory that accounted for the approbation did not *ipso facto* account for the obligation. He might have said that, if he showed why one course of conduct was regarded as good and another as bad, he implicitly showed why one course was felt to be right and the other to be wrong – why it was felt that one course ought to be followed and the other course ought to be avoided. For the feeling of authority and obligation is involved in the fact of approbation. As it has been well put by Brown, 'The very conceptions of the rectitude, the obligation, the approvableness (of certain actions) are involved in the feeling of the approbation itself. It is impossible for us to have the feeling, and

---

[4] *Introduction to Ethics;* translation, vol. ii., p. 147.

not to have these. . . . To know that we should feel ourselves unworthy of self-esteem, and objects rather of self-abhorrence, if we did not act in a certain manner, is to feel the moral obligation to act in a certain manner, as it is to feel the moral rectitude of the action itself. We are so constituted that it is impossible for us, in certain circumstances, not to have this feeling; and having the feeling, we must have the notions of virtue, obligation, merit.'[5]

Moreover, Adam Smith expressly pointed out that the difference between *moral* approbation and approbation of all other kinds lay in the impossibility of our being as indifferent about *conduct* as about other things, because conduct, either directly or by our imagination, affected ourselves; so that the additional strength thus conferred on the feeling of *moral* approbation was quite sufficient to account for that feeling of the imperative and obligatory force which inculcates obedience to moral rules. If there is no authority in an instinct *per se*, it may nevertheless be so constituted and may so operate that the strictest sense of duty may ultimately grow from it and upon it. The obligation is none the less real because it can be accounted for; nor are the claims of duty any the less substantial because they are capable of being traced to so humble a beginning as an instinctive desire for the sympathy of our fellows.

It may therefore be said, on behalf of Adam Smith, that it is not to weaken the basis of morality, nor the authority of conscience, to trace either of them to their sources in sentiments of sympathy, originally influenced by pleasure and pain. The obligatory nature of moral rules remains a fact, which no theory of their origin can alter or modify; just as benevolent affections remain facts of our moral being, irrespective of their possible superstructure on instincts of self-interest. If conscience is explicable as a kind of generalization or summary of moral sympathies, formed by the observation of the distribution of praise or blame in a number of particular instances and by personal experience of many years, its influence need be none the less great nor its control any the less authoritative than if it were proved to demonstration to be a primary principle of our moral consciousness.

It is also necessary to remember that Adam Smith carefully

[5] *Lectures on Ethics*, p. 13.

restricted the feeling of obligation to the one single virtue of justice, and throughout his treatise avoided generally the use of words which, like 'right' and 'wrong,' seem to suggest the idea of obligation. By the use of the words 'proper' and 'improper,' or 'meritorious,' as applied to sentiments and conduct, he seems to have wished to convey the idea that he did regard morality as relative to time, place, and circumstance, as to a certain extent due to custom and convention, and not as absolute, eternal, or immutable. Properly speaking, justice, or the abstinence from injury to others, was, he held, the only virtue which, as men had a right to exact it from us, it was our *duty* to practise towards them. The consciousness that force might be employed to make us act according to the rules of justice, but not according to the rules of any other virtues, such as friendship, charity, or generosity, was the source of the stricter obligation felt by us in reference to the virtue of justice. 'We feel ourselves,' he said, 'to be in a peculiar manner tied, bound, and obliged to the observation of justice,' whilst the practice of the other virtues 'seems to be left in some measure to our own choice.' 'In the practice of the other virtues, our conduct should rather be directed by a certain kind of propriety, by a certain taste for a particular tenor of conduct, than by any regard to a precise rule or maxim;' but it is otherwise with regard to justice, all the rules of which are precise, definite, and certain, and alone admit of no exception.

As to the authority of our moral faculties, of our perception, howsoever derived, of different qualities in conduct, it is, in Adam Smith's system, an ultimate fact, as indisputable as the authority of other faculties over their respective objects; for example, as the authority of the eye about beauty of colour, or as that of the ear about harmony of sounds. 'Our moral faculties, our natural sense of merit and propriety,' approve or disapprove of actions instantaneously, and this approval or judgment in their peculiar function. They judge of the other faculties and principles of our nature; how far, for example, love or resentment ought either to be indulged or restrained, and when the various senses ought to be gratified. Hence they cannot be said to be on a level with our other natural faculties and appetites, and endowed with no more right to restrain the latter than the latter are to restrain them. There can be no more appeal from them about their objects than there is from the eye, or the ear, or the taste with regard to the objects of their several jurisdictions. According as anything is agreeable or not to them, is it fit, right, and proper, or unfit, wrong, and improper. 'The sentiments which they approve of are graceful and becoming; the contrary, ungraceful and unbecoming. The very words, right, wrong, fit, proper, graceful, or becoming, mean only what pleases or displeases those faculties.'

Hence the question of the authority of our moral faculties is as futile as the question of the authority of the special senses over their several objects. For 'they carry along with them the most evident badges of this authority, which denote that they were set up within us to be the supreme arbiter of all our actions, to superintend all our senses, passions, and appetites, and to judge how far either of them was either to be indulged or restrained.' That is to say, it is impossible for our moral faculties to approve of one course of conduct and to disapprove of another, and at the same time to feel that there is no authority in the sentiment which passes judgment either way.

Perhaps the part of Adam Smith's theory which has given least satisfaction is his account of the ethical standard, or measure of moral actions. This, it will be remembered, is none other than the sympathetic emotion of the impartial spectator – which seems again to resolve itself into the voice of public opinion. It will be of interest to follow some of the criticism that has been devoted to this point, most of which turns on the meaning of the word *impartial*.

If impartiality means, argues Jouffroy, as alone it can mean, impartiality of judgment, the impartiality of a spectator must be the impartiality of his reason, which rises superior to the suggestions of his instincts or passions; but if so, a moral judgment no longer arises from a mere instinct of sympathy, but from an operation of reason. If instinct is adopted as our rule of moral conduct, there must be some higher rule by which we make choice of some impulses against the influence of others; and the impartiality requisite in sympathy is itself a recognition of the insufficiency of instinctive feelings to supply moral rules.

It may be said, in reply to this, that by impartiality Adam Smith meant neither an impartiality of reason nor of instinct, but simply the indifference or coolness of a mind that feels not the full strength of the original passion, which it shares, and which it shares in a due and just degree precisely because it feels it not directly but by reflection. If the resentment of A.

can only fairly be estimated by the power of B. to sympathize with it, the latter is only impartial in so far as his feeling of resentment is reflected and not original. His feeling of approbation or disapprobation of A.'s resentment need be none the less a feeling, none the less instinctive and emotional, because he is exempt from the vividness of the passion as it affects his friend. It is simply that exemption, Adam Smith would say, which enables him to judge; and whether his judgment is for that reason to be considered final and right or not, it is, as a matter of fact, the only way in which a moral judgment is possible at all.

The next objection of Jouffroy, that the sympathy of an impartial spectator affords only variable rules of morality, Adam Smith would have met by the answer, that the rules of morality are to a certain extent variable, and dependent on custom. Jouffroy supposes himself placed as an entire stranger in the presence of a quantity of persons of different ages, sexes, and professions, and then asks, how should he judge of the propriety of any emotion on his part by reference to the very different sympathies which such an emotion would arouse. Lively sensibilities would partake of his emotions vividly, cold ones but feebly. The sympathies of the men would be different from those of the women, those of the young from those of the old, those of the merchant from those of the soldier, and so forth. To this it might fairly be replied, that as a matter of fact there are very few emotions with which different people do not sympathize in very different degrees, and of which accordingly they do not entertain very different feelings of moral approbation or the reverse. Each man's sympathy is in fact his only measure of the propriety of other men's sentiments, and for that reason it is that there is scarcely any single moral action of which any two men adopt the same moral sentiment. That morality is relative and not absolute, Adam Smith nowhere denies. Nevertheless, he would say, there is sufficient uniformity in the laws of sympathy, directed and controlled as they are by custom, to make the rule of general sympathy or of the abstract spectator a sufficiently permanent standard of conduct.

It is moreover a fact, which no one has explained better than Adam Smith, in his account of the growth in every individual of the virtue of self-command, that though our moral estimate of our own conduct begins by reference to the sympathy of particular individuals, our parents, schoolfellows, or others, we yet end by judging ourselves, not by reference to any one in particular so much as from an abstract idea of general approbation or the contrary, derived from our experience of particular judgments in the course of our life. This is all that is meant by 'the abstract spectator,' reference to whom is simply the same as reference to the supposed verdict of public opinion. If we have done anything wrong, told a lie, for example, the self-condemnation we pass on ourselves is the condemnation of public opinion, with which we identify ourselves by long force of habit; and had we never heard a lie condemned, nor known it punished, we should feel no self-condemnation whatever in telling one. We condemn it, not by reference, as Jouffroy puts it, to the feelings of John or Peter, but by reference to the feelings of the general world, which we know to be made up of people like John and Peter. There is nothing inconsistent therefore in the notion of an abstract spectator, 'who has neither the prejudices of the one nor the weaknesses of the other, and who sees correctly and soundly precisely because he is abstract.' The identification of this abstract spectator with conscience, is so far from being, as Jouffroy says it is, a departure from, and an abandonment of the rule of sympathy, that it is its logical and most satisfactory development. There is no reason to repeat the process by which the perception of particular approving sympathies passes into identification with the highest rules of morality and the most sacred dictates of religion. By reference to his own experience, every reader may easily test for himself the truth or falsity of Adam Smith's argument upon this subject.

It is said with truth, that to make the judgment of an impartial or abstract spectator the standard of morality is to make no security against fallibility of judgment; and that such a judgment is only efficacious where there is tolerable unanimity, but that it fails in the face of possible differences of opinion. But this objection is equally true of any ethical standard ever yet propounded in the world, whether self-interest, the greatest possible happiness, the will of the sovereign, the fitness of things, or any other principle is suggested as the ultimate test of rectitude of conduct. This part of the theory may claim, therefore, not only to be as good as any other theory, but to be in strict keeping with the vast amount of variable moral sentiment which actually exists in the world.

In further disproof of Adam Smith's theory, Jouffroy appeals to consciousness. We are not conscious, he says, in judging of the acts of others, that we measure them by reference to our ability to sympathize with them. So far are we from doing this, that we consider it our first duty to stifle our emotions of sympathy or antipathy, in order to arrive at an impartial judgment. As regards our own emotions, also, there is no such recourse to the sympathies of others; and even when there is, we often prefer our own judgment after all to that which we know to be the judgment of others. Consciousness therefore attests the falsity of the theory that we seek in our own sensibility the judgments we pass upon others, or that we seek in the opinions of others the principle of estimation for our own sentiments and conduct.

The truth of the fact stated in this objection may evidently be conceded, and yet the validity of the main theory be left untouched. The latter is a theory mainly of the origin of moral feelings, and of their growth; and emotions of sympathy which originally give rise to moral feelings may well disappear and be absent when long habit has once fixed them in the mind. It is quite conceivable, for instance, that if we originally derived our moral notions of our own conduct from constant observation of the conduct of others, we might yet come to judge ourselves by a standard apparently unconnected with any reference to other people, and yet really made up of a number of forgotten judgments passed by us upon them. Children are always taught to judge themselves by appeals to the sentiments of their parents or other relations about their conduct; and though the standard of morality, thus external at first, may in time come to be internal, and even to be more potent than when it was external, it none the more follows that recourse to such sympathy never took place because it ceases to take place or to be noticed when the moral sentiments are fully formed. In learning to read and write, an exactly analogous process may be traced. The letters which so painfully affected our consciousness at first, when we had to make constant reference to the alphabet, cease at last to affect it at all; yet the process of spelling really goes on in the mind in every word we read or write, however unconscious we may be of its operation. Habit and experience, says Adam Smith, teach us so easily and so readily to view our own interests and those of others from the standpoint of a third person, that 'we are scarce sensible' of such a process at all.

Then again, the question has been raised, Is it true that sympathy with an agent or with the object of his action is a necessary antecedent to all moral approbation or the contrary?

It is objected, for instance, by Brown, that sympathy is not a perpetual accompaniment of our observation of all the actions that take place in life, and that many cases occur in which we feel approval or disapproval, in which consequently moral estimates are made, and yet without any preceding sympathy or antipathy. 'In the number of petty affairs which are hourly before our eyes, what sympathy if felt,' he asks, 'either with those who are actively or with those who are passively concerned, when the agent himself performs his little offices with emotions as slight as those which the objects of his actions reciprocally feel? Yet in these cases we are as capable of judging, and approve or disapprove – not with the same liveliness of emotion indeed, but with as accurate estimation of merit or demerit – as when we consider the most heroic sacrifices which the virtuous can make, or the most atrocious crimes of which the sordid and the cruel can be guilty.' There must be the same sympathy in the case of the humblest action we denominate right as in that of the most glorious action; yet such actions often excite no sympathy whatever. Unless therefore the common transactions of life are to be excluded altogether from morality, from the field of right and wrong, it is impossible to ascribe such moral qualities to them, if sympathy is the source of our approval of them.

To this objection, founded on the non-universality of sympathy, and on its not being coextensive with feelings of moral approbation, Adam Smith might have replied, that there was no action, howsoever humble, denominated right, in which there was not or had not been to start with a reference to sentiments of sympathy. It is impossible to conceive any case in the most trivial department of life in which approbation on the ground of goodness may not be explained by reference to such feelings. Brown himself lays indeed less stress on this argument than on another which has, it must be confessed, much greater force.

That is, that the theory of sympathy assumes as already existing those moral feelings which it professes to explain. If, he says, no moral sentiments preceded a feeling of sympathy, the latter could no more produce them than a mirror, without pre-existence and pre-supposition of light, could reflect the beautiful colours of a landscape.

If we had no principle of moral approbation previous to sympathy, the most perfect sympathy or accordance of passions would prove nothing more than a mere agreement of feeling; nor should we be aware of anything more than in any case of coincidence of feeling with regard to mere objects of taste, such as a picture or an air of music. It is not because we sympathize with the sentiments of an agent that we account them moral, but it is because his moral sentiments agree with our own that we sympathize with them. The morality is there before the sympathy. If we regard sentiments which differ from our own, not merely as unlike our own, but as morally improper and wrong, we must first have conceived our own to be morally proper and right, by which we measure those of others. Without this previous belief in the moral propriety of our own sentiments, we could never judge of the propriety or impropriety of others, nor regard them as morally unsuitable to the circumstances out of which they arose. Hence the sympathy from which we are said to derive our notions of propriety or the contrary assumes independently of sympathy the very feelings it is said to occasion.

A similar criticism Brown also applies to that sympathy with the gratitude of persons who have received benefits or injuries which is said to be the source of feelings of merit and demerit. If it is true that our sense of the merit of an agent is due to our sympathy with the gratitude of those he has benefited – if the sympathy only transfuses into our own breasts the gratitude or resentment of persons so affected, it is evident that our reflected gratitude or resentment can only give rise to the same sense of merit or demerit that has been already involved in the primary and direct gratitude or resentment. 'If our reflex gratitude and resentment involve notions of merit and demerit, the original gratitude and resentment which we feel by reflexion must in like manner have involved them. . . . But if the actual gratitude or resentment of those who have profited or suffered imply no feelings of merit or demerit, we may be certain, at least, that in whatever source we are to strive to discover those feelings, it is not in the mere reflexion of a fainter gratitude of resentment that we can hope to find them. . . . The feelings with which we sympathize are themselves moral feelings or sentiments; or if they are not moral feelings, the reflexion of them from a thousand breasts cannot alter their nature.'

Unless therefore we already possessed moral feelings of our own, the most exact sympathy of feelings could do no more than tell us of the similarity of our own feelings to those of some other person, which they might equally do whether they were vicious or virtuous; and in the same way, the most complete dissonance of feeling could supply us with no more than a consciousness of the dissimilarity of our emotions. As a coincidence of taste with regard to a work of art pre-supposes in any two minds similarly affected by it an independent susceptibility of emotions, distinguishing what is beautiful from what is ugly, irrespectively of others being present to share them; so a coincidence of feeling with regard to any moral action pre-supposes an independent capacity in the two minds similarly affected by them of distinguishing what is right from what is wrong, a capacity which each would have singly, irrespectively of all reference to the feelings of the other. There is something more that we recognize in our moral sentiments than the mere coincidence of feeling recognized in an agreement of taste or opinion. We feel that a person has acted not merely as we should have done, and that his motives have been similar to those we should have felt, but that he has acted rightly and properly.

It is perhaps best to state Brown's criticism in his own words: 'All which is peculiar to the sympathy is, that instead of one mind only affected with certain feelings, there are two minds affected with certain feelings, and a recognition of the similarity of these feelings; a similarity which far from being confined to our moral emotions, may occur as readily and as frequently in every other feeling of which the mind is susceptible. What produces the moral notions therefore must evidently be something more than a recognition of similarity of feeling which is thus common to feelings of every class. There must be an independent capacity of moral emotion, in consequence of which we judge those sentiments of conduct to be right which coincide with sentiments of conduct previously recognized as right – or the sentiments of others to be improper, because they are not in unison with those which we previously recognized as proper. Sympathy then may be the diffuser of moral sentiments, as of various other feelings; but if no moral sentiments exist previously to our sympathy, our sympathy itself cannot give rise to them.'

The same inconsistency Brown detects in Adam Smith's theory of moral sentiments relating to our own conduct, according to which it would be impossible for us to distinguish without reference to the feelings of a real or imaginary spectator any difference of propriety or impropriety, merit or demerit, in our own actions or character. If an impartial spectator can thus discover merit or demerit in us by making our case his own and assuming our feelings, those feelings which he thus makes his own must surely speak to us to the same purpose, and with even greater effect than they speak to him. In no case then can sympathy give any additional knowledge: it can only give a wider diffusion to feelings which already exist.

It is therefore, according to Brown, as erroneous in ethics to ascribe moral feelings to sympathy, or the mental reflection by which feelings are diffused, as it would be, in a theory of the source of light, to ascribe light itself to the reflection which involves its existence. 'A mirror presents to us a fainter copy of external things; but it is a copy which it presents. We are in like manner to each other mirrors that reflect from breast to breast, joy, sorrow, indignation, and all the vivid emotions of which the individual mind is susceptible; but though, as mirrors, we mutually give and receive emotions, these emotions must have been felt before they could be communicated.'

The objection contained in this analogy of the mirror is perhaps more fatal to the truth of Adam Smith's theory than any other. If a passion arises in every one analogous to, though weaker than, the original passion of the person primarily affected by it; if, for instance, by this force of fellow-feeling we enter into or approve of another person's resentment or gratitude; it seems clear that the original gratitude or resentment must itself involve, irrespective of all sympathy, those feelings of moral approbation, or the contrary, which it is asserted can only arise by sympathy. It is impossible to state this objection more clearly than in the words already quoted from Brown. But when the latter insists on the irregular nature of sympathy as the basis of morality – on its tendency to vary even in the same individual many times in the day, so that what was virtuous in the morning might seem vicious at noon, it is impossible to recognize the justice of the criticism. Adam

Smith might fairly have replied, that the educational forces of life, which are comprised in ordinary circumstances and surroundings, and which condition all sympathy, were sufficiently uniform in character to ensure tolerable uniformity in the result, and to give to our notions of morality all that appearance of certainty and sameness which undoubtedly belongs to them.

Adam Smith seems himself to have anticipated one of the difficulties raised in Brown's criticism, namely, the relation of moral approbation to the approbation of another person's taste or opinions. Why should the feeling of approbation be of a different kind when we sympathize with a person's sentiments or actions than when we sympathize with his intellectual judgments? The *feeling* of sympathy being the same in either case, why should the feeling of resultant *approbation* be different?

No one could state more clearly than does Adam Smith the analogy there is between coincidence of moral sentiment and coincidence of intellectual opinion; nor is anything more definite in his theory than that approval of the moral sentiments of others, like approval of their opinions, means nothing more than their agreement with our own. The following are his words: 'To approve of another man's opinions is to adopt those opinions, and to adopt them is to approve of them. If the same arguments which convince you convince me likewise, I necessarily approve of your conviction; and if they do not, I necessarily disapprove of it; neither can I possibly conceive that I should do the one without the other. To approve or disapprove, therefore, of the opinions is acknowledged by everybody to mean no more than to observe their agreement or disagreement with our own. But this is equally the case with regard to our approbation or disapprobation of the sentiments or passions of others.'

Whence, then, comes the stronger feeling of approbation in the case of agreement of sentiments than in that of agreement of opinion? Why do we esteem a man whose moral sentiments seem to accord with our own, whilst we do not necessarily esteem him simply for the accordance of his opinions with our own? Why in the one case do we ascribe to him the quality of rightness or rectitude, and in the other only the qualities of good taste or good judgment? To quote Brown once more: 'If mere accordance of emotion imply the feeling of moral excellence of any sort, we should certainly feel a moral regard for all whose taste coincides with ours; yet, however gratifying the sympathy in such a case may be, we do not feel, in consequence of this sympathy, any morality in the taste which is most exactly accordant with our own.'

Adam Smith's answer is, that matters of intellectual agreement touch us much less nearly than circumstances of behaviour which affect ourselves or the person we judge of; that we look at such things as the size of a mountain or the expression of a picture from the same point of view, and therefore that we agree or disagree without that imaginary change of situation which is the foundation of moral sympathy. The stronger feeling of approbation in the one case than in the other arises from the personal element, which influences our judgment of another person's conduct, and which is absent in our judgment of his opinions about things. It will be best again to let Adam Smith speak for himself.

'Though,' he says, 'you despise that picture, or that poem, or even that system of philosophy which I admire, there is little danger of our quarrelling upon that account. Neither of us can reasonably be much interested about them. They ought all of them to be matters of great indifference to us both; so that, though our opinions may be opposite, our affections may still be very nearly the same. But it is quite otherwise with regard to those objects by which either you or I are particularly affected. Though your judgments in matters of speculation, though your sentiments in matters of taste, are quite opposite to mine, I can easily overlook this opposition; and, if I have any degree of temper, I may still find some entertainment in your conversation, even upon those very subjects. But if you have either no fellow-feeling for the misfortunes I have met with, or none which bears any proportion to the grief which distracts me; or if you have either no indignation at the injuries I have suffered, or none that bears any proportion to the resentment which transports me, we can no longer converse upon these subjects. We become intolerable to one another. I can neither support your company, nor you mine. You are confounded at my violence and passion, and I am enraged at your cold insensibility and want of feeling.'

Accordingly, we only regard the sentiments which we share as moral, or the contrary, when they affect another person or ourselves in a peculiar manner; when they bear no relation to either of us, no moral propriety is recognized in a mere agreement of feeling. It is obvious that this explanation, to which Brown pays no attention whatever, is satisfactory to a certain point. A plain, or a mountain, or a picture, are matters about which it is intelligible that agreement or difference should give rise to very different feelings from those produced by a case of dishonesty, excessive anger, or untruthfulness. Being objects so different in their nature, it is only natural that they should give rise to very different sentiments. Independently of all sympathy, admiration of a picture or a mountain is a very different thing from admiration of a generous action or a display of courage. The language of all men has observed the difference, and the admiration in the one case is with perfect reason called *moral*, to distinguish it from the admiration which arises in the other. But when Adam Smith classes 'the conduct of a third person' among things which, like the beauty of a plain or the size of a mountain, need no imaginary change of situation on the part of observers to be approved of by them, he inadvertently deserts his own principle, which, if this were true, would fail to account for the approbation of actions done long ago, in times or places unrelated to the approver.

But, even if Adam Smith's explanation with regard to the difference of approbation felt where conduct is concerned from that felt in matters of taste or opinion be accepted as satisfactory, it is strange that he should not have seen the difficulty of accounting by his theory for the absence of anything like moral approbation in a number of cases where sympathy none the less strongly impels us to share and enter into the emotions of another person. For instance, if we see a man in imminent danger of his life – pursued by a bull or seeming to fall from a tight rope – though we may fully sympathize with his real or pretended fear, in neither case do we for that reason morally approve of it. In the same way, we may sympathize with or enter into any other emotion he manifests – his love, his hope, or his joy – without any the more approving them or passing any judgment on them whatever. Sympathy has been well defined as 'a species of involuntary imitation of the displays of feeling enacted in our presence, which is followed by the rise of the feelings themselves.'[6] Thus we become affected with whatever the mental state may be that is manifested by the expressed feelings of another person; but unless his emotion

---

[6] Bain, *Mental and Moral Science*, p. 277.

already contains the element of moral approbation, or the contrary, as in a case of gratitude or resentment, the mere fact of sympathy will no more give rise to it than will sympathy with another person's fear give rise to any moral approval of it. It is evident, therefore, that sympathy does not necessarily involve approbation, and that it only involves *moral* approbation where the sentiments shared by sympathy belong to the class of emotions denominated *moral*.

What, then, is the real relation between sympathy and approbation? and to what extent is the fact of sympathy an explanation of the fact of approbation.

It is difficult to read Adam Smith's account of the identification of sympathy and approbation, without feeling that throughout his argument there is an unconscious play upon words, and that an equivocal use of the word 'sympathy' lends all its speciousness to the theory he expounds. The first meaning of the word sympathy is fellow-feeling, or the participation of another person's emotion, in which sense we may be said to sympathize with another person's hope or fear; the second meaning contains the idea of approval or praise, in which sense we may be said to sympathize with another person's gratitude or resentment. Adam Smith begins by using the word sympathy in its first and primary sense, as meaning participation in another person's feelings, and then proceeds to use it in its secondary and less proper sense, in which the idea of approbation is involved. But the sympathy in the one case is totally different from the sympathy in the other. In the one case a mere state of feeling is intended, in the other a judgment of reason. To share another person's feeling belongs only to our sensibility; to approve of it as proper, good, and right, implies the exercise of our intelligence. To employ the word 'sympathy' in its latter use (as it is sometimes employed in popular parlance) is simply to employ it as a synonym for 'approbation;' so that sympathy instead of being really the source of approbation, is only another word for that approbation itself. To say that we approve of another person's sentiments when we sympathize with them is, therefore, nothing more than saying that we approve of them when we approve of them – a purely tautological proposition.

It cannot therefore be said that Adam Smith's attempt to trace the feeling of moral approbation to emotions of sympathy is altogether successful, incontestable as is the truth of his application of it to many of the phenomena of life and conduct. Yet although sympathy is not the only factor in moral approbation, it is one that enters very widely into the growth of our moral perceptions. It plays, for instance, an important part in evolving in us that sense of right and wrong which is generally known as Conscience or the Moral Faculty. It is one of the elements, just as self-love is another, in that ever-forming chain of association which goes to distinguish one set of actions as good from another set of actions as bad. Our observation in others of the same outward symptoms which we know in our own case to attend joy or grief, pleasure or pain, leads us by the mere force of the remembrance of our own pleasures and pains, and independently of any control of our will, to enter into those of other people, and to promote as much as we can the one and prevent the other.

Sympathy accordingly is the source of all disinterested motives in action, of our readiness to give up pleasures and incur pains for the sake of others; and Adam Smith was so far right, that he established, by reference to this force of our sympathetic emotions, the reality of a disinterested element as the foundation of our benevolent affections. In the same way, self-love is the source of all the prudential side of morality; and to the general formation of our moral sentiments, all our other emotions, such as anger, fear, love, contribute together with sympathy, in lesser perhaps but considerable degree. None of them taken singly would suffice to account for moral approbation.

Although any action that hurts another person may so affect our natural sympathy as to give rise to the feeling of disapprobation involved in sympathetic resentment, and although an action that is injurious to ourselves may also be regarded with similar feelings of dislike, the constant pressure of authority, exercised as it is by domestic education, by government, by law, and by punishment, must first be brought to bear on such actions before the feeling of *moral* disapprobation can arise with regard to them. The association of the pain of punishment with certain actions, and the association of the absence of such pain (a negative pleasure) with certain others, enforces the natural dictates of our sympathetic or selfish emotions, and impresses on them the character of morality, of obligation, and of duty. The association is so close and constant, that in course of time the feeling of the approbation or disapprobation of certain actions becomes perfectly independent of the various means, necessary at first to enforce or to prevent them; just as in many other cases our likes and dislikes become free of the associations which first permanently fixed them.

In this way the feeling of moral approbation is seen to be the product of time and slow growth of circumstance, a phenomenon to which both reason and sentiment contribute in equal shares in accordance with the laws that condition their development. Moral approbation is no more given instantaneously by sympathy than it is given instantaneously by a moral sense. Sympathy is merely one of the conditions under which it is evolved, one of the feelings which assist in its formation. It is indeed the feeling on which, more than on any other, the moral agencies existing in the world build up and confirm the notions of right and wrong; but it does of itself nothing more than translate feelings from one mind to another, and unless there is a pre-existent moral element in the feeling so translated, the actual passage will not give rise to it. Sympathy enables one man's fear, resentment, or gratitude to become another man's fear, resentment, or gratitude; but the feeling of moral approbation which attends emotions so diffused, arises from reference to ideas otherwise derived than from a purely involuntary sympathy – from reference, that is, to a standard set up by custom and opinion. A child told for the first time of a murder might so far enter by sympathy into the resentment of the victim as to feel indignation prompting him to vengeance; but his idea of the murder itself as a wrong and wicked act – his idea of it as a deed morally worse than the slaughter of a sheep by a butcher, would only arise as the result of the various forces of education, availing themselves of the original law of sympathy, by which an act disagreeable to ourselves seems disagreeable in its application to others. And what is true in this case, the extreme form of moral disapprobation, is no less true in all the minor cases, in which approbation or the contrary is felt.

The feeling of moral approbation is therefore much more complex than it is in Adam Smith's theory. Above all things it is one and indivisible, and it is impossible to distinguish our moral judgments of ourselves from our judgments of others. There is an obvious inconsistency in saying that we can only judge of other people's sentiments and actions by reference to our own power to sympathize with them, and yet that we can only judge of our own by reference to the same power in them. The moral standard cannot primarily exist in ourselves, and yet, at the same time, be only derivable from without. If by the hypothesis moral feelings relating to ourselves only exist by prior reference to the feelings of others, how can we at the same time form any moral judgment of the feelings of others by reference to any feelings of our own?

But although the two sides of moral feeling are thus really indistinguishable, the feeling of self-approbation or the contrary may indeed be so much stronger than our feeling of approval or disapproval of others as to justify the application to it of such terms as Conscience, Shame, Remorse. The difference of feeling, however, is only one of degree, and in either case, whether our own conduct or that of others is under review, the moral feeling that arises is due to the force of education and opinion acting upon the various emotions of our nature. For instance, a Mohammedan woman seen without a veil would have the same feeling of remorse or moral disapprobation with regard to herself that she would have with regard to any other woman whom she might see in the same condition, though of course in a less strong degree. In either case her feeling would be a result of all the complex surroundings of her life, which is meant by education in its broadest sense. Sympathy itself would be insufficient to explain the feeling, though it might help to explain how it was developed. All that sympathy could do would be to extend the dread of punishment associated by the woman herself with a breach of the law, to all women who might offend in a similar way; the original feeling of the immorality of exposure being accountable for in no other way than by its association with punishment, ordained by civil or religious law, or by social custom, and enforced by the discipline of early home life. It is obvious that the same explanation applies to all cases in which moral disapprobation is felt, and conversely to all cases in which the sentiment of moral approbation arises.

KEY ISSUES

Series Editor: **Andrew Pyle,** *University of Bristol*

The *Key Issues* series makes available the contemporary reactions that met important books and debates on their first appearance.
Examining the range of contemporary literature – journal articles and reviews, book extracts, public letters, sermons and pamphlets – *Key Issues* gives the reader an essential insight into the historical, social and political context in which a key publication or particular topic emerged.
Each text has a new editorial introduction to supply the necessary historical background.

Liberty
Contemporary Responses to John Stuart Mill
Edited and introduced by **Andrew Pyle,** *University of Bristol*

PHILOSOPHY, POLITICS
ISBN 1 85506 244 5 : 466pp : Hb : 1994 : £45.00 $24.95
ISBN 1 85506 245 3 : 466pp : Pb : 1994 : £14.95 $72.00

Population
Contemporary Responses to Thomas Malthus
Edited and introduced by **Andrew Pyle,** *University of Bristol*

ECONOMICS, POLITICS, SOCIAL HISTORY
ISBN 1 85506 344 1 : 320pp: Hb : 1994 : £40.00 $24.95
ISBN 1 85506 345 X: 320pp : Pb: 1994 : £13.95 $72.00

Group Rights
Perspectives Since 1900
Edited and introduced by **Julia Stapleton,** *University of Durham*

SOCIOLOGY, POLITICS
ISBN 1 85506 403 0 : 360pp : Hb : 1995 : £45.00 £24.95
ISBN 1 85506 402 2 : 360pp : Pb : 1995 : £14.95 $72.00

Agnosticism
Contemporary Responses to Spencer and Huxley
Edited and introduced by **Andrew Pyle**, *University of Bristol*

PHILOSOPHY, THEOLOGY
ISBN 1 85506 405 7 : 328pp : Hb : 1995 : £45.00 **$24.95**
ISBN 1 85506 404 9 : 328pp : Pb 1995 : £14.95 **$72.00**

Leviathan
Contemporary Responses to the Political Theory of Thomas Hobbes
Edited and introduced by **G. A. J. Rogers**, *Keele University*

PHILOSOPHY, POLITICS
ISBN 1 85506 407 3 : 317pp : Hb : 1995 : £45.00 **$24.95**
ISBN 1 85506 406 5 : 317pp : Pb : 1995 : £14.95 **$72.00**

The Subjection of Women
Contemporary Responses to John Stuart Mill
Edited and introduced by **Andrew Pyle**, *University of Bristol*

PHILOSOPHY, POLITICS, HISTORY OF FEMINISM
ISBN 1 85506 409 X : 340pp : Hb : 1995 : £45.00 **$24.95**
ISBN 1 85506 408 1 : 340pp : Pb : 1995 : £14.95 **$72.00**

The Origin of Language
Edited and introduced by **Roy Harris**, *University of Oxford*

LANGUAGE, ANTHROPOLOGY
ISBN 1 85506 438 3 : 344pp : Hb : £45.00 **$24.95**
ISBN 1 85506 437 5 : 344pp : Pb : £14.95 **$72.00**

Pure Experience
The Response to William James
Edited and introduced by **Eugene Taylor** and **Robert H. Wozniak**,
Harvard University & Bryn Mawr College, Pennsylvania

PSYCHOLOGY, PHILOSOPHY
ISBN 1 85506 413 8 : 294pp : Hb : £45.00 **£24.95**
ISBN 1 85506 412 X : 294pp : Pb : £14.95 **$72.00**

Gender and Science
Late Nineteenth-Century Debates on the Female Mind and Body
Edited and introduced by **Katharina Rowold,**
Wellcome Institute, London

GENDER, HISTORY OF SCIENCE
ISBN 1 85506 411 1 : 310pp : Hb : £45.00 **$24.95**
ISBN 1 85506 410 3 : 310pp : Pb : £14.95 **$72.00**

Free Trade
The Repeal of the Corn Laws
Edited and introduced by **Cheryl Schonhardt-Bailey,** LSE

POLITICS, ECONOMICS, BRITISH HISTORY
ISBN 1 85506 446 4 : 340pp : Hb : £45.00 **$24.95**
ISBN 1 85506 445 6 : 340pp : Pb : £14.95 **$72.00**

Hume on Miracles
Edited and introduced by **Stanley Tweyman,** *York University, Toronto*

PHILOSOPHY, THEOLOGY
ISBN 1 85506 444 8 : 190pp : Hb : £45.00 **$24.95**
ISBN 1 85506 443 X : 190pp : Pb : £14.95 **$72.00**

Hume on Natural Religion
Edited and introduced by **Stanley Tweyman,** *York University, Toronto*

PHILOSOPHY, THEOLOGY
ISBN 1 85506 451 0 : 352pp : Hb : £45.00 **$24.95**
ISBN 1 85506 450 2 : 352pp : Pb : £14.95 **$72.00**

Herbert Spencer and the Limits of the State
Contemporary Responses to Spencer's The Man Versus the State
Edited and introduced by **Michael Taylor,** *London Guildhall University*

POLITICS, PHILOSOPHY, SOCIOLOGY
ISBN 1 85506 453 7 : 296pp : Hb : £45.00 **$24.95**
ISBN 1 85506 452 9 : 296pp : Pb : £14.95 **$72.00**

Race: The Origins of an Idea, 1760–1850
Edited and introduced by **Hannah Augstein,**
Wellcome Institute, London

ANTHROPOLOGY, POLITICS
ISBN 1 85506 455 3 : 294pp : Hb : £45.00 $24.95
ISBN 1 85506 454 5 : 294pp : Pb : £14.95 $72.00

Religious Scepticism
Contemporary Responses to Gibbon
Edited and introduced by **David Womersely,** *Jesus College, Oxford*

THEOLOGY, PHILOSOPHY, HISTORY, LITERATURE
ISBN 1 85506 509 6 : 250pp : Hb : £45.00 $29.95
ISBN 1 85506 510 X : 250pp : Pb : £14.95 $75.00

John Locke and Christianity
Contemporary Responses to the Reasonableness of Christianity
Edited and introduced by **Victor Nuovo,** *Middlebury College, Vermont*

ANTHROPOLOGY, POLITICS
ISBN 1 85506 539 8 : 250pp : Hb : £45.00 $24.95
ISBN 1 85506 540 1 : 250pp : Pb : £14.95 $72.00

Mill and Religion
Contemporary Responses to Three Essays on Religion
Edited and introduced by **Alan P.F. Sell,**
United Theological College, Aberystwyth

ANTHROPOLOGY, POLITICS
ISBN 1 85506 541 X : 250pp : Hb : £45.00 $24.95
ISBN 1 85506 542 8 : 250pp : Pb : £14.95 $72.00